COLOR PSYCHOLOGY AND
COLOR THERAPY

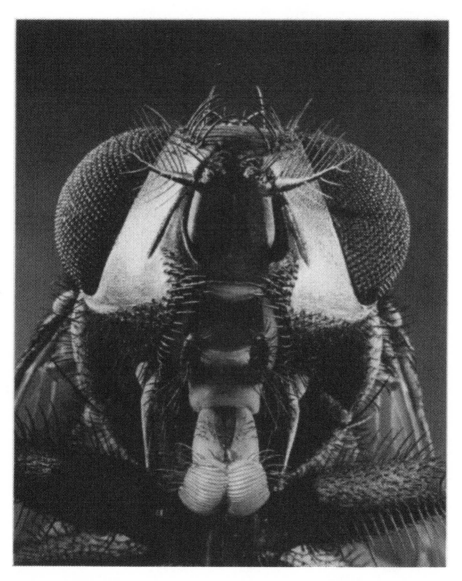

Enlarged view of the eyes and head of the common house fly. The color vision of insects differs from that of man and is vital to their survival. (Courtesy, American Museum of Natural History.)

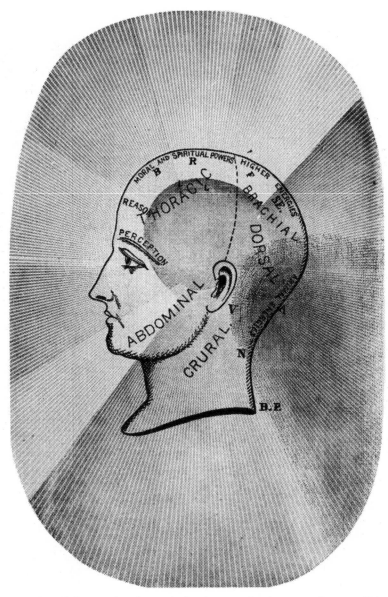

The psychic lights and colors of the human brain according to Edwin D. Babbitt (1878). Emanations were dark red in low natures and yellowish in high natures. Blue predominated where intellectual powers were great.

Faust in his Study, by Rembrandt. In the mysteries of life and death, the conflicts of good and evil, the mystic presumed to insights and powers unknown to the common man. But were these forces from celestial or nether regions? (Courtesy, Metropolitan Museum of Art.)

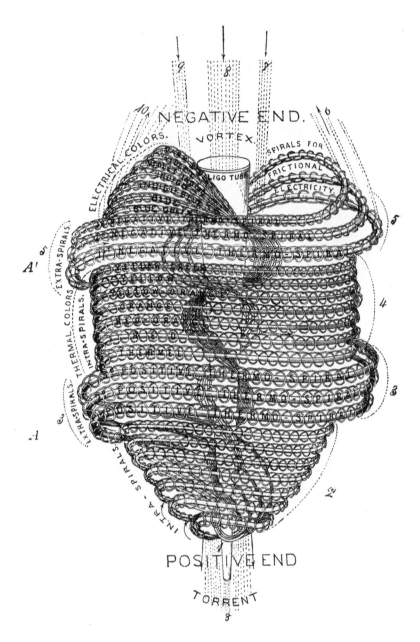

In 1878, Edwin D. Babbitt wrote of his atom: "If such an atom should be set in the midst of New York City, it must create such a whirlwind that all its palatial structures, ships, bridges and surrounding cities, with nearly two millions of people, would be swept into fragments and carried into the sky."

The Sorcerer of Mallaghem, by Peter Bruegel the Elder. Here the great Flemish painter burlesques the magic healers of his day, shows their paraphernalia, methods and apparently greedy ways. (Courtesy, Metropolitan Museum of Art.)

Color discrimination is an endowment of apes and men, but of few other mammals. It serves a fundamental purpose in vision that is less concerned with beauty than practical orientation to the world. (Courtesy, American Museum of Natural History.)

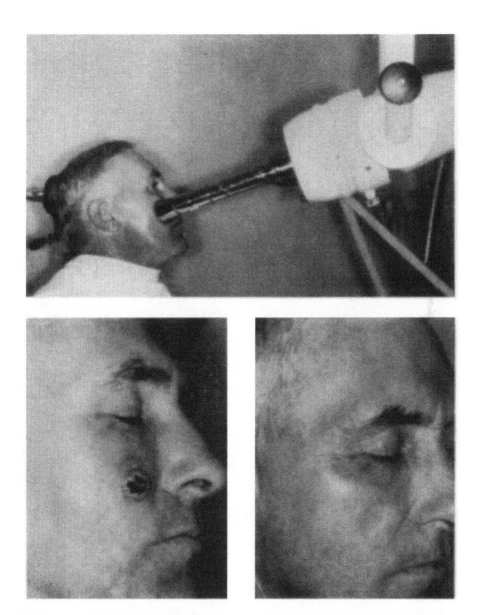

Treatment of skin cancer by X ray. (Reprinted by permission from "Treatment of Cancer and Allied Diseases," edited by George T. Pack and Edward M. Livingston, Paul Hoeber, New York, 1940. "Treatment of Malignant Tumors of the Skin," by George T. Pack and William O. Wuester, Vol. III.

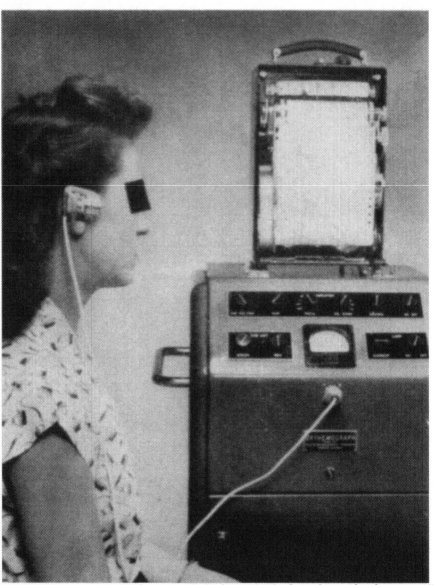

The Oxyhemograph. This unusual device, attached to the patient's ear, will react to the color of human blood and provide a quick record of oxygen content. It has been found useful in long operations and in operations on the heart. (Courtesy, Dr. Roy D. McClure, Henry Ford Hospital, Detroit.)

In safety, color serves an effective purpose in attracting the eye and calling attention to hazards. Cutting and forming devices, shown here, have brilliant orange at critical points. The body of machinery is a nondistracting gray, with projecting parts in yellow and switch controls in blue.

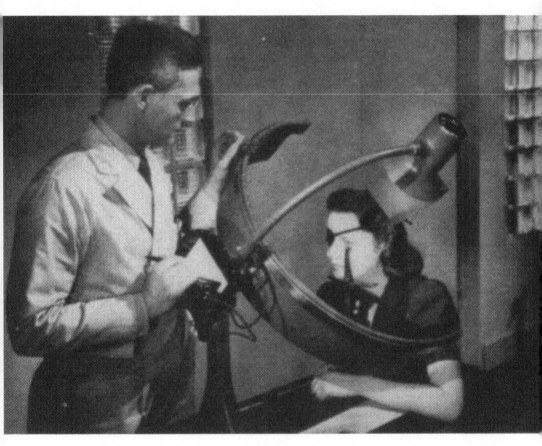

The retina of the human eye may be affected by fatigue, "eyestrain," and by many diseases and disorders of the body. Sensitivity to color may undergo a change of area, the boundaries of which may be readily measured with a perimeter such as shown here. (Courtesy, Bausch & Lomb.)

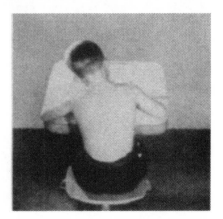

Good illumination and good color are vital to child welfare in schools. Where conditions are right—without glare and extreme contrast—there is balanced posture and straight spine. Bad conditions cause unbalanced posture, bent head, tilted shoulders, muscular strain. (Courtesy, Dr. D. B. Harmon.)

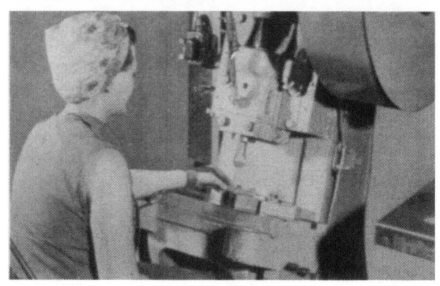

Before and after view of a punch press. Through a functional application of color it is possible to concentrate attention, relieve eyestrain and fatigue and contribute to human efficiency, comfort and well being. Color has definite relation to good production, industrial harmony and safety.

Eyes closed

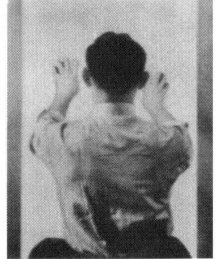

Influence of yellow

Influence of red

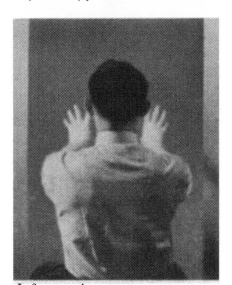

Influence of green

Even though the reaction may be a subtle one, the outstretched arms of a subject will tend to deviate away from each other under the influence of a warm color such as red, and toward each other under the influence of a cool color such as green or blue. (After Kurt Goldstein.)

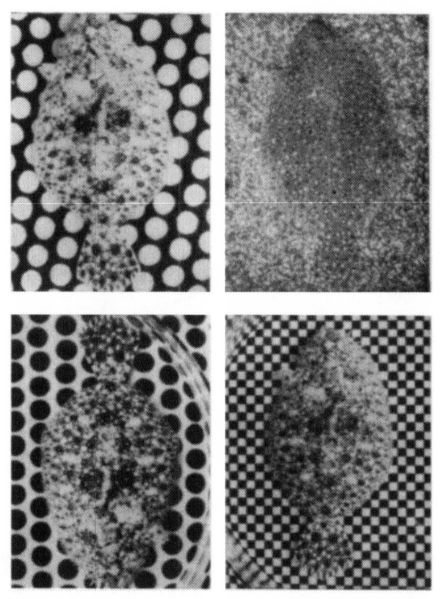

Color change in animals is regulated by vision. Response to environment, however, is less dependent on light intensity than on color of local background. These views of a flounder show remarkable adaptation, despite unnatural pattern. (Courtesy, U. S. Fish and Wildlife Service.)

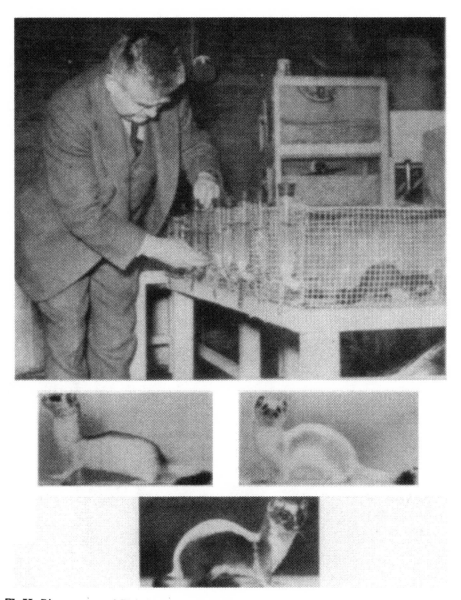

T. H. Bissonnette of Trinity College, Hartford, has induced abnormal coloration in weasels (American ermine) by regulating length of day. In the illustrations shown here, the weasel, normally white in winter, has had its coat
white in May and vari-colored in July through control of light.

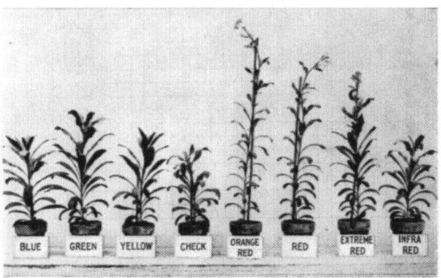

Upper illustration shows effects of supplementary light on growth of asters. Plants flowered almost as abundantly under 0.3 foot-candles as under 100 foot-candles. Lower illustration shows effects of colors of different wave length on growth of the stock plant. (Courtesy, Smithsonian Institution.)

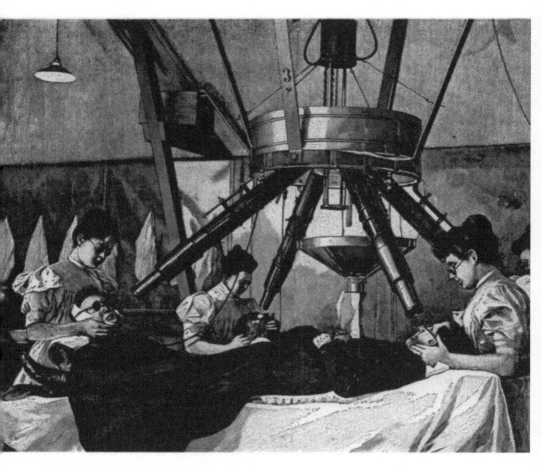

Treatment with ultraviolet (carbon arc) light at the Finsen Institute, Copen-hagen, during the latter part of the nineteenth century. This pioneering work in the use of radiant energy to relieve many human ills, had a rather difficult course before its complete scientific acceptance. (Courtesy, Bettman Archive.)

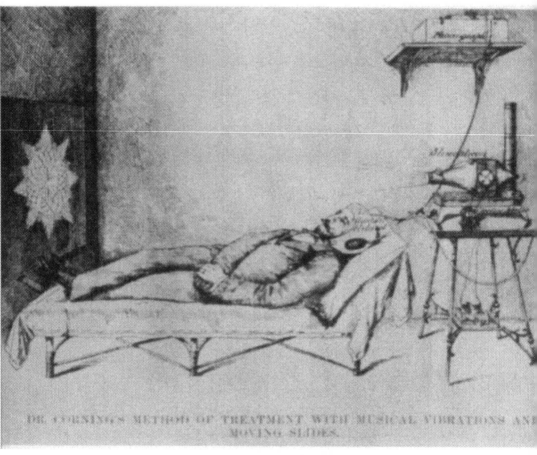

DR. OVENING'S METHOD OF TREATMENT WITH MUSICAL VIBRATIONS AND MOVING SLIDES.

A graphic portrayal of chromopathy during the 1890's. Music and slides of "enchanting beauty" were used to cure just about every affliction known to humankind. If the quack failed in his cures, he found the public gullible to color and willing dupes to it. (Courtesy, Bettman Archive.)

An American Indian medicine man. Headdress and mask worn by the native Alaskan doctor. Color has always played an impressive role in amulets and charms. It has symbolized divine forces, spiritual and bodily harmony with God and the universe. (Courtesy, American Museum of Natural History.)

The Alchemist, by Peter Bruegel the Elder. The great Flemish artist has depicted the paraphernalia of the alchemist, presumably in the concoction of the Elixir of Life. Although the Philosopher's Stone was never found, chemistry had its weird beginnings. (Courtesy, Metropolitan Museum of Art.)

Manic—red

Hysterical—green

Schizophrenic—yellow

Paranoid—brown

Manic patients prefer red, a symbol of blood. Hysterical patients prefer green, perhaps as an "escape." The schizophrenics are sensitive to yellow. The color associated with paranoia is brown. (Courtesy, Hans Huber, Publishers, Berne, Switzerland, Dr. Lipot Szondi, Experimentelle Triebdiagnostik.)

In the abstract study of color and form, certain shapes, proportions, sequences seem to have universal appeal and order. Mobile color effects projected by an instrument such as the Chromoton have great significance to the artist, the psychologist and the psychiatrist. (Courtesy, Tom Douglas Jones.)

COLOR PSYCHOLOGY
and COLOR THERAPY

A Factual Study of the INFLUENCE OF COLOR ON HUMAN LIFE

By Faber Birren

UNIVERSITY BOOKS, Inc. *New Hyde Park, New York*

Typography and illustrations
By *RAYMOND LUFKIN*

To DEANE B. JUDD

Contents

Preface to the Revised Edition

When COLOR PSYCHOLOGY AND COLOR THERAPY first appeared in 1950, it was fairly well reviewed in the medical press. There were reservations, of course, especially where I launched into mysticism, but for the most part the medical reviewers found the text not without a measure of interest.

What is now saving the day for color therapy is the rising science of psychosomatic medicine, which admits that man has a psyche that cannot be divorced from his body. The fears and tensions that cause the ulcer (or the asthma or the allergy) must be relieved or the person never will be well. The value of color therapy in psychosomatic disease cannot be denied. However, as this book strives to show, the influence of color is by no means limited to the psychological realm; its direct biological and physiological effects are rapidly becoming more evident as new research data accumulate.

In the years since the publication of the first edition of this book, I have continued my own studies and engaged in correspondence with other workers all over the world. A review of some of the more important research results from 1950 to the present is included in a new section of the present edition, Part 5, *New Biological and Psychological Findings*. Thus brought up to date, it is my hope that this volume will be accepted as a standard reference work in the field of color psychology.

FABER BIRREN

New York
1961

Introduction to the Revised Edition

Faber Birren is not a theorist but a very practical craftsman. Whether he is reading the works of mystics, or of biologists, or of psychologists, he is reading and studying them not for their theoretical structures, and one might say not even to know whether what they're saying is true but, quite simply, in order to find something to use in picking the colors for a mental hospital or a battleship, or a missile base, or to make new kinds of colored paper to print on, or to make a new home attractive, or to make new kinds of colored bricks for buildings.

Most of us bring our preconceptions and prejudices wherever we go. We are like horses with blinders on, going only in the direction we have been set to go. What is so extraordinary and so fruitful about Faber Birren's practicality is that it goes everywhere quite utterly without prejudice. Unlike most of us, Faber Birren, now just as when he was a young man, is willing to learn from anybody. He has learned from the most diverse people, from people who contradict each other, from people who denounce each other, from the occultists and mystics as well as from the biologists and agnostic scientists. He *dares* to learn from the occultists and mystics as well as the scientists.

It is necessary to emphasize this because otherwise Part One of this book, "The Historical Aspects," may appear to the reader to be a speedy commentary on a dead past, to be read as mere background after which one can turn to the rest of the book for some really scientific knowledge. Faber Birren does speak of "superstitions," "cults," and similar invidious terms, as if to show that he is not being taken in. But these terms should not obscure the full extent of his acknowledged debt to the mystic arts. Unfortunately, too, the first section of his book is much too short for what it contains and—to take but one example—the reader will hardly grasp from the one quotation from E. A. W. Budge's great work on amulets how much one can learn from this book. One of the fullest sections in this first part is on the work of Edwin D. Babbitt, but the reader will find it difficult to be sure what Birren has accepted, and what not. (It is pleasant to report that Birren has promised an abridged edition of Babbitt's THE PRINCIPLES OF LIGHT AND COLOR.) The reader whose appetite has been whetted should understand that he will do best if he takes this first part of Faber Birren's book as a guide to the literature which is mentioned rather than a substitute for it.

Birren entered the University of Chicago in 1920, majoring in education. Soon he decided to make color his lifework. There was no institution which gave instruction in this subject. He left the university after two years and set up his own system of study. He read all the books on light and color he could obtain from the Chicago Public Library and the Library of the American Medical Association, and entered into correspondence with various European psychologists, physicists, and ophthalmologists. He also made color experiments of his own.

To test the truth of the old quotation, "paint the dungeon red and drive the prisoner mad," he painted the walls, floor and ceiling of his room vermilion, curtained the windows with red glassine, and installed red light bulbs. He spent weeks in this room and found the red surroundings only made him feel "quite comfortable and cheerful."

To support himself during these early years of research, Birren worked for a publishing firm and occasionally wrote articles on color for medical and technical journals. In 1934 he rented an office in Chicago and set up as a color consultant. But it was not until he solved a problem for the Brunswick-Balke-Collender Company, that manufacturers took an interest in his work.

The public was not buying billiard tables for basement rumpus rooms. Birren found it was largely a matter of color psychology. American women would not have the green-topped billiard tables in their homes, he had learned, because they associated this color with cheap pool halls and gambling dens. Birren recommended changing the color of the table covering to a soft purplish tone. The company complied and home sales of the purple-topped tables climbed quickly.

By 1935 Birren was called to New York City so frequently that he decided to move his offices there.

In the Southern textile mills of Marshall Field & Company, Birren reduced fatigue by giving workers light green end-walls He relieved monotony for thousands of telephone girls by introducing yellow into the decoration of exchanges. He reduced accidents in the Caterpillar Tractor Company by devising a new color scheme for its 72-acre plant. The advent of fluorescent lights brought Birren many new accounts, because special color treatment was needed to spare employees eyestrain and keep objects from looking ghastly.

To understand Faber Birren's full debt to the occultists, compare their views as given in the first part of this book with Faber Birren's own views as he gives them in chapter 20 on "the prescription of color" (page 255 *et seq.*). I will give but one example.

For the Pawnee priest, red is the color of life. For the Egyptians, red was for themselves; their rites and ceremonies are written in red ink, and since then the formulas of the magician are usually written in red ink. In the fashioning of amulets the favorite color was red. "Red is the most interesting of all colors in magic healing." See especially Faber Birren's summary on this point on pages 35 and 36.

Turn now to page 258. Faber Birren is prescribing in his own name. I quote only the first of several paragraphs: "Red is perhaps the most dominant and dynamic of colors. Its energy has a strong influence on the growth of plants. It has been found to accelerate the development of certain lower animals, to increase hormonal and sexual activity and to heal wounds."

In between, Faber Birren has given us a great deal of science which buttresses his position. But to the science he adds—when he speaks for himself—a daring firmness of statement which he learned from the occultists.

Faber Birren does not try to explain away the inexplicable. He says very well: "Explanations of psychological and psychical phenomena are not always easy—and indeed unnecessary. There are in man many strange and inexplicable mysteries regarding color" (page 199).

Remember Birren's practical bent and his debt to occult literature and this book will be more illuminating to you.

I now have the pleasant duty to tell the reader how well all this has served Faber Birren. He has proved it in life and the competition of the market place.

Faber Birren makes his living by prescribing color. He prescribes it to government, to education, to the armed forces, to architecture, to industry and commerce.

Faber Birren is one of three children of Joseph P. and Crescentia (Lang) Birren. His father came from Luxembourg and was a successful landscape painter. As a child, Birren revealed a talent for drawing and mixing colors. Later, he decorated the walls of his home with murals depicting family scenes. In 1918 he graduated from the Nicholas Senn High School in Chicago and attended classes in life drawing and painting at the Art Institute of Chicago.

Millions of inexperienced men and women entered industrial jobs after the outbreak of World War II; the accident rate rose rapidly. Birren surveyed scores of plants, often two in one day, and at night dictated his suggestions. The plants then rushed in paint gangs to put his advice into effect, and the accident toll began to fall.

By using a safety color code devised by Birren, according to the U. S. Army Service Forces, some government plants during the war cut their accident frequencies from 46.14 to 5.58 per thousand.

His work for the United States Navy has been described as the "largest single color-coordination job ever undertaken." He laid out color specifications for almost everything found in or on a naval shore establishment, even to altering the color scheme of the helmet worn by men who work on ships and docks. In three years the Navy lowered its accident frequency from 6.4 to 4.6—a drop of twenty-eight per cent.

Birren's color code for safety has become internationally accepted in countries as remote from each other as England, Japan, Italy, Argentina, Uruguay.

He maintains an office in London where his specifications for color are being applied to paints, tile, plastics for use in industrial, commercial and institutional buildings.

His work has been acknowledged and recommended by the Council on Industrial Health of the American Medical Association.

In 1955 the U. S. State Department sent him to an international congress in Rome on work productivity, safety and industrial health. He went as the only—and the world's leading—authority on color.

Among his present clients are Du Pont, the Hoover Company, General Electric, Masonite, Minnesota Mining, National Lead, House & Garden Magazine, the West Virginia Pulp & Paper Company.

Inevitably, Faber Birren has to answer the question what is his favorite color. It is maroon.

FELIX MORROW

Preface

Two desires have prompted the writing of this book. The first has been to assemble a wealth of data on color psychology and color therapy which has a credible basis in fact rather than fancy. Color readily lends itself to hyperbole and outright charlatanry. Too many books have put rapture before reason and have thus added little more than confusion to the subject. If color is to cure human ills, physical or mental, greater proof of its efficacy will be required than mere exuberance.

A first desire then, has been to search the literature of science and to assemble—probably for the first time—a full array of tenable research data. With good evidence so brought together, a second desire has been to appeal to science and the medical profession to abandon old prejudices and to give color its honest due. Many true values have been lost simply because honest men have disdained the pretenders and in so doing have washed their hands of the whole subject.

I am convinced that a fair appraisal of color will restore its prestige in the eyes of modern medicine and will lead to great human benefits. If this book in any way encourages a new tolerance and interest it will serve a happy purpose.

FABER BIRREN

NEW YORK, N. Y.
January, 1950

Part 1

THE HISTORICAL ASPECTS

CHAPTER 1

The Inspired Mystics

NEARLY ALL of early color expression concerned mysticism and the enigmas of life and death. It is perhaps a mistaken notion that man in his love of color was impelled by some æsthetic urge. The greatest weight of evidence points to the fact that color was involved with the supernatural and therefore had significance that went beyond what might be thought of as mere sensuous delight.

Man at the dawn of civilization recognized that sunlight was essential to life. Color, being a manifestation of light, held divine meaning. Historical records of color show little interest in the physical nature of color, nor yet in its abstract beauty, but in a symbolism that attempted to resolve the strange workings of creation and give it personal and human meaning.

In the Zoroastrian scriptures one reads: "We sacrifice unto the undying, shining, swift-horsed Sun. When the light of the sun waxes warmer, when the brightness of the sun waxes warmer, then up stand the heavenly Yazatas, by hundreds and thousands: they gather together its glory, they make its glory pass down, they pour its glory upon the earth made by Ahura, for the increase of the world of holiness, for the increase of the creatures of holiness, for the increase of the undying, shining swift-horsed Sun."

Sun worship is as old as antiquity. The Egyptian Ra, self-created, once dwelt upon earth. Driven into the sky through man's iniquity, his eye became the sun.

In many instances the sun represented the masculine virtues of the deity and the moon the feminine. The Egyptians, in truth, had an expressive color symbolism which pervaded all their art and culture. The hues of the rainbow were as significant as language and were generally a part of hieroglyphics. Temples, talismans and charms, burial trappings, all were rich in the color tokens prescribed by the magicians who themselves wore breastplates of blue to mark the sacredness of their judgments.

The Greeks likewise identified color with universal harmony. In the conception of a god, his body was his virtue and his garments his achievement. Athena wore a golden robe. The red poppy was sacred to Ceres. In presenting *The Odyssey*, purple was worn to signify the sea wanderings of Ulysses. When reciting *The Iliad*, scarlet was worn as a token of the bloody encounter mentioned in the poem.

The Druids of England, who likewise built temples to the sun and whose culture antedated the Roman conquest, were equally superstitious. Eliphas Levi in his *History of Magic* writes, "The

4

Druids were priests and physicians, curing by magnetism and charging amulets with their fluidic influence. Their universal remedies were mistletoe and serpents' eggs, because these substances attracted astral light in a special manner." (Further data in regard to this book, as well as others cited, will be found in the bibliography on page 267.)

In the orient, Brahmanism recognized yellow as a sacred color. Of man himself, the Hindu Upanishads relate, "There are in his body the veins called Hita, which are as small as a hair divided a thousandfold, full of white, blue, yellow, green, and red."

Buddha's color was similarly yellow or gold. However, he wore red when he pondered over the vicissitudes of man. "And the Blessed One, putting on a tunic of double red cloth, and binding on his girdle, and throwing his upper robe over his right shoulder, would go thither and sit down, and for a while remain solitary, plunged in meditation."

Confucius, who also is identified with the color yellow, wore black and white. According to the book *Heang Tang,* "The superior man did not use a deep purple, or a puce color, in the ornaments of his dress. . . . Over lamb's fur he wore a garment of black, over fawn's fur one of white; over fox's fur one of yellow." His dislike for purple is very well expressed in his own writings. "I hate the purple color, because it confuses us with the red color. I hate the goody-goodies because they confuse us with the virtuous people."

To the Mohammedan, however, the color of all colors is green. In the Koran one reads, "As to those who believe and do good works . . . for them are prepared gardens of eternal abode. . . . They shall be adorned therein with bracelets of gold, and shall be clothed in green garments of fine silks and brocades, reposing themselves therein on thrones."

5

In Hebrew and Christian lore, color symbolism is no less glorified. Blue is the hue of the Lord Jehovah. In Exodus: "Then up went Moses, and Aaron, and Nadab, and Abihu, and seventy of the elders of Israel; and they saw the God of Israel; and there was under his feet as it were a paved work of sapphire stone, and as it were the very heaven for clearness."

In Judaism the divine hues are red, blue, purple, and white. Josephus wrote: "The veils, too, which were composed of four things, they declared the four elements; for the plain [white] linen was proper to signify the earth, because the flax grows out of the earth; the purple signified the sea, because the color is dyed by the blood of a sea shellfish; the blue is fit to signify the air; and the scarlet will naturally be an indication of fire."

To the Christian, however, blue is less significant than green and is seldom used in church ritual. The Holy Grail was emerald. According to St. John the Divine, "He that sat was to look upon like a jasper and a sardine stone; and there was a rainbow round about the throne, in sight like unto an emerald."

THE RACES OF MAN

The Pawnee priest of America chanted, "The morning star is like a man; he is painted red all over; that is the color of life."

Among the peoples of the world, color has always been associated with racial pride. The art of cosmetics, in truth, originated in ancient Egypt where red dyes were used to emphasize race distinction. Darwin wrote, "We know . . . that the color of the skin is regarded by the men of all races as a highly important element in their beauty." Extreme whiteness of skin among northern peoples, extreme yellowness or goldenness among the orientals, extreme blackness among Negroes became emblematic of the ideal racial type.

6

The Egyptians recognized four races. Red was for themselves, yellow for the Asiatics, white for the peoples across the Mediterranean, black for the Negroes. The Assyrians held to the same designations. The Arabs, however, accepted two races, one red or ruddy, the other black. In African mythology the descendants of those who ate the lungs and blood of the first ox slaughtered for food established the red race. Those who feasted on the liver begot the black race.

In India the four original castes were associated with colors. As the story goes, mankind once comprised four races. From the mouth of the creator came the Brahmans, whose color was white and who were to be priests. From his arms came the Kshatriyas, whose color was red and who were to be soldiers. From his thighs came the Vaisyas, the yellow ones of the mercantile class. From his feet came the lowly, black Sudras of the servile class. These were the four varnas, "varna" being a word which means "color" in the Sanskrit language.

In *The Arabian Nights*, "Tale of the Ensorcelled Prince," the evil wife of the Prince cast this spell upon the inhabitants of the Black Islands: "And the citizens, who were of four different faiths, Moslem, Nazarene, Jew, and Magian, she transformed by her enchantments into fishes; the Moslems are the white, the Magians red, the Christians blue, and the Jews yellow."

THE QUARTERS OF THE EARTH

Belief in the divine healing properties of color pervades all ancient symbolism, religious or otherwise. Obviously man's survival was beset by countless hazards. His was a struggle against visible and invisible forces, a trek out of misery and ignorance.

Practically all civilizations identified color with the supposed four quarters of the earth. In Egypt, the Pharaoh wore a white

7

crown to symbolize his dominion over Upper Egypt and a red crown to proclaim his authority over Lower Egypt. The ceilings of temples were usually blue and embellished with drawings of the constellations. The floors were often green like the meadows of the Nile.

Among the peoples of Tibet in Central Asia, the world was conceived as being a high mountain called Sumur. As the earth grew from the beginning of time, its summit rose into the sky and provided a convenient dwelling-place for the gods. The mountain of Sumur was shaped like a pyramid with its top broken off. The sides facing the four quarters were hued and shone like jewels. To the north was yellow, to the south blue, to the east white, to the west red. In each of these directions was a continent within a salty sea, inhabited by different races of people having square, oval, crescent-shaped, and round faces.

Such symbolism has been found in lands as remote from each other as Egypt, Ireland, China, and America. In ancient Ireland black represented the north, white the south, purple the east, and dun color the west. In China, black was a token of the north, red of the south, green of the east, and white of the west.

In America similar traditions have existed. Thousands of years ago, according to a Navaho legend, men dwelt in a land surrounded by high mountains. The rise and fall of these mountains created night and day. The southern mountains were blue and caused the dawn. The eastern mountains were white and caused the day. The western mountains were yellow and brought twilight. The northern mountains were black and covered the earth in darkness.

The American Indian also had color designations for a lower world, which was generally black, and for an upper world, which had many colors. The tattooing on his face, the colors on his

8

masks, effigies, and huts were full of mystical significance. He related colors to his songs, ceremonies, prayers, and games. Life and death were somehow influenced by them.

THE PLANETS

Man has always been convinced that his destiny is ruled by divine forces within the sky. The macrocosm of the universe, the microcosm of the individual soul, all came out of darkness into light. All knowledge was with the gods who dwelt in the firmament; the sun, the planets, and the stars held answers to the secrets of life.

Over two thousand years before Christ, astrology was an important science. The Egyptian called time "the everlasting green one." The Chaldean gazed into the sky and saw the movement of the planets and the sun. Eternal laws were written here. The planets controlled the earth and all upon it. Each had its hour of ascendency during which it ruled men, formed their minds and spirits, and brought health and fortune, disease, adversity, or death to them.

Much of early architecture involved color symbolism referring to the sun and planets. C. Leonard Woolley in his *Ur of the Chaldees* has written of the "Mountain of God" unearthed between Bagdad and the Persian Gulf in modern times. One of the oldest buildings of history, it dates back to 2300 B.C. and was thought to be the original home of Abraham.

The tower was built in four stages. The lowest was black, the uppermost red. The shrine was covered with blue glazed tile, the roof with gilded metal. Woolley writes, "These colors had mystical significance and stood for the various divisions of the universe, the dark underworld, the habitable earth, the heavens and the sun."

9

Of other such towers, or ziggurats, Herodotus wrote in the fifth century B.C., "The Medes built the city now called Ecbatana, the walls of which are of great size and strength, rising in circles one within the other. . . . The number of the circles is seven, the royal palace and the treasury standing within the last. . . . On this wall the battlements are white, of the next black, of the third scarlet, of the fourth blue, of the fifth orange; all these are colored with paint. The last two have their battlements coated respectively with silver and gold."

To all indications Herodotus referred to the great temple of Nebuchadnezzar at Barsippa. Uncovered in recent years, its bricks bear the stamp of the Babylonian monarch. James Fergusson has given a lucid description of the building and translated its astrological symbolism: "This temple, as we know from the decipherment of the cylinders which were found on its angles, was dedicated to the seven planets or heavenly spheres, and we find it consequently adorned with the colors of each. The lower, which was also richly panelled, was black, the color of Saturn; the next, orange, the color of Jupiter; the third, red, emblematic of Mars; the fourth, yellow, belonging to the Sun; the fifth and sixth, green and blue respectively, as dedicated to Venus and Mercury; and the upper probably white, that being the color belonging to the Moon, whose place in the Chaldean system would be uppermost."

CHINESE ASTROLOGY

Yet not all astrology was devoted to the intangible and inexplicable mysteries of human fate. The Chinese, for example, were quite practical about the messages they read in the heavens. In his *Outlines of Chinese Symbolism,* C. A. S. Williams writes, "The appearance of comets, the eclipse of the sun and moon, are believed to have a malign influence over the affairs of men." Superstitions, though of ancient origin, still trouble the hearts of living Asiatics.

Mars ruled the summer season, was the author of punishment and the producer of sudden confusion.

Saturn represented earth, and when it met Jupiter in the same "house," it brought good fortune to the empire. However, if Saturn appeared white and round, mourning and droughts were in store. If the planet was red, disturbances were to be expected and troops might take to the battlefield. If it was green, there would be floods. If it was black, sickness and death would descend upon the land. If it was yellow, China would see prosperity.

Mercury when white forecast the drought. When it was yellow the crops would be scorched. When it was red, the enemy would attack. When it was black, floods were imminent. If it was large and white in the east, the troops beyond the frontier would disperse. If it was red in the east, the Middle Kingdom would be victorious.

Green clouds in the sky were omens of a plague of locusts. Red clouds meant calamity or warfare. Black clouds brought floods. Yellow clouds heralded prosperity.

THE ZODIAC

The word "zodiac" derives from the Greek *zodiakos kuklos*, meaning "circle of little animals." Astrology and the zodiac held the secrets of divination, of life and death. Manly P. Hall in his monumental book on symbolism writes, "It is difficult for this age to estimate correctly the profound effect produced upon the religions, philosophies and sciences of antiquity by the study of the planets, luminaries, and constellations." Astrology, in truth, still fascinates the world today and, credulously accepted by many devotees, continues to be looked upon by these devotees as a ruling factor in human life.

The zodiac presumes the existence of a zone in the sky through which the sun, the moon, and the planets travel. The twelve constellations were twelve "houses" which the sun visited each year. Each sign of the zodiac thus had its own symbol and color: red for Aries, dark green for Taurus, brown for Gemini, silver for Cancer, gold for Leo, variegated hues for Virgo, clear green for Libra, vermilion for Scorpio, sky-blue for Sagittarius, black for Capricorn, gray for Aquarius, sea-blue for Pisces.

While there may be good reason to doubt that the planets rule human destiny, such skepticism cannot reject the ancient science of astrology entirely. The astrologer was a sober man and his work was carefully founded on a study of human beings—literally millions of them. These "case histories" perhaps gave him his clues, his averages, and from them he may have reached conclusions which had a higher percentage of verity than chance alone could have assured.

Today modern scientific investigators are lending support to many of the astrologer's contentions, even though the planets and the stars are not the point of attention. Dr. Ellsworth Huntington of Yale, for example, has discussed a possible relationship between the season of a person's birth and his character, a view that is as old as history. It may be that the month of conception holds major significance.

Many geniuses, imbeciles, and criminals have birthdays in February, March, and April, the months of conception being May, June, and July. Spring conceptions presumably follow a definite "urge of nature," resulting in more impulsive offspring. The Hall of Fame gives preference to birthdays in February, March, and April—as well as do most jails! From a record of

3,000 persons suffering from dementia praecox, more birthdays were in February and March than in any other months. *Who's Who* shows a predominance of September and October birthdays, the months of conception being December and January. A January birth seems to influence a person toward the clergy, August toward chemistry. Multiple births occur chiefly in May, June, and July. June and July births are the lowest in number.

THE GOLDEN AGE

To ancient man, color less expressed the æsthetic than the mystical. He was superstitious and frightened. He knew so little of the nature of things, of the universe. He was sure that he would survive or die as he succeeded or failed in effecting harmony with divine forces.

Color provided hopeful symbols of unity, of command over nature, of regeneration within himself. Though life went on endlessly, great ages were to be built. These ages might be of gold or iron, colorful or drab, as man directed. To the Greeks, a Golden Age once was upon the earth. Saturn ruled, evil did not exist, and humanity dwelt unaging in piety and contentment. But man acquired the knowledge of evil and because of it went from an age of gold to one of silver. Now Jupiter ruled. Nature rebelled, no longer making gifts of her fruits, and agriculture was born. Evil increased. As man grew more savage he entered the Copper Age where Mars was all-powerful. From virtue to sin he fell into the Iron Age of despair, marked by the decadence still known today.

How to regain the Golden Kingdom? Man must strive for the perfection of old. He must don the white robe of purity, the red robe of sacrifice and love, the blue robe of truth and integrity, as did the noble gods.

CHAPTER 2

The Bewildered Philosophers

THE WORD "SCIENTIST" in its present connotation did not become a part of language until the modern era. In ancient and medieval times philosophy was everything, and the philosopher was the custodian of human wisdom. He knew of the moral law, of religion, government, natural history, alchemy, mathematics, healing, and all knowledge. Indeed, the sedulous scholar at one time had been able to master the entire sum of academic learning. This is in striking contrast with the world of today, in which a man may devote a lifetime to a single type of microbe and still consider his subject vast and complex enough for a full generation of profound study. Having few details to bother about in his pursuit of knowledge, the ancient could think in broad and encompassing terms.

According to legend, Hermes Trismegistus, the Thrice Great-est, Master of All Arts and Sciences, founded the art of healing—together with just about every branch of learning that interested mankind. The famous Emerald tablet, said to have been found in the valley of Ebron, epitomized the teachings of the fabulous Egyptian. It contained an alchemical formula and involved color simply because color was part of alchemy and in turn obedient to one supreme and divine entity associated with light. Hermes unquestionably tried to heal with color. One papyrus exclaims, "Come verdigris ointment! Come then verdant one!"

Numerous Egyptian surgical and medical works have been unearthed. One of these is the Ebers Papyrus dating back to about 1500 B.C. and said to be "the oldest [complete] book the world possesses." The manuscript, beautifully preserved, unrolls to a length of 68 feet and comprises a collection of medical pre-scriptions. In the introduction to his translation, Bryan writes, "Throughout the manuscript the heading of the different chap-ters, the names of the diseases, the directions for treatment, and in many cases the weights and dosages of the drugs are written in vivid red."

Here one unquestionably finds the first advice to apply raw meat to a black eye!

Colored minerals—malachite, red and yellow ochre, hematite (a red clay)—are endowed with efficacy, apparently because of their hue. For constipation, white or red cakes are advised.

Vermilion writing fluid mixed with goat's fat and honey is prescribed as a salve.

For other ailments there are other colored substances, organic and inorganic, including the blood of a black cat.

15

Another ancient Egyptian papyrus deals with the age-old speculation as to the sex of an unborn child: "Another time: if thou seest her face green . . . she will bring forth a male child, but if thou seest things upon her eyes, she will not bear ever."

The Egyptian carried a purple amulet to thwart adversity. He had an involved ritual of death. The Egyptian *Book of the Dead* states, "And behold, thou shalt make a scarab of green stone, which shall be placed in the breast of a man, and it shall perform for him 'the opening of the mouth.' " Thus would the speech of the deceased be restored.

The Tjet, a red stone, gave the dead the virtue of the blood of Isis. The Ab, or heart amulet, also red, preserved the soul of the physical body. The Udjat, of gold, afforded health and protection. The Sma amulet was brownish and enabled the dead man to breathe again.

ANCIENT REMEDIES

It is an acknowledged fact today that many ancient remedies were excellent curatives, despite the mysticism that originally surrounded them. Egyptian papyri which prescribed the eating of liver for certain afflictions associated with anemia and poor eyesight established a therapy that is still being used after four thousand years. Hippocrates also mentioned the efficacy of liver, as did Pliny the Elder.

In *Germs and Man,* Justina Hill refers to the ancient use of compounds of mercury, silver, and copper. "These dyes exhibit marked preferences in their antiseptic action for different groups of organisms." Cinnabar (the red sulfide of mercury), "ye blood of ye dragon," was prescribed for eye diseases, burns, and pustules. In the form of mercurochrone in aqueous solution, it still continues to be used.

16

In some instances the ancient credited his miracles to color rather than to the chemical properties of his substances. Thus the purple dye extracted from murex shells was used to check the overgrowth of granulation tissue and to draw pus from boils. What the ancient failed to realize was "that this efficacy was unrelated to the glorious color of the purpura, but due to the formation of calcium oxide, one of the first compounds which was to lead to Dakin's solution 2,000 years later."

PRINCIPAL COLORS

In Asia Minor the Persians practiced a form of color therapy based on the emanations of light. The Greeks, however, attempted to take a more practical view. Modern medicine traces its ancestry to Hippocrates in the fourth century B.C. Yet if the Greeks contributed to the progress of medicine they also invented a system of logic that kept human intelligence in a maze for several centuries.

It was not perhaps until the time of the Greeks that much thought was given to the physical rather than metaphysical nature of color. Previously the ancients had looked upon color as a phenomenon associated with things spiritual rather than mundane. Light was the emanation of a great deity. It fell from heaven and permeated all space. It entered the bodies of men and in turn shone forth as an aura. Metaphors were more important than explanations. What was the significance of the colors which the gods had created? What profound meanings did they have?

One of the earliest known references to a rational "science" of color is found in the works of Democritus. In an effort to explain the hues of nature he regarded black, red, green, and white as primary. Other colors resulted from mixtures of these four.

To Aristotle, black and white were primary. "The different shades of crimson and violet depend upon differences in the strength of their constituents, whilst blending is exemplified by mixture of white with black which gives crimson. For observation teaches us that black mixed with sunlight or firelight always turns crimson, and that black objects heated in the fire all change to a crimson color, as *e.g.* smoky tongues of flame, or charcoal when subjected to intense heat, are seen to have a crimson color. But a vivid bright violet is obtained from a blend of feeble sunlight with a thin dusky white."

Pliny held to a different view. He wrote, "I remark that the following are the three principal colors; the red, that of kermes, for instance, which, beginning in the tints of the rose, reflects, when viewed sideways and held up to the light, the shades that are found in the Tyrian purple; the amethystine color, which is borrowed from the violet; . . . and a third properly known as the 'conchyliated' color, but which comprehends a variety of shades, such, for instance, as the tints of the heliotropium, and others of a deeper color, the hues of the mallow, inclining to a full purple, and the colors of the late violet."

To find a place for golden yellow, Pliny turned rather abruptly from his observations of nature and contrived the following strange bit of reasoning: "I find it stated that, in the most ancient times, yellow was held in the highest esteem, but was reserved exclusively for the nuptial veils of females; for which reason it is perhaps that we do not find it included among the principal colors, these being used in common by males and females: indeed, it is the circumstance of their being used by both sexes in common that gives them their rank as principal colors." Here is ancient logic stretched to odd limits. The great Pliny seemed willing to let custom encroach upon nature.

Science had a good start (though a curious one) in the conception of the world as comprised of elements. And from the very first, these elements were symbolized by colors.

In the Hindu Upanishads, which date back to the seventh or eighth century B.C., one reads, "The red color of burning fire is the color of fire, the white color of fire is the color of water, the black color of fire the color of earth. . . . Great householders and great theologians of olden times who knew this have declared the same, saying, 'No one can henceforth mention to us anything which we have not heard, perceived, or known.' Out of these they knew all. Whatever they thought looked red, they knew was the color of fire. Whatever they thought looked white, they knew was the color of water. Whatever they thought looked black, they knew was the color of earth. Whatever they thought was altogether unknown, they knew was some combination of these three beings."

Pythagoras believed in four elements—earth, water, fire, and air—as did the Greek philosophers who followed. Aristotle assigned colors to them. "Simple colors are the proper colors of the elements, i.e., of fire, air, water, and earth. Air and water when pure are by nature white, fire (and the sun) yellow, and the earth is naturally white. The variety of hues which earth assumes is due to coloration by tincture, as is shown by the fact that ashes turn white when the moisture that tinged them is burnt out. It is true that they do not turn a pure white, but that is because they are tinged afresh, in the process of combustion, by smoke, which is black. . . . Black is the proper color of elements in process of transmutation. The remaining colors, it may easily be seen, arise from blending by mixture of these primary colors." All colors, thus concluded the great Aristotle, were derived from mixtures of white and black—an idea that persisted for centuries.

Chinese elements were five in number: yellow for earth, black for water, red for fire, green for wood, and white for metal. (The elements of certain American Indian tribes were fire, wind, water, and earth.)

HIPPOCRATES AND AFTER

Man's belief in the elements lasted for many centuries, until well after the Renaissance. Da Vinci, in fact, wrote as follows: "We shall set down white for the representative of light, without which no color can be seen; yellow for earth; green for water; blue for air; red for fire; and black for total darkness."

In the centuries of the Greeks, however, white garments were worn by the afflicted to cause pleasant dreams. Pythagoras is described as having used music, poetry, and color to cure disease. Yet it was the great Hippocrates who abandoned mysticism, cast suspicious eyes on the habits and dissipations of men, listened to the beating of their hearts, and founded that critical and diagnostic attitude which has become a part of modern medicine.

At this point in history the story of color in medicine leads into two divergent paths, the mystics and the clinicians. As the centuries followed there were some who would pursue the secrets of life in the divine workings of the Creator, and others of more incredulous bent who would cope with disease through an investigation of wholly natural causes. These two groups were to wrangle with each other from generation to generation, at last finding some harmony and reconciliation in the present century through the work of the psychologist and psychiatrist.

Celsus, who lived at the beginning of the Christian era, followed the doctrines set forth by Hippocrates the clinician.

His attitude toward color was also practical rather than occult, although superstition did influence him at times. For example, he prescribed medicines with color in mind—white violets, purple violets, the lily, iris, narcissus, rose, saffron. The plasters he used to relieve wounds were black, green, red, and white. Of red he wrote, "There is one plaster almost of a red color, which seems to bring wounds very rapidly to cicatrize."

Celsus declared spring to be the most salubrious season, then winter, summer, with autumn most inimical. Regarding the insane he wrote, "It is best . . . to keep him in light who dreads darkness; and to keep him in darkness who dreads light." One of his potions was yellow: "Saffron ointment with iris-oil applied on the head, aids in procuring sleep, and also in tranquilizing the mind."

Galen, a famous Greco-Roman physician (A.D. 130–200), also a clinician, bitterly attacked the medical men of his day. Next to Hippocrates he was perhaps the most distinguished doctor of antiquity. He was attracted to motion and change as significant in diagnosis. "Thus, if that which is white becomes black, or that which is black becomes white, it undergoes motion in respect to *color*." He worked out an elaborate theory in which these visible changes were reckoned with. One of his queries in this connection is amusing. "How, then, could blood ever turn into bone without having first become, as far as possible, thickened and white? And how could bread turn into blood without having gradually parted with its whiteness and acquired redness?"

AVICENNA, THE ARABIAN

During the Dark Ages progress in medicine passed from Rome to Islam and found its greatest leader in Avicenna, an Arabian (980–1037?). In his *Canon of Medicine,* one of the most venerable of medical documents, he pays rare tribute to color both as a guide in diagnosis and as an actual curative. Avicenna's attitude was more searching and passionate than that of Hippocrates, Celsus, or Galen. Color was of vital importance, worthy of profound study. In consequence the Arabian dealt freely with it and wrote it into almost every page of his *Canon*.

Avicenna was an acknowledged disciple of Aristotle. The world to him comprised certain elements which he allied to the senses, the mind, and the emotions. These elements created tendencies which formed the body and soul of man. Too, a man's breathing had different phases, strong and weak, and the vibration rates of breath were related to the elements. The breath of earth was slow, the breath of ether fine and quick.

Avicenna diagnosed the diseases of his patients with an eye for hue. The color of hair and skin, of eyes, of excrement and urine, were significant. "In jaundice, if the urine becomes of a deeper red until it is nearly black, and if its stain on linen can no longer be removed, it is a good sign—the better the deeper red. But if the urine becomes white or slightly reddish, and the jaundice is not subsiding, the advent of dropsy is to be feared."

If the skin of the patient changed to yellow, he suspected a disorder of the liver. If the change was to white, the disorder was probably in the spleen. All these hues must be carefully observed.

Avicenna devoted much study to the fluids and humors of the body. He developed an unusual chart in which color was related to temperament and to the physical condition of the body.

The predecessors of the great Arabian had also noted that color was an observable symptom in disease. But Avicenna was more of a mystic. Color was not only the sign of affliction—it might also be the cure! First of all, the innate temperaments of men might be found written in the color of their hair. People with black hair had hot temperaments, while those with brown hair had cold temperaments. The temperament of the tawny-headed or red-headed person was equable. Here there was an excess of "unburnt heat"; hence there was proneness to anger. The temperament of the fair-haired was cold and very moist; that of the gray-headed was cold and very dry. In both instances Avicenna saw weakness and physical degeneracy. Men, like plants, lost color when they dried!

Of humors he wrote: "Even imagination, emotional states and other agents cause the humors to move. Thus, if one were to gaze intently at something red, one would cause the sanguineous humor to move. This is why one must not let a person suffering from nose-bleeding see things of a brilliant red color." He also declared red and yellow to be injurious to the eye. Blue light soothed the movement of the blood; red light stimulated it. The clear light of morning aided nutrition.

Avicenna thus had every confidence in the therapy of color. Because he believed that red moved the blood, this hue was used profusely and prescribed in numerous medicines. White, conversely, was a refrigerant. Potions of red flowers cured disorders of the blood. Yellow flowers cured disorders of the biliary system, reducing pain and inflammation.

THE ALCHEMISTS

After the fall of Rome and during the time of Avicenna, Europe lay buried in the Dark Ages. Philosophers, cut apart from each other, trudged through the intellectual bogs of the mighty Aristotle. When progress in the healing art made its way again during the early part of the Renaissance, it found its chief glory in the mysteries and secrets of alchemy.

In Europe, alchemy became the most important of the sciences, all jumbled up with paganism, Christianity, and occultism in general. Among its exponents were men such as Albertus Magnus, Roger Bacon, Thomas Aquinas, Nicholas Flamel, Raymond Lully, Paracelsus, Jakob Böhme, and Ben Jonson. In the fifteenth century the alchemists banded together into a religious and political organization whose initiates penetrated the sanctuaries of nature, prophesied the future, cured disease, concealed their formulas in secret writings, and did their best to preserve their necks against the wrath of the church.

While some of these men devoted themselves to the transmutation of metals, all saw in alchemy a universal panacea. The philosopher's stone, the elixir of life, would cure all ills. They were said to embody salt, sulfur, mercury, and azoth, all special substances which could be concocted into a magic potion through laborious and intricate methods.

PARACELSUS

Among the greatest of alchemists—-and the greatest of healers —was Theophrastus Bombastus von Hohenheim (1493–1541), known to history as Paracelsus. He declared that the true purpose of alchemy was not to make gold but to prepare efficacious medicines. Poor and contaminated blood was the root of all disease. Good blood, the true nostrum, was to be generated by nourishing the sick with "digested heat." In illness the natural heat of the body was impeded; food was not digested. The heat of the sun and the moon must be given the patient. Such "heat" was to be extracted from nature through a wonderful and occult art. He wrote, "Heat acting on moisture generates blackness, and, acting on dryness, generates whiteness, in which red is hidden."

Paracelsus freely prescribed his "potable gold." The adult received eight drops, the child one drop. He was said to have cured an endless list of afflictions: apoplexy, epilepsy, headache, insomnia, paralysis, melancholy, fever, pains in the stomach and kidneys, ulcers, palpitation of the heart, fainting spells, worms, colds, rupture, gangrene, plague.

The clinicians were virulently condemned by Paracelsus. He endeavored to lead medicine back again to things spiritual and divine. The Sun ruled the heart of man, the Moon his brain, Saturn his spleen, Mercury his lungs, Venus his kidneys, Jupiter his liver, and Mars his gall.

On one occasion, preceding a series of lectures at Basel, Paracelsus publicly burned the works of Galen and Avicenna, thereby showing his contempt for past and contemporary medicine. Disease was caused by inharmony. Color and light were vital. He wrote: "Whatever tinges with a white color has the nature of life, and the properties and power of light, which produces life. Whatever, on the other hand, tinges with blackness, or produces black, has a nature in common with death, the properties of darkness, and forces productive of death."

Paracelsus relied upon invocations, the vibrations of music and color, divine elixirs, talismans and charms, herbs and the regulation of diet, and bleeding and purging. These cures of his were hailed as miraculous by his contemporaries, and his genius was known throughout Europe.

THE AGE OF ENLIGHTENMENT

Today many an occultist believes that Paracelsus is still the greatest healer of all times. However, his theories failed to have any lasting influence on the progress of medicine. After him came Vesalius the anatomist, Leeuwenhoek and his microscope, then

men like Pasteur and Koch. Disease was caused by the attack of
an army of microbes. To argue about the harmony of natural
and supernatural forces seemed childish in view of the evidence
of squirming germs. Man at last could foresee his mastery over
the forces that destroyed him. The power lay within his being
and not alone within the inscrutable cosmos.

CHAPTER 3

The Amulet Wearers

REGENERATE MAN, the demigod of the alchemists, is alluringly described in the Song of Solomon: "My beloved is white and ruddy, the chiefest among ten thousand. His head is as the most fine gold, his locks are bushy, and black as a raven. His eyes are as the eyes of doves by the rivers of waters, washed with milk, and fitly set. His cheeks are as a bed of spices, as sweet flowers: his lips like lilies, dropping sweet smelling myrrh. His hands are as gold rings set with beryl: his belly is as bright ivory overlaid with sapphires. His legs are as pillars of marble, set upon sockets of fine gold: his countenance is as Lebanon, excellent as the cedars. His mouth is most sweet: yea, he is altogether lovely. This is my beloved, and this is my friend, O daughters of Jerusalem."

An occult and mystical view of life is still cherished in modern times. Believers in astrology still look to the heavens for answers to human destiny. Although the traditions of Hippocrates and the clinicians dominated medicine after Paracelsus—and continue to do so—the mystics have also flourished.

PHLOGISTON AND ETHER

The chief purpose of this book is to present the story of color therapy as developed through research methods acknowledged and accepted by modern science. The occult aspects of color therapy will be encountered in dozens of books in any sizable library. In the main such works are disappointing, both because they are highly empirical in content and because they fail to show much consistency, one book to the next.

Perhaps it is easy to write a book on the efficacy of color if, for testimony, the writer deals with abstruse generalities. To review such literature is of little avail, for there is practically nothing to be found beyond things vague and esoteric.

However, the clinician is not to be championed beyond his due. The history of formal science also has had its false pretensions. A classical example is found in the term "phlogiston," which once was current in the scientific field. All substances that could be kindled by fire were said to contain phlogiston. If a substance burned readily, it contained much phlogiston; if not, phlogiston was missing. It was not until the work of Lavoisier in the latter part of the eighteenth century that the caloric theory of heat was evolved and phlogiston cast aside as being nothing more than an empty word.

Much today can likewise be said about ether, the "substance" through which light is supposed to travel. Although science assumes the existence of the ether, men have failed to detect it.

Sir James Jeans, himself an eminent physicist, has remarked that, "The ethers and their undulations are in all probability fictitious." Writing almost like an alchemist, he added, "We must always remember that the existence of the ether is only an hypothesis, introduced into science by physicists who, taking it for granted that everything must admit of a mechanical explanation, argued that there must be a mechanical medium to transmit waves of light, and all other electrical and magnetic phenomena."

THE DEVOTIONALISTS

The mystical aspects of color, however, make for interesting reading. Thus in this and the remaining chapters of this section the reader will find a review of superstitions and practices that lie quite outside the realm of recognized medical science. The rest of the book, however, will be found devoted to clinical and research studies and to evidence which has behind it the weight of controlled investigation and measurable result.

The ancient had an insatiable desire to peer into the future. He was forever in terror of death. He was convinced that just as there were divine gods to reward him for virtue, there were evil gods and demons to curse and destroy him. To win the favor of just gods the ancient gave himself to good works.

One of the most primitive fears of men was of the evil eye. One glimpse of it and a man was likely to be cursed with misfortune, insanity, or disease. The evil eye was the fabulous witch that went about wrecking the life, love, labor, and sanity of men.

Some primitives wore round blue disks strung together with beads and painted with the symbol of an eye. In Persia a bit of turquoise was placed in the eye of a sacrificial lamb, the animal roasted, and the stone then put in an amulet case and sewn into a child's headdress.

Pliny states that the magicians once protected themselves with jet. In India the Hindu mother put daubs of black on the nose and forehead or on the eyelids of her babe. She also tied a piece of white or blue cloth to her dress. In Jerusalem the "hand of might," almost always blue, was worn as a bracelet. In Scotland the newborn was made safe from the evil eye by a piece of red ribbon tied about its neck. In parts of England a ring or amulet of red chalcedony was worn. In Italy a piece of coral held the needed power.

AMULETS AND CHARMS

Color was important to magic. First of all, the formulas of the magician were usually written in red ink. This is true of the rites and ceremonies found in the famous Egyptian *Book of the Dead.* Color had potent force in the resistance of evil and the overthrow of demons. And where it was a natural product of nature, permanently resisting fading, as in precious and semiprecious stones, its power was thought to be supreme.

From Egyptian and Babylonian inscriptions it is known that amulets of certain gems and hues were worn to bless their wearers with the favor of the gods and to bring them into daily contact with divine beings. Some of these stones had curious markings like veins. Others resembled eyes. They were to be worn next the scalp or forehead, against the ear, heart, genital organs, wrist, spine. Some were to be fastened to poles in the field, attached to the horns of cattle, tied to the beds of the sick. Color was to bring success in commerce, to prevent disease, to afford safety from shipwreck, lightning, the attack of animals, to assure abundant harvests and favorable control of the elements.

One is reminded that the ancients revered color for its divine significance and not because it was "pretty" as a decoration or ornament. Rings, necklaces, and bracelets held meaning. Budge in his *Amulets and Superstitions* writes, "In the bazaars of Cairo and Tanttah large blue-glazed pottery beads, fully half an inch in diameter, used to be sold to caravan men, who made bandlets of them and tied them to the foreheads of their camels before they set out on their journeys across the desert. The natives believed that the baleful glances of the evil eye would be attracted to the beads, and averted from the animals. . . . It is tolerably certain that the brass bosses and ornaments which decorate the harness of cart horses and shire-stallions were, like the great brass horns which rise from their collars, originally intended to protect the animal from the evil eye; but this fact has been forgotten, and amulets have degenerated into mere ornaments."

In the fashioning of amulets the preferred colors were red, blue, yellow, green, and white. Red stones were efficacious in the treatment of disease and in protecting their wearers from fire and lightning. Blue and violet stones were associated with virtue and faith. They were hung about the necks of children not only to assure the watchfulness of heaven but to make the youngsters obedient to their parents. Yellow stones brought happiness and prosperity. Green stones caused fertility in man and beast and had mysterious connection with vegetation, rain, and strength generally. White stones averted the evil eye and, because they were thought to come from heaven, carried with them the protection of heaven.

THE EFFICACY OF GEMS

Because disease came mysteriously out of nature, the most potent hues to combat it must also come out of nature. Thus precious and semiprecious stones were considered particularly therapeutic.

Brown agate drove away fevers, epilepsy, madness. It stopped the flow of rheum in the eye, reduced menstruation, dispersed the water of dropsy.

Amber was mixed with honey for earache or failure of sight. Amber dust relieved pains in the stomach and helped the kidneys, liver, and intestines. The smell of burnt amber aided women in labor. An amber ball, held in the palm of the hand, reduced fever and even kept a man cool on the hottest of days. Amber beads preserved the wearer from rheumatism, toothache, headache, rickets, jaundice. A bit placed in the nose stopped bleeding. About the neck it made the largest goiter disappear. The Arab physician used powdered amber to prevent miscarriage, to overcome boils, carbuncles, ulcers.

Amethyst was used to cure the gout. Placed under the pillow, it supposedly gave the sleeper pleasant dreams.

Asphalt, or bitumen, supposedly preserved a man from sprains, fracture of the bones, blows, headache, epilepsy, dizziness, palpitation of the heart.

Green beryl, through sympathetic magic, overcame diseases of the eye. Yellowish beryl was prescribed for jaundice and a bad liver.

Carnelian, the "blood stone," was thought to restrain hemorrhage and remove blotches, pimples, and sores from the flesh.

The cat's-eye, according to Budge, was washed in milk and the liquid drunk by a husband. Should his wife commit adultery after his departure, no child would be born of the illicit union.

Chalcedony lowered fever and eased the passage of gallstones.

Crystal in powder form was a cure for swellings of the glands, diseased eyes, heart disease, fever, intestinal pains. Mixed with honey it increased the milk of a mother.

Coral was presumed to overcome sterility.

The diamond fortified mind and body. It was said to cure practically everything. Dipped in water and wine, it created an elixir that reduced gout, jaundice, and apoplexy.

The emerald was prescribed for diseases of the eyes.

The garnet was worn to relieve skin eruptions.

Hematite cleared bloodshot eyes, stopped hemorrhages of the lungs and uterus, prevented sunstroke and headaches.

Jade assisted in childbirth. It cured dropsy, quenched the thirst, relieved palpitation of the heart.

Jasper was helpful in pregnancy.

Jet healed epilepsy, toothache, headache, glandular swellings.

Lapis lazuli was believed to prevent miscarriage.

Opal cured diseases of the eye.

Peridot was a palliative for various diseases of the liver.

The ruby was dipped in water for a stomachic and ground into powder to check the flux of blood.

Sapphire was used to thwart disease and plague.

Turquoise protected its wearer from poison, the bites of reptiles, diseases of the eyes. Dipped or washed in water it supposedly charged the liquid and made it a palliative for those who suffered from the retention of urine.

These superstitions have not entirely disappeared. Robert Branson, United Press correspondent, has reported the present-day use of jewels and precious metals in the Unani Hospital of Hyderabad City, India (*New York World-Telegram*, September 28, 1948). Medicines are mixed in a huge "pharmacy" and include such prescriptions as crushed gold and pearls as a general tonic as well as for rheumatism, bronchitis, epilepsy; emeralds for diabetes; rubies for the heart and brain; dried lizards for anemia; rose water for bowel diseases. Dr. Falurrahman Kahn of the hospital stated to the correspondent: "We make use of medical secrets that have been proved successful by the ages. Our theories are the siftings of Mogul, Persian, Greek, Roman, Egyptian, Hindu and Arab medical knowledge. We ourselves cannot always explain why our medicines work. But they have been working for centuries."

According to Branson, the Unani Hospital is by no means a medieval or ancient den of magic. "In many ways, Unani resembles the most modern hospital. Its wards are spacious and well ventilated. The nurses wear crisp white uniforms. Everything is spotlessly clean."

PLANTS AND HERBS

In old Teutonic magic one reads, "Then took Wodan nine magic twigs, smote then that serpent that in nine bits she blew apart. Now these nine herbs avail against nine spirits of evil, against nine venoms and against nine winged onsets."

Plants and herbs were also among the earliest of remedies. Many of these brought actual physical benefit and were perhaps discovered through trial and error. Yet in many instances the magic was based on weird associations alone. Almost any substance might be used—fungus from a grave, dew from grass, noxious concoctions that were often fantastic. Again, the healer would associate the form of a plant with the affliction itself. The juices of fern and moss were good for the hair. The palma Christi, shaped like a hand, cured the hand. Another plant, tooth-shaped, relieved the ache of a tooth. The onion, with its rings and layers, was said to possess healing virtues because it was supposed to be designed like the world itself. The strong odor of garlic was thought to exude powers that chased away illness. There were special stones that drove men mad, stopped the barking of dogs, expelled demons or turned black in the hands of false witnesses.

34

Most of the symbolism of color in healing was quite direct. Colors were associated with disease because disease produced color. Plants, flowers, minerals, elixirs were presumably efficacious when· their hues resembled the pallor of the flesh or the sores upon it. Thus red, yellow, and black had great medicinal value, for they were identified respectively with fever, plague, and death.

THE SYMBOLISM OF RED

Red is the most interesting of all colors in magic healing. It is found not only in the lore of ancient medicine but in the superstitions of modern times. Scarlet cloth has for many centuries been used to stop bleeding. Avicenna in the eleventh century dressed and covered his patients with red. The physician to Edward II, to thwart smallpox, directed that everything about the room be red. Francis I was treated in a scarlet blanket for the same affliction. The children of one of the Mikados were surrounded by red in all furnishings during an attack of the disease.

At times the physician would go to the extremes of prescribing red medicines and foods so that everything the patient ate or saw was crimson. The custom was so persistent that English physicians once wore scarlet cloaks as a distinguishing mark of their profession. In the rural districts of Massachusetts a red flag was once displayed to call the doctor as he made his rounds.

In Ireland and Russia red flannel was a remedy for scarlet fever. Red wool was applied to relieve sprains in Scotland, sore throat in Ireland, and to prevent fevers in Macedonia. Red thread was thought necessary in the teething of English children. The breath of a red ox was relied upon as a palliative in convulsions. Red sealing wax held strange powers in certain eruptions. Red coral kept teeth from loosening in England and relieved head troubles in Portugal. Red overcame nightmares in Japan. In Macedonia red yarn was tied on the bedroom door after the birth of a child to bind evil.

In China the ruby was worn to promote long life. A ribbon of red cloth was tied to the pigtail of the child for the same reason. The garnet in India and Persia similarly protected its wearers. Roman coral and red carnelian drove away the evils of disease.

Budge has written of these red amulets which were common also in Egypt centuries ago: "A considerable number of rings made of red jasper, red faïence, and red glass have been found in the tombs of Egypt; all are uninscribed and all have a gap in them. How and why they were used is not known, but a recent view about them is that they were worn as amulets by soldiers and by men whose work or duties brought them into conflict with their enemies, to prevent them from being wounded, or if wounded, to stop the flow of blood. It is possible that they were worn by women to prevent bleeding."

OTHER COLORS

Yellow cured jaundice because jaundice was yellow. In Germany the disease was attacked with yellow turnips, gold coins, saffron, and a dozen other yellowish things. Yellow spiders rolled in butter were English remedies. In one part of Russia gold beads were worn. In another section the patient gazed at a black surface, this being the presumed opposite of yellow and therefore capable of drawing the jaundice from the system. In India jaundice was banished to yellow bodies, creatures, and things such as the sun, where it properly belonged. The red, vigorous color of health was then "drawn" from a bull after certain recitations by a priest.

In Greece an affliction called "gold disease" was treated by having the patient drink wine in which a gold piece had been placed and exposed to the stars for three nights. Bits of gold were also sprinkled on food as a safeguard against poisoning. In one of the Malay states disease and plague were driven away in a yellow ship—or a buffalo covered with red pigment lumbered out of the village with the scourge upon him.

Among the ancient Greeks it was believed that the eggs of a raven would restore blackness to the hair. So effective was the remedy thought to be that the Greek kept his mouth filled with oil while the egg was rubbed into his hair in order to keep his teeth from turning black. Black threads from the wool of black sheep cured earache in Ireland, England, and parts of Vermont. Black snails were rubbed on warts.

In France the skins of black animals, applied while warm to the limbs of the body, relieved rheumatism. To the superstitious, a black fowl, if buried where caught, would cure epilepsy. The blood of a black cat has been prescribed for pneumonia in places as remote from each other as England and South Africa.

Plutarch mentioned that a white reed found on the banks of a river while one journeyed to sacrifice at dawn, if strewn in a wife's bedroom, drove an adulterer mad and forced him to confess his unspeakable sin.

Few other colors are found in charms meant to cure disease. Blue and green have been used mostly as preventives, to ward off the evil eye, and to spare the wearer from the visitation of demons. However, in Ireland blue ribbon was used for the croup, and indigestion was relieved when a person measured his waist with a green thread in the name of the Trinity and then ate three dandelion leaves on a piece of bread and butter for three consecutive mornings.

Among the Indians of America color was an intimate part of religion. Like the races of Africa, Europe, and Asia the primitive American had a hue for the universal deity. The Mexicans, for example, gave the name Kan to a god who supported the sky. The word itself meant yellow. One easily comprehends the symbolism of the Indian's pipe, or calumet. The smoke of fire reached to the sky and was seen by the gods. And even the gods smoked, for they built fires of petrified wood, used a comet for a flame, and blew clouds into the wind to be seen by man. The calumet was the Indian's altar, its smoke a proper offering. And he almost invariably sought a red stone from which to make it. For the sun god was red, the underworld god black, and the fire god varicolored.

When human sacrifice was practiced among the Aztecs, on the eve of the yearly festival (in July), a young woman portraying the goddess of the young maize was adorned with the upper part of her face red and the lower part yellow. Her legs and arms were covered with red feathers. Her shoes were striped with red. She it was who died for the gods on the summit of the temple, her head chopped off and her heart torn from her breast.

In Haran, the priest, clothed in red and smeared with blood, offered a red-haired, red-cheeked youth in sacrifice within a temple painted red and draped with red hangings.

How vital to rule nature and control the elements! In Egypt redheaded youths and red oxen were sacrificed to the gods to assure an abundant harvest. The Bavarian sower wore a gold ring to endow his grain with a rich color. In Ireland the storm was quelled by burning the pelt of a black dog and scattering the ashes down the wind. In provinces of Central India a twin saved the crops from the ravages of rain or hail by standing in the direction of the wind with his right buttock painted black and his left buttock of some other hue. The sacrifice of black animals, like the black cloud, drew water from the sky. White beasts brought forth the sun.

In Scotland, Hungary, Portugal, Norway, Denmark, Germany, red strings and bits of cloth were tied to animals to protect them from death. In Afghanistan, Syria, and Macedonia, blue performed the same magic.

There were also good-luck tokens to bless the households of mankind. The Syrians used special red designs. The red hand in Ireland, India, Constantinople, and Mexico shielded the family from harm. In Jerusalem a blue hand was painted on the doors or walls of dwellings.

Many of these superstitions linger to this day and no doubt follow traditions that date back many centuries. And just as color brought security to man so also did it warn him of impending tragedy. In Spain the black insect was portentous, the black cat and white insect omens of good fortune. In parts of Castile and Galicia the white moth was a harbinger of death.

Cats—the Japanese dreaded red or pinkish brown most of all. The all-black cat had divine powers, one of which was to foretell the weather.

How to explain these curious beliefs? Even today it is said that Yorkshire fishermen dread white, while their Northumberland neighbors only fifty miles distant fear black. In America the black cat is generally accused of bringing bad luck. Yet it is supposed to assure the success of a new theatrical production. Yellow, however, is treacherous in the theater and must not appear on posters, trunk labels, or even in a clarinet in the orchestra pit; it may cancel the good token of the black cat.

Magic, sorcery, and divination survive today in the abstruse mysticism of the fortuneteller, crystal-gazer, and spiritualist. Much but not all of the significance of color has been left at the waysides of the years. Once a divine art, the invocation of the supernatural degenerated into what has been called "black art." Christianity disdained the amulet and the esoteric rite. Those who were drawn to it were said to be creatures of the devil.

Superstition and sentimentality often stride along hand in hand. Strange and enticing voices seem to whisper to many human beings that elixirs of life do exist. Patent medicines, special mineral waters, powders and pills, still are stocked on drugstore shelves and still are foisted upon the public over the radio. Ill health and ill luck often beget faith in things obviously spurious. Man continues to be a mystic at heart.

Perhaps it is not always easy to decide where right and wrong differ, where the art of healing is and should be factual and where it may be fanciful. To say, for example, that acts of prayer cannot cure a broken leg may leave a salient point overlooked. People with troubled minds frequently are prone to accidents and frequently break their bones. If faith cannot cure an actual broken leg, surely it may be presumed that faith can lead to peace of mind and to the prevention of accidents in mentally disturbed and upset persons.

CHAPTER 4

The Aural Healers

To CONTINUE THE story of the mystics, just as charms and amulets were often thought to hold magical properties, so too was the being of man frequently likened to a celestial body. The microcosm of man emitted light as did the sun, the planets, and the stars. This conception usually referred to a supreme deity whose rays gave life and spirit to human beings. The halos, robes, insignia, jewels, and ornaments used by mortals on their own persons and on the effigies of their gods symbolized the spiritual energies that radiated from the body. The elaborate headdress of the Egyptian and the nimbus of the Christian saint represented the auric bodies of the elect. These streams were supposed to pour from the surface of the flesh, and their colors were a gauge of cultural development, spiritual perfection, and physical health. Artists of all ages have tried to express this divine luminosity of gods and demigods.

ASTRAL LIGHT

To the mystic all plants and animals emitted an aura. In man the aura was as much a part of his entity as his body. Celebrated men like Benvenuto Cellini had noted it. "Ever since the time of my strange vision until now an aureole of glory (marvelous to relate) has rested on my head. This is visible to every sort of men to whom I have chosen to point it out; but there have been very few. This halo can be observed above my shadow in the morning from the rising of the sun for about two hours, and far better when the grass is drenched with dew."

Just as the brain was said by the occultist to be the central organ for the circulation of nerve fluid, and as the heart was the central organ for the circulation of the blood, the spleen was the organ from which the astral elements drew their vitality. The emanations, in consequence, were affected by the physical, emotional, and spiritual state of the body. Colors differed as individuals differed and also as the mood and thought of any one person underwent change. Hartmann writes: "The quality of psychic emanations depends on the state of activity of the center from which they originate, for each thing and each being is tinctured with that particular principle which exists at the invisible center, and from this center receives the form of its own character or attributes."

This may be rather involved and may stretch human credulity to ridiculous limits. Yet the mystic insisted that the true character of men was shown in their auras. In persons of low nature the predominating color was said to be dark red. In persons of high nature the hues were white and blue, gold and green, in various tints. Red indicated strong desire. Blue indicated love. Green indicated benevolence.

Panchadasi writes: "The human aura may be described as a fine, ethereal radiation or emanation surrounding each and every human being. It extends from two to three feet, in all directions from the body." It may be likened to the rising of heat from a stove. The colors of the aura are said to be best seen by those having psychic insight. They fluctuate and change. They may be tranquil like water or impulsive like flames. They will reveal peace of heart and flash deep rays of anger and hatred. All this, of course, is visible only under special conditions and then only to very special persons.

In form, some of the hues are soft and misty. Others shoot out in straight lines. Still others unfold like coils. C. W. Leadbeater in his *Man, Visible and Invisible* describes the significance of these emanations:

Black clouds indicate hatred and malice.

Deep flashes of red on a black ground show anger. A sanguine red exposes an unmistakable sensuality.

A dull brown means avarice. A grayish brown means selfishness. A greenish brown means jeolousy.

Gray is to be associated with depression and fear.

Crimson shows a loving nature.

Orange reveals pride and ambition.

Yellow emanates from the aura of the intellectual person.

A grayish green signifies deceit and cunning. An emerald green shows versatility and ingenuity. A pale, delicate green means sympathy and compassion.

Dark blue shines forth from the person having great religious feeling. Light blue indicates devotion to noble ideals.

Thus the character of human beings reads like a neon sign for the elect. The aura of the savage is said to be dull yellow over his head and shows rays of grayish blue, dull orange and the brownish red of sensuality. All the colors are irregular in outline. The average person emits hues of a higher octave, more yellow, pure red, and clear blue. In anger black swirls and flashes of red are seen. In fear there is a livid gray mist. In devotion the colors are bluish.

Floating specks of scarlet issue from the irritable man. The miser is exposed by deep brownish bars of light. The depressed soul sends forth dull gray rays. The devotional type has an aura greatly developed in blue.

Finally, the aura of the superman is filled with iridescent hues: "All the colors of an Egyptian sunset and the softness of an English sky at eventide." There is a yellow nimbus about his head which shines like the rays of the sun.

THE ASTRAL WORLD

Some occultists tell of an astral world where spiritual culture reigns supreme. It is inhabited by the nature spirits of Paracelsus, the undines (water spirits), the sylphs (air spirits), the gnomes (earth spirits), and the salamanders (fire spirits). Fortunately or unfortunately they seldom choose to visit the mortal haunts of men. Leadbeater says, "Under ordinary conditions they are not visible to physical sight at all, but they have the power of making themselves so by materialization when they wish to be seen."

The astral world itself, which is likened to the celestial realms of the Atlanteans, Greeks, and Christians, is indeed beautiful to behold in fancy. Hartmann says, "Wherever a man's consciousness is, there is the man himself, no matter whether his physical body is there or not." In Panchadasi's book this world is described as having seven planes graded according to degrees of

44

vibration. These planes are to be attained by those having an astral sense. Hartmann declares, "He who can see the images existing in the Astral Light can read the history of all past events and prophesy the future!" For here he reaches the true Golden Age that has been the dream of mystics since the beginning of time. Nirvana has been revealed.

THE MODERN VIEWPOINT

Admittedly the astral side of color therapy is the most fantastic and therefore the most dubitable. The glorious sight of rainbow hues emanating from the bodies of men is almost too much to expect. In truth, because the occultists differ so much among themselves as to what is seen in the human aura, one has good reason to believe that the best of them see very little.

Yet despite aural healers and their ilk, one is not to doubt the efficacy of psychic forces. The will to live is in itself an aid to good physical well being. The close relationship existing between mental troubles and organic troubles is well known in the medical profession. In the study of amulets and charms, aural healing and the like, one suspects that optimism and exuberance, not color, have been the "good fairy" at work. Even in this century and decade, doctors and scientists of fair reputation have willingly taken the witness stand to attest to "faith cures."

After all, the human body does have an aura—whether or not such an aura signifies a man's sickness or health, and whether or not it has any remote relation to healing. The human aura not only may be sensed as heat or odor, but under proper conditions it may be seen. Sir Oliver Lodge, who had a definite belief in the psychic, wrote, "All evidence tends to convince me that we have an Etheric body as well as a physical body . . . it is the organized entity that builds up the body."

45

Paracelsus credited the body with having two substances, invisible and visible. The latter substance, the etheric shadow, was said to be beyond disintegration. Derangements of it produced disease. He therefore sought to reharmonize the substance by bringing it in contact with healthy bodies whose vital energy might supply the elements needed to overthrow the affliction.

The auric healer of the occult school works in three ways, by thought transference, by influencing the aura of the patient, and by encouraging the right emanations. In short, he attempts to set up vibrations in the mind of his patient through concentration; his thought on certain hues will (so he hopes) build up his own aura and thence act directly on the aura of his patient; and this in turn will arouse corresponding vibrations in the mind of the patient—and thereupon effect the cure.

This auric healing is mental and spiritual rather than physical. No colored lights or colored mediums are employed. The whole process is a psychic one and, like most things psychic, is not very defensible to those of rational and skeptical mind.

For the nervous system, the auric colors used in mental concentration are violet and lavender for a soothing effect, grass greens for an invigorating effect, and medium yellows and oranges for an inspiring effect.

For the blood and organs of the body, clear dark blues are soothing, grass greens are invigorating, and bright reds are stimulating. Blue is the hue to invoke in cases of fever, high blood pressure, or hysteria. Red is the hue in cases of chill or lack of sufficient bodily warmth.

Panchadasi writes: "A nervous, unstrung patient may be

treated by bathing him mentally in a flood of violet or lavender auric color; while a tired, used up, fatigued person may be invigorated by flooding him with bright reds, followed by bright, rich yellows, finishing the treatment with a steady flow of warm orange color."

The concluding vibration will then be the Great White Light. "This will leave the patient in an inspired, exalted, illuminated state of mind and soul, which will be of great benefit to him, and will also have the effect of reinvigorating the healer by cosmic energy."

And lest the skeptical physician frown haughtily upon the therapy of auric healing, one stout champion utters this warning: "The purblind atheist scientists who practice vivisection, the injection of disgusting lymph and other abominable iniquities in the vain hope of annihilating disease by propagating it, must, sooner or later, be brought to see the error of their ways."

BORDERLINE SCIENCE

There have been a number of devout investigators of aural phenomena who have been satisfied to report less spectacular sights and to refrain from losing themselves too much in the vagaries of imagination. All admit that simple colors are visible to the eye. If a full array of hues, rivaling the sunset or the rainbow, is to be seen, one must indeed be psychic and a prodigy among men.

One book, *The Story of the Human Aura,* written by George Starr White, takes a fairly middle course between the eloquent viewpoint of the mystic and the modest viewpoint of the more liberal-minded scientist. White declares that a magnetic atmosphere surrounds animals and plants. These emanations differ and are subject to change. Accepting them, one may account for the mysteries of thought transference, the weird prescience of strange happenings that often strike a person. He states that health and disease make themselves evident in the aura. And the rays change in appearance when a person is turned toward different points of the compass. "No matter what form life or vital force may take, no matter what vehicle life is carried in—be it animate or inanimate—its magnetic atmosphere must be characteristic of the vehicle."

White's viewpoint has not been very well received by the medical profession. He concludes that the magnetic emanations from the forefinger of the left hand and the thumb of the right hand are positive, and that the emanations from the forefinger of the right hand and the thumb of the left hand are negative. He describes an auric cabinet to study the phenomenon. The color of the average aura is grayish blue.

THE WORK OF KILNER

An even more restrained attitude, however, is to be found in Walter J. Kilner's book, *The Human Atmosphere*. Kilner very deliberately shunned the mystic aspects of auric light and made his investigation with all the sedulity of an enthusiastic laboratory worker. His conclusions: surrounding the human body is a visible envelope having three definite parts. First is a narrow dark band, a quarter of an inch wide, which is adjacent to the skin. Beyond this, and projecting from two to four inches outward, is a second aura. This is the clearest of all. And beyond this is a third aura, misty in aspect and without sharp outline on its farther edge. This is generally about six inches across.

Normally the radiations shoot out at right angles from the body. These rays are electric in appearance and have a fugitive quality shifting and changing. Longer rays project from the fingers, the elbows, the knees, the hips, the breasts. The color of health is a bluish gray, according to Kilner, and tinged with yellow and red. A grayer and duller color is typical to a diseased body. Kilner, however, preferred to base his diagnoses on the shape of the aura rather than on its chromatic qualities.

THE WORK OF BAGNALL

Kilner's work has been extended by Oscar Bagnall. In *The Origin and Properties of the Human Aura* a number of engaging theories are set forth, and also a detailed explanation as to the procedure to follow in making the aura visible. Some may observe it merely by gazing at a person in a dimly illuminated room. Bagnall, however, following the example of Kilner, makes use of a special screen.

He divides the aura into two parts, an inner and an outer. The inner aura, about three inches across, is marked by a clear brightness and rays that shoot out in straight lines. This aura is approximately the same in all persons. It may also be supplemented by special bundles of rays emanating from various parts of the body and not necessarily being parallel to the other rays.

The outer aura, according to Bagnall, is more filmy, enlarges with age, and generally has greater dimension in women than in men. Its average width is about six inches. Color is best seen here—bluish or grayish. The bluer the hue, the finer the intellect. The grayer the tone, the duller the intellect. The aura of a Negro is likely to be brownish and coarse in texture. The aura of a newborn baby is slightly greenish. A rather clear blue is a good token of intelligence. Bagnall, after some investigation, believes that this bluish color is as innate to an individual as any other inherited quality—and that it will follow the laws of heredity. The outer aura is subject to radical change brought about by mood or disease. Bagnall declares that no aura shines from any dead thing.

In studying the aura, the eye is first sensitized by gazing at the sky through a special dicyanin (blue) filter. The observer then sits with his back to the window. A feeble illumination is permitted to enter the room. The patient, naked, stands before a neutral screen.

To Bagnall auric light is ultraviolet and has definite wave lengths that lie beyond the visible spectrum (in the region extending from 400 millimicrons to about 310). And because blue and violet rays are seen better by the rods of the eye than by the cones, the blue filter tends to eliminate the longer red and orange rays of light and to emphasize the violet. Sensitizing of the eye can also be achieved by first gazing at areas of yellow paper which fatigue the retinal nerves to red and green and at the same time bring out a stronger response to blue.

In a rather fetching theory Bagnall credits nocturnal birds and animals with ultraviolet vision. Rod vision, so prevalent in animals, may add dimension to the sense of sight in many creatures, enabling them to see emanations which to the human eye are invisible. All this, of course, is largely a matter of conjecture and does not check very well with research to be described in later parts of this book. Indeed, the eyes of many birds are particularly sensitive to the *red* end of the spectrum!

But to return to mankind—organic diseases seem to affect the inner aura. The emanating rays may lose their sparkle and appear dull or limpid. Intellectual and nervous disorders, puberty, menstruation, seem to affect the outer aura. Bagnall says that the aura of a strong person will apparently flow into the aura of a weak person. While some therapeutic "healing" may be possible here, he does not venture to make any bold assertions.

In disease certain dark patches may appear. More telling, however, will be the general shape of the aura.

An aura that falls away suddenly in the neighborhood of the thigh may indicate that a person suffers from nervous complaint.

An outward bulge, away from the spine, is a typical sign of hysteria.

Neurotics usually have a poor outer aura and a dull inner aura.

Physical disturbances seem to affect brightness. Nervous conditions seem to affect the quality of hue.

Bagnall diagnoses pregnancy as follows: The aura becomes broader and deeper over the breasts. There is a widening of the haze in the area immediately below the navel. There is a slight decrease in the clearness of the bluish color, a phenomenon that changes as pregnancy advances.

He feels that medicine and surgery may some day be served through a further clinical study—and it seems likely that his plea will not go unattended. The body of man undoubtedly has an aura. Heat in itself is an emanation. Apparently these emanations have profound significance.

CHAPTER 5

The Eager Chromopaths

WITH THE ADVENT of modern surgery, the development of antiseptics, the findings of the microbe hunters, interest in the therapy of color lay dormant for many generations. Then in America in the latter part of the nineteenth century a resurrection occurred. Through the efforts of S. Pancoast and notably Edwin D. Babbitt the world again stormed the ethereal realm of light to find the universal panacea. All the mysterious fascination of alchemy, of the philosopher's stone, and the elixir of life, known to other generations, now charmed a more modern world. Color therapies and color practitioners sprang up everywhere. Medicine was clumsy and unwieldy. Its cures were too laborious and dull, particularly to the more credulous and superstitious of heart. In color there was not only romance but a divine unity and harmony that revealed great powers, beyond the ken of diligent but uninspired men.

In 1877 S. Pancoast published his *Blue and Red Light*. He turned abruptly from the rational teachings of the medical profession and hailed the wisdom of ancient philosophers and cabalistic literature. After writing vehemently on the secrets of mysticism he said, "Our reader has, we trust, learned to respect, as we do, the Ancient Sages, at whom modern Scientists, in their overweening self-esteem, their ignorant vainglory, are wont to scoff."

Pancoast believed that "White is the color of the quintessence of Light; toward its negative pole, White is condensed in Blue, and fixed in Black; toward its positive pole, White is condensed in Yellow, and fixed in Red. Blue invites to repose, or to slumber, Black is absolute rest, the sleep of death; Yellow is activity, Red is absolute motion, the motion of life; and White is the equilibration of motion, healthful activity." And again, "In Life-unfoldment, the progress is from Black to Red—Red is the Zenith of manhood's prime; in the decline of Life the course is from Red to Black; in both unfoldment and decline, White is traversed, the healthful, elastic period of first maturity and of the medium stage of old age."

Though his words were eloquent and his claims extraordinary, Pancoast worked in a rather simple way. Sunlight was made to pass through panes of red or blue glass—the two chief therapeutic agents. "To *accelerate* the Nervous System, in all cases of relaxation, the *red* ray must be used, and to *relax* the Nervous System, in all cases of excessively accelerated tension, the *blue* ray must be used." According to his own far from modest word

53

he effected a great number of miraculous cures and quoted numerous startling case histories.

THE WORK OF BABBITT

Edwin D. Babbitt was the curious combination of scientist, mystic, physician, artist, and essayist. His viewpoint was far more panoramic than Pancoast's. He had a cosmic interest in life and the world and confidently assumed an attitude that made him at once (in his own opinion) an initiate of the most complex mysteries of ancient philosophy as well as the intricacies of modern science. In his famous book, *The Principles of Light and Color,* published in a first edition in 1878 and a second edition in 1896 he won world-wide fame. His doctrines were translated into many languages. His theories founded cults that still survive to this day. He brought red, yellow, and blue window panes to Victorian homes. He dealt with the most treacherous afflictions. For many exciting years an anxious but fickle world paid homage to him as the miracle man of his day.

First of all, Babbitt was an enthusiast and quite entranced by hyperbole. He wrote: "Light reveals the glories of the external world and yet is the most glorious of them all. It gives beauty, reveals beauty and is itself most beautiful. It is the analyzer, the truth-teller and the exposer of sham, for it shows things as they are. Its infinite streams measure off the universe and flow into our telescopes from stars which are quintillions of miles distant. On the other hand it descends to objects inconceivably small, and reveals through the microscope objects fifty millions of times less [*sic*] than can be seen by the naked eye. Like all other fine forces, its movement is wonderfully soft, yet penetrating and powerful. Without its vivifying influence, vegetable, animal, and human life must immediately perish from the earth, and general ruin take place. We shall do well, then, to consider this potential and beautiful principle of light and its component colors, for the more deeply we penetrate into its inner laws, the more will it present itself as a marvelous storehouse of power to vitalize, heal, refine, and delight mankind."

Within light and color Babbitt saw unity. He developed an all-encompassing harmonic law and declared: "Unity exists in absolutely all unimpeded natural growth." Contrast was masculine; gradation was feminine. The unity of the two meant perfection.

The atom was the epitome of the universe; color was produced by its miraculous workings. Gold was yellow, for example, "because it has one spiral of the right grade to *repel* or *reflect* the yellow-forming ether, while it has other spirals which receive the other color ethers more or less within themselves and thus hide them." Like so many faddists, he resorted to effusion that ran roughshod over semantics.

THE THERAPEUTIC PRIMARIES

Babbitt chose three primaries. To him red was the center of heat, the ruling spectrum of hydrogen, a thermal or heat-producing color. Yellow was the center of luminosity. Blue was the center of electricity, the ruling spectrum of oxygen. In color therapy there must be unity and affinity. Thus any one hue had its complement—red with blue, red-orange with indigo-blue, orange with indigo, yellow-orange with violet-indigo, yellow with violet, yellow-green with dark violet. "Substances in which thermal colors predominate must affinitize with those in which the electrical colors rule."

He summed up his major doctrine by describing a strange "series of graduations in the peculiar potencies of colors, the center and climax of electrical action, which cools the nerves, being in violet; the climax of electrical action, which is soothing to the vascular system, being in blue; the climax of luminosity being in yellow; and the climax of thermism or heat being in red. This is not an imaginary division of qualities, but a real one, the flamelike red color having a principle of warmth in itself; the blue and violet, a principle of cold and electricity. Thus we have many styles of chromatic action, including progression of hues, of lights and shades, of fineness and coarseness, of electrical power, luminous power, thermal power, etc."

Pancoast's use of sunlight and a mere pane of glass was insufficient for the mighty Babbitt. Instead he developed and sold a special cabinet, the "Thermolume." This made use of natural sunlight. Then to be less dependent on nature, another cabinet of similar type was employed, this one getting its light source from the electric arc. He also employed a "Chromo Disk," a funnel-shaped affair which localized light and which could be fitted with special color filters. Blue light, for example, was localized on inflamed parts, wounds, and hemorrhages. Yellow light was localized on the brain, the liver, the abdomen.

BABBITT'S THEORIES

To take up babbitt's hues in order, here are their powers and some of the diseases and ills they were supposed to cure. Red stimulated and increased "the action of the warm red principle in the human system, as for instance, the *arterial blood,* and also acts as the harmonizing affinitive element of the cold blue principle, which causes blueness of veins, paleness of countenance, etc." Red was prescribed for paralysis, consumption of the third stage, physical exhaustion, and chronic rheumatism. Practically any cure could be effected.

Babbitt, like Avicenna, saw a relationship between color and the efficacy of a medicine. "Red light, like red drugs, is the warming element of sunlight, with an especially rousing effect upon the blood, and to some extent upon the nerves, especially as strained through some grades of red glass which will admit not only the red but the yellow rays, and thus prove valuable in paralysis and other dormant and chronic conditions."

Yellow and orange stimulated the nerves. "Yellow is the central principle of nerve stimulus as well as the exciting principle of the brain which is the foundation head of the nerves." It was a laxative, an emetic, and a purgative. It was used by Babbitt in costiveness, bronchial difficulties, and hemorrhoids. Yellow with considerable red was a diuretic. With a little red it was a cerebral stimulant. About half and half, it was a tonic and helped the human system in general.

Blue and violet had "cold, electrical and contracting potencies." The colors were soothing to all systems in which inflammatory and nervous conditions predominated—sciatica, hemorrhage of the lungs, cerebrospinal meningitis, neuralgic headache, nervousness, sunstroke, nervous irritability.

Blue and white were particularly effective in sciatica, rheumatism, nervous prostration, baldness, and concussion.

To review all this in grandiloquent style: "Substances combine in a harmonizing union with those substances whose colors form a chemical affinity with their own and thus keep up that law of equilibrium which is the safety of all things. This law having been so abundantly explained, it is obvious beyond all guesswork, that if the red arterial blood should become overactive and inflammatory, blue light or some other blue substance must be the balancing and harmonizing principle, while again, if the yellow and to some extent the red and orange principle of the nerves should become unduly excited, the violet and also the blue and indigo would be the soothing principles to have applied. This applies to the nerves of the cranium, stomach, bowels, and kidneys, as well as elsewhere, in which the heating and expansive action of these thermal principles may beget the condition of delirium, emesis, diarrhoea, diuresis, etc., that can be assuaged only by the cooling and contracting influence of substances possessing the electrical colors. Can this law, which thus stands out clearly and simply like a mathematical demonstration, be shown to have a basis in actual practice in harmony with the experience of the medical world for ages back?"

SOLAR DRUGS

Babbitt's spirit was perhaps too exuberant. One begins to squirm when he devotes considerable space to his elixirs—cerule, rubi, amber, purpur, verd, viole. Not only were the colored rays of the sun beneficial when showered upon the human body, but equal magic could be caught within a bottle of water! He developed a special "Chromo Lens" for this purpose. It was a glass flask, holding about 42 ounces and capable of being hung before a light source. He wrote, "In the course of thousands of experiments made by my students and myself with bottles and chromo lenses of different colors, it has been demonstrated that a new and remarkable healing power has been brought before the world." Here is one of his case histories: "Having been costive for a few days I held a small half-ounce amber colored vial of water close to a kerosene lamp for seven minutes, before retiring, and then drank it. In the morning I had two gentle passages without any pain, and for weeks experienced no return of costiveness. This is a good example to show the enduring character of the cures wrought by the finer elements."

Babbitt's contention was that these flasks of his retained the vital elements of light. With red, one caught iron, zinc, barium, and so on. With blue, one caught sulphur, copper, nickel, cobalt, cadmium, manganese. These metals and elements were of a special, high order. "The solar rays are never poison, but their drug forms often are."

BABBITT'S DISCIPLES

The work of Pancoast and Babbitt has been elaborated upon by disciples of this century (and bitterly attacked by such agencies as the American Medical Association). Medical science still looks skeptically at the rainbow and acknowledges potency in "light" only at those far regions of the electromagnetic spectrum which are invisible to the eye—the rays of infrared, ultraviolet, X rays, radium. The energy found here has an evident effect upon the human body. It will raise temperature, penetrate tissue, tan the skin, destroy bacteria and certain malignant growths. Colors like red, yellow, or blue are not so obvious in their action. Visible light, however, has a definite, physiological effect upon the human body, as will be described in later pages.

The "chromopath" is not discouraged. He frequently accepts his persecution with the ecstasy of a martyr. He looks upon color as a curative, because to his way of thinking disease involves bodily inharmony just as much as it involves microbes. J. Dodson Hessey, who is not without honor in his own country, England, writes, "The great importance of Color lies in the fact that it can influence all the different aspects of man—physical, emotional, mental and spiritual, and so help to produce that harmony which in itself implies perfect health."

Hessey reasons as follows: The human body is composed of cells. The basis of life is the atom. Within the atom are vibrating particles—negatively charged electrons circling around positively charged protons. Beyond this, color therapy postulates a rhythmic order of vibrations of several degrees, the lowest and coarsest being the physical, then the emotional, and then the mental. Health is harmony and disease is discord. Illness may arise in the physical, emotional, or mental sphere. "Is it too visionary to imagine a time when diseases will be classified by their wave length and the counteracting of them become a mathematical certainty?"

HESSEY'S THEORIES

Hessey believes in the efficacy of three main colors, blue, green, and orange, and five secondaries, yellow, rose, amethyst, red, and violet. The red end of the spectrum is inflammatory; the blue end is cooling. Working with equipment similar to Babbitt's, he relies upon a color "bath" and the mental cooperation of the patient. In short, while the light is being used, the patient remains passive and color is "forced into" him.

Blue, according to Hessey, contracts the arteries and raises the blood pressure. It is a blood tonic, an antiseptic and has a beneficial effect in skin diseases, rheumatism, and various forms of inflammation.

Green lowers the blood pressure. It affects the nervous system and is a sedative and hypnotic. It is useful in cases of nervous irritability, exhaustion, neuralgia, headaches, anxieties, neurotic fears, and shell shock.

Orange, the third main hue, is considered to be a stimulant and increases the blood pressure only slightly. It has an enlivening effect upon the emotions.

Yellow is a mental stimulant. In Hessey's opinion its primary effect is cheerful but it leads the patient into a state of somno-

60

lence. It may be used in cases of mental deficiency and tuberculosis.

Red is too strong; a soft rose is better and beneficial in cases of melancholia and general debility.

Amethyst (purple) combines the stimulating effect of red with the tonic effect of blue.

Violet acts specifically upon the heart, lungs, and blood vessels.

Like Babbitt and Avicenna, Hessey claims therapeutic benefits for the *color* of medicines such as iodine. He mentions the effect of color upon the glands of the human body: the activity of male sex glands is said to be increased by red, and female sex glands by violet. Blue has the best effect on the posterior pituitary gland. The thyroid is little affected except by yellow. All colors have a diminishing effect upon the pancreas. He refers to one investigator who claims that the visualization of red causes an increased respiratory effort in the upper part of the chest, while visualization of violet produces deep abdominal respiration. Most of the other hues are neutral in this particular regard.

THE PRESCRIPTION OF COLOR

C. G. Sander and others have studied human ailments and prescribed colors to cure them. Practically all these men, however, dwell on the wrong side of the tracks set up by the medical profession. Choleric and nervous people are supposed to need green or blue. Lymphatic and melancholy people need red, orange, or yellow. Consumptive and anemic people need red. Sanguine people need blue or green. Those of dark complexion, eyes, and hair frequently have poor circulation and need red. Fair persons often suffer from lethargy and pessimism and need the beneficial radiation of yellow.

The following ailments and prescriptions summarize the diagnostic views of many of today's chromopaths. They are presented to satisfy the curiosity of those readers who may wonder what rituals are followed in the use of color. However, to quote from the six-point type often printed on the labels of patent medicines, "Use at your own risk. If pains persist, call your doctor."

Neurosis

Neuralgia: Blue over the temples, face, ears, or where pain is felt.

Paralysis: Blue over the head. Yellow for the paralyzed part. Ruby over solar plexus. Yellow over spine.

Sciatica: Blue over back of leg or where pain is felt. Lumbar region of spine may be treated with a short exposure of yellow followed by blue.

Hysteria: Blue over head, solar plexus, and abdomen.

Convulsion: Blue over head and spine.

Apoplexy: Blue over forehead.

Neuritis: Blue locally and over spine.

Epilepsy: Blue over head, spine, and over the solar plexus.

Heart and Circulation

Red stimulates and blue soothes.

Palpitation: Short exposure of blue over heart, ruby over solar plexus.

Goiter: Red and yellow, except in inflamed condition; then blue is advised.

Rheumatism: Inflammatory stages need blue; otherwise yellow, red, and especially purple. Blue will alleviate pain. Yellow will stimulate the spinal nerves and bowels.

Arthritis: Short exposure of red, full exposure of blue.

Respiratory Organs

Tuberculosis: Yellow over chest, at times ruby. Cervix may be stimulated with ruby. "Violet light destroys the bacillus of tuberculosis."

Asthma: Short exposures of yellow and blue alternately over the throat and chest.

Bronchitis: Blue to allay inflammatory state. Short exposure of yellow. Ruby over cervix.

Pleurisy: Exposure to blue.

Nasal catarrh: Blue and yellow in order.

Diphtheria: Blue locally and over solar plexus. Cervix stimulated with yellow.

Whooping cough: Yellow and blue to be used alternately.

Digestive Organs

Gastritis, nausea, indigestion: Blue for inflamed condition. Ruby is good for the stomach. Green has a calmative action.

Sluggish liver: Ruby or yellow.

Diarrhea: Blue over abdomen.

Constipation: Yellow over colon and abdomen.

Kidney trouble: Nephritis is to be treated with blue.

Dormant kidneys: Yellow and red.

Inflammation of the bladder: Blue with short alternate exposure of yellow.

Skin Diseases

Eczema: Ruby or violet and blue—or blue alone.

Erysipelas: Ruby and blue alternately.

Scabies, ringworm: Violet and ruby to be superimposed.

Wounds, scalds, burns: Exposures to blue.

63

Fevers

Typhoid fever: Blue over head and abdomen. Yellow over intestines in cases of constipation.

Smallpox, scarlet fever, measles: Red and yellow, with blue alternately to reduce fever.

Malaria: Blue during feverish state, yellow and purple during chill. Blue always to be kept on the head.

Yellow fever: Blue over head and yellow over bowels to relieve constipation.

Eyes and Ears

Inflammation of eyes treated with blue. Cervix and cerebellum exposed to ruby.

Atrophied optic nerves stimulated by red or by blue and red superimposed.

Yellow helpful in cases of deafness, red to stimulate circulation, blue for any form of inflammation.

Cancer

Sander advises the use of green, alternately with violet and ruby. Blue is used to ease pain and distress.

C. E. Iredell prescribes green to begin and end the treatment. Royal blue is employed after green, then yellow, then violet and back to green. Orange and red are seldom used.

Other Ailments

Chromopaths see blue as a magic cure for burns, headache, fatigue.

Indigo is to be employed in cases of vomiting and toothache. Magenta is prescribed for masculine impotency and feminine

64

apathy. Violet is excellent in insomnia. Scarlet relieves melancholia. Orange is the right tonic for baldness and colic. Yellow is recommended for the weak memory. Lemon yellow relieves the pangs of heartburn.

PRELUDE TO MODERN THINKING

So much for the more turgid and esoteric aspects of color therapy. Thus far the reader has encountered notes on mysticism, the cosmic laws of the occultists, traditions established by the founders of medicine, superstitions regarding amulets, charms, the human aura, the theories of eager chromopaths.

That much supposition has attended the therapy of color is unfortunate, for many in the medical profession have been led to disdain the power of color altogether. There has been a general unwillingness on the part of conservative researchers to deal with phenomena which have been so ecstatically treated by others. Because of this, much that is of therapeutic value in color has been slighted or deliberately ignored.

All electromagnetic energy — including visible color — will affect the human organism. It is the purpose of the remaining sections and chapters of this book to discuss visible and invisible light, not in an obscure or mystical way, but from a more sober and objective viewpoint. The evidence to be presented has had its basis in well-organized research, in studies and investigations which should be acceptable because they have been ably and fairly conducted by men of recognized standing in the medical and scientific world.

Part 2

THE BIOLOGICAL ASPECTS

CHAPTER 6

Electromagnetic Energy

As discussed in the first chapters of this book, the ancients held strange views as to the nature of light and color. Aristotle, who had stated that "simple colors are the proper colors of the elements; *i.e.,* of fire, air, water, and earth," dominated human thinking for many centuries. Bruno, who visited Oxford in 1583, wrote: "Masters and Bachelors who did not follow Aristotle faithfully were liable to a fine of five shillings for each divergence." As late as the seventeenth century, men continued to look upon color as had the mighty Greek.

BOYLE AND NEWTON

The enlightenment took place in the seventeenth and eighteenth centuries. Descartes (1596–1650) spoke of the "plenum" and declared that light was essentially a pressure transmitted through a dense mass of invisible particles. The "diversities of color and light" were due to different ways in which the matter moved.

Robert Boyle (1627–1691) wrote, "I have not found that by any Mixture of White and True Black . . . there can be a Blew, a Yellow, or a Red, to name no other color."

Anticipating Newton, Boyle believed that all hues were contained in white light. It was Isaac Newton (1642–1727), however, who became the father of modern physics. His observations on the refraction of light through a prism in 1666 led to the formulation of a new doctrine: white light was not simple; it was a mixture of rays which the prism separated. He chose seven hues—red, orange, yellow, green, blue, indigo, and violet—and allied them to seven planets and the notes of the diatonic scale.

AFTER NEWTON

Being an atomist, Newton supposed that light was generated by particles which spun about and moved forward in a straight line. Though he was opposed in this contention by Robert Hooke (1635–1703), who championed a wave theory, science was faithful to Newton for a full century and a half.

The physical nature of electromagnetic energy, of light, has been ably discussed in many books. Yet a satisfactory answer to the phenomena is still to come. LeGrand H. Hardy writes, "A wave theory, an electrical theory of matter, or an atomic theory of energy can be made perfectly legitimate and defensible."

Through the efforts of such men as Planck, Bohr, and Einstein, however, scientists today are in pretty fair agreement. Radiant energy is said to be propagated through space in the form of electromagnetic waves. The visible portion of this energy is seen as light. A substance excited to luminosity radiates certain waves, depending on its composition. This collection of waves is characteristic of the substance and may be analyzed in a spectroscope. In addition, the waves that a substance radiates when excited will be identical with those it will absorb when radiant energy falls upon it.

Radiant energy, however, not only has a wave structure but a corpuscular structure as well. This means that radiant energy has tangible substance. It has mass and may be "bent," for example, by the force of gravity.

THE ELECTROMAGNETIC SPECTRUM

The complete spectrum of electromagnetic energy, to be described, contains sixty or seventy "octaves." It begins, at one end, with radio waves of exceedingly great wave lengths, proceeds through infrared rays, visible light, ultraviolet—the wave lengths getting shorter—and reaches its other extreme in X rays, gamma rays, and cosmic rays.

All this energy travels at the same rate of speed—about 186,000 miles a second—and differs in length of waves as measured from crest to crest. Though mathematics of a rather fabulous order may be involved, measurements of the speed of light, of frequencies and wave lengths, are extremely accurate and are accepted throughout the scientific world.

The following notes offer a quick review of the various forms of electromagnetic energy and are supplemented by a few facts on their medical applications.

Radio Rays

The longest of all electromagnetic waves are employed for "wireless," high power transoceanic communication, ship-to-shore calling, direction finding, and the like. Such waves may measure several thousand feet from crest to crest.

In the form of induction heat, long radio rays are employed in industry to raise the temperature of metals for hardening purposes in the period of a mere instant.

Commercial broadcasting rays fall next in order. Because they "bounce" back from the ionosphere of the sky they will travel completely around the earth.

Next is the so-called "short-wave band," used for certain distance broadcasting, for police, ship, amateur, and government.

Here also are the waves used in diathermy. By clamping electrodes to certain parts of the body, heat may be generated to relieve rheumatism, arthritis, neuralgia.

Next follow FM radio, television, radar, the wave lengths getting shorter and ranging from several meters to a fraction of a meter. This energy, however, penetrates the ionosphere and is not reflected back. It follows a straight path, requires rebroadcasting points, and may be sent out in controlled directions.

Infrared Rays

Next in order, long waves in the infrared region (invisible) have the power of penetrating distance and heavy atmosphere. Photographic plates sensitive to them are used to take pictures where the human eye has difficulty in seeing.

Radiant heat comes next as wave lengths shorten. Such energy is used for heating and drying purposes, and is emitted by steam radiators, electric heaters, and infrared lamps.

Visible Light

The sun's spectrum extends from relatively long waves of infrared light, through the entire gamut of visible light (red, orange, yellow, green, blue, violet), into the shorter waves of ultraviolet light. This energy, the chief concern of this book, will be given special attention in later chapters. Visible light rays measure about 1/33,000 inch at the red end of the visible spectrum and about 1/67,000 inch at the violet end.

Ultraviolet Radiation

The longer waves of ultraviolet produce fluorescence in many substances.

Next follow the erythemal rays. This is the energy which produces sun tan and which is employed for the synthetic production of vitamin D.

Still shorter ultraviolet energy has bactericidal properties. It is used to destroy certain microorganisms and for the sterilization of materials, water, air.

X Rays

On up the electromagnetic spectrum are the Grenz rays, or soft X rays, used therapeutically for many skin diseases. This energy does not have much power of penetration.

X rays of higher voltage and shorter frequency are used for diagnostic purposes and for certain forms of cancer.

Hard X rays, next in order, are used medically for deep-seated afflictions—as well as to take radiographic pictures to detect flaws in metal.

X-ray frequencies may measure 1/2,500,000 inch where high voltages are involved.

Gamma Rays and Cosmic Rays

Next follow the radium rays, discovered by Pierre and Marie Curie and given therapeutic application in the early part of the

73

twentieth century. They are used to cure many forms of cancer.

Toward the short-wave end of the electromagnetic spectrum are the emanations from nuclear fission associated with the atom bomb and the bombardment of the atom nucleus. Such energy is rapidly finding its way into medicine.

Lastly, and of highest wave lengths, are the cosmic rays. Still a mystery, they probably are produced beyond the earth's atmosphere and spread their waves throughout the universe.

THE EFFECTS OF INVISIBLE LIGHT

The laboratories of physicians and hospitals are well equipped with devices for the production of electromagnetic energy *of shorter and longer wave length than that of visible light.* Rays of color, however, red, yellow, blue, are seldom found. Yet visible light, as will be indicated in following chapters, is of vital significance in the growth and development of plants and animals. Friedrich Ellinger writes, "Knowledge of the significance of visible light as a healing agent is inversely proportional to the universal importance of visible light in biology." It would appear from this observation that inconsistencies exist in the study of color and that its value to human life has not been fairly evaluated by medical science.

Of waves longer than visible light (infrared), there is little to be told. Such energy obviously produces heat within the human body—as do the still longer radio rays of diathermy. Harold F. Blum in his remarkable book, *Photodynamic Action and Diseases Caused by Light,* remarks that "it cannot be assumed this part of the spectrum [infrared] is very active biologically."

However, the heating effect of invisible rays at the red end of the spectrum is known to everyone who has ever used a hot-water bottle.

74

Infrared rays are also thought to weaken the bactericidal action of ultraviolet rays. They also seem to destroy the antirachitic effect of vitamin D. While such "heat" rays may be generally beneficial, they represent a great hazard to the human eye. While ultraviolet waves are strongly absorbed by the eye media, infrared waves are not. The latter may be responsible for the development of cataracts. Ellinger writes, "On the basis of animal experiments, A. Vogt believes that cataracts in workers exposed to fire (welders, glass blowers, etc.) are due to the action of infrared rays."

HELIOTHERAPY

The energy most frequently and extensively used in medicine is that of shorter wave length than visible light: ultraviolet, X rays (Roentgen rays), and the gamma rays of radium. Yet not until the twentieth century did science build equipment capable of utilizing it therapeutically.

Heliotherapy is perhaps as old as civilization. In his excellent book, *The Biologic Fundamentals of Radiation Therapy,* Friedrich Ellinger writes, "Knowledge of the therapeutic action of light is one of mankind's oldest intellectual possessions. The earliest experiences depended of course upon nature's own light source, the sun. Sun-bathing was practiced even long ago by the Assyrians, Babylonians and Egyptians. A highly developed sun- and air-bathing cult existed in ancient Greece and Rome. The old Germans regarded the healing power of sunlight very highly and worshipped the rising sun as a deity. The Incas of South America also practiced a sun cult."

However, the sun worshipers, together with the alchemists and mysticists, lost prestige after the Middle Ages. Though there were a few obscure champions from time to time, it was not until the nineteenth century that heliotherapy was again recognized.

75

NIELS R. FINSEN

The pioneer of light research was Niels R. Finsen of Denmark. In his early years he held a strong interest in color and believed in the treatment of smallpox with visible red light to prevent scar formation. Later (1896) he wrote of the actinic properties of sunlight and founded a Light Institute for the cure of tuberculosis. He was awarded a Nobel prize in 1903 and later reported startling cures among some 2,000 patients using both sunlight and artificial ultraviolet light.

Credit is also due Downs and Blunt of England, who, in 1877, discovered the bactericidal action of ultraviolet radiation. This gave full evidence that sunburn was not produced by heat rays alone and that in waves of higher frequency than visible light, science had a great therapeutic medium.

PHOTOSENSITIVITY

The scientist associates photosensitivity with heliotherapy and both with the energy of sunlight which ranges from infrared through visible light to ultraviolet. On the other hand, radiosensitivity is the term associated with radiotherapy and is concerned with the high-frequency radiation of X rays and gamma or radium rays.

To deal with photosensitivity first, the human body is particularly responsive to ultraviolet light. Blonds, however, are more sensitive than brunets. Infants are not very sensitive. According to Ellinger, the influencing factors are the color of hair, age, sex, and season. In girls, photosensitivity increases during adolescence. "Endocrine influences play an important part and are probably bound up with the sex function," for with menopause photosensitivity tends to diminish.

There are two interesting observations to be noted regarding sunlight and human life. In India, rickets is a common affliction among higher caste Hindus, no doubt because the religious system requires mothers and children to dwell in complete indoor isolation. Hence, because the body is deprived of sunlight, it suffers from vitamin D deficiency. Among Eskimo women, menstruation may cease during the long Arctic night, and the libido of Eskimo men may also be dormant at that time. Here, in effect, lack of sunlight leads to nature's form of human hibernation.

EFFECTS OF ULTRAVIOLET LIGHT

Ultraviolet radiation is essential to human welfare. It prevents rickets, keeps the skin in a healthy condition, is responsible for the production of vitamin D, destroys germs, and effects certain necessary chemical changes in the body. It is used in the treatment of certain skin diseases, in erysipelas, and in skin tuberculosis.

It may be employed to irradiate foodstuffs such as lard, oil, and milk to form vitamin D. Curiously, however, cod-liver oil loses its better properties after irradiation. Although ordinary window glass and many materials will absorb it, ultraviolet light is effectively scattered by the atmosphere, and its benefits are found even in smoky cities.

After exposure to ultraviolet, human skin becomes pigmented. A tanned complexion is perhaps nature's method of building up protection, even though protection against ultraviolet is often achieved without pigmentation.

Yet a glowing tan is by no means a sign of vigorous health. Overexposure to sunlight may make the complexion wrinkled and old in time. More serious, Blum points out that prolonged exposure to sunlight "may stimulate the production of malignant tumors of the skin." Apparently the old adage of moderation in all things must include the beach and the sun deck.

FLUORESCENCE

In the phenomenon of fluorescence certain substances are made luminous by the action of ultraviolet light. This offers many aids to science and medicine. Foods may be examined and many facts known about them. Butter, for example, glows yellow, while margarine glows blue. As little as 15 per cent adulteration may be noted. Fungi in cheese fluoresce a brilliant green, natural ripening being detected from artificial. Healthy potatoes show color; those affected by ring rot do not. Fresh eggs fluoresce a pale red, while older eggs become more bluish.

The skin of Caucasians fluoresces more than the skin of Negroes. Live teeth glow; dead ones or artificial ones do not. The same test distinguishes between natural hair and dyed hair or wigs. Aspirin when taken orally will make the urine appear purplish; quinine will make the urine appear greenish. Tuberculosis germs in human sputum will fluoresce yellow.

A fluorescent dye injected into the blood stream has been used as an aid to surgery. Cancer tissue will glow a vivid yellow. In amputations, the blood stream will carry the dye to the infected area. By making an examination under ultraviolet light the surgeon can perform his work more accurately.

RADIOSENSITIVITY

The first cure by Roentgen rays (X rays) was effected by Tor Stenbeck of Sweden in 1900. This was the successful removal of a tumor from the tip of a woman's nose. Since then X-ray and radium therapy have been therapeutically applied throughout the world and have performed countless miracles.

78

It should be understood that radiotherapy cures because of certain reverse effects. In brief, the diseased tissue or cell is more easily destroyed than the healthy tissue. After the radiation has had its effect, breaking down the diseased area, the healthy, recuperative powers of the human body take over and restore things to normal.

The cell and cell nucleus are most sensitive. Again children and blonds are more readily affected than adults and brunets. A long list of afflictions responds to radiotherapy, from superficial eczema to deep-seated cancer of the inner organs, bones, and joints. Malignant tumors are particularly sensitive. As Ellinger states, "And so for many, the concept of radiotherapy is synonymous with the fight against cancer."

THE EFFECTS OF RADIOACTIVE ENERGY

The white corpuscles of the blood are radiosensitive; the red corpuscles are not. The muscles of the body, the brain, the eye are little affected. However, cartilage and bone, the stomach and liver, all respond actively to irradiation.

Overdoses of X rays or radium rays may cause serious damage. There may be a depressant or destructive result, depending on the health of the body and the sensitivity of its tissue and cells. This high-frequency energy may cause the hair to fall out; it may decrease the function of the sweat glands, produce inflammation and discoloration of the skin, cause sexual sterility.

Worst of all, it may lead to anemia and to the dreaded Roentgen carcinoma. Amputations may be necessary, although recurrences may develop; making death inevitable.

Equally macabre, misuse of irradiation in the first months of pregnancy may result in abortion. In later months it may produce monsters and imbeciles.

The hazards of high-frequency radiation are being brought to mind these days in discussions of the atom bomb. As yet science has no sure defense. Once spread, this energy has a deadly and lasting effect. Yet because this potential menace, like that of cancer, involves similar phenomena, one may hope that successful research will one day conquer both. The preservation of human life is among the highest of the arts. Man, who has generated the forces of electromagnetic energy, has now to control them to assure security and lengthen the days of his life.

CHAPTER 7

The Growth of Plants

SCIENCE GENERALLY RECOGNIZES
that visible light is essential to the growth of plants. Infrared
light has much the same action as darkness, is detrimental to
plant growth, and may inhibit the development of chlorophyll.
Ultraviolet light alone is harmful and will destroy the plant.

Although rays longer and shorter than visible light are found
in sunlight, it is apparent that nature has effected a practical balance and that visible light is the chief requirement for sound
growth and development. The philosopher has good cause to
note that men and plants have endured and survived under the
same conditions and in the same world. Why should visible light
be imperative to plants and of negative value to human beings?
And why should infrared and ultraviolet, both of which destroy

the plant, be declared therapeutic to human beings? It is the conviction of the writer that the benefits of visible light to human life are not properly understood and that time and research will eventually divulge them.

GENERAL A. J. PLEASANTON

One of the earliest investigators of the growth of plants under colored light was Tessier of France (1783). Working with colored screens, he noted marked differences for various hues. However, it was General A. J. Pleasanton of Philadelphia who, during the period between 1860 and 1870, expounded a series of startling theories that both inspired and enraged the botanists and horticulturists of his day.

Pleasanton in his book, *Blue and Sun-Lights,* declared that the blue sky held the secret to the bounty of life. Blue "for one of its functions, deoxygenates carbonic acid gas, supplying carbon to vegetation and sustaining both vegetable and animal life with its oxygen." He constructed a special greenhouse which had one pane of blue glass for every eight panes of clear. With grapes he claimed a growth of 45 feet (with 1-inch stems) for the first year, a crop of 1,200 pounds of grapes for the second, and 2 tons for the third. Grapevines not so treated under blue light required five or six years to be productive at all. His facts, however, must have been exaggerated.

The work of Pleasanton later fired Edwin D. Babbitt and did much to found the cult of the later chromopaths. From experiments with hogs and a bull calf, Pleasanton reported to the Philadelphia Society for Promoting Agriculture: "If by a combination of sunlight and blue light from the sky, you can mature quadrupeds in 12 months with no greater supply of food than would be used for an immature animal in the same period, you can scarcely

82

conceive of the immeasurable value of this discovery to an agricultural people!"

Pleasanton's rapture over blue light was not shared by other researchers who followed him. In 1895 C. Flammarion reported best effects for red light. He grew plants in hothouses under red, green, blue, and clear glass, attempting in a crude way to equalize light intensities. Red seemed to produce taller plants but with thinner leaves. Blue created weak, undeveloped plants.

In 1902 L. C. Corbett supplemented daylight with artificial green, blue, and red illumination in a greenhouse at night. He witnessed a markedly stimulating effect for red upon the growth of lettuce.

These biological effects of radiation became something of a "rage" at the turn of the century. Yet from the reports of numerous students it seems obvious that unusual results were brought about, not by any positive action of colored light, but rather by the negative effect of reduced light and lack of radiation.

Thus Fritz Schanz in 1918 conducted tests in which he withheld certain energy in the sun's spectrum. He attempted to prove that ultraviolet light checked plant growth. His plants, indeed, grew tallest when blue-violet energy was cut off. Schanz therefore concluded that light of short wave length was detrimental— yet he, too, did little to equalize intensities.

H. W. Popp in more recent times (1926) carefully worked with colored lights of approximately equal intensity. He grew plants in five small greenhouses, each covered with a special type of glass. His most startling effects occurred when short wave lengths were eliminated. Yet he also believed that a balance of light was best. "The results as a whole indicate that the blue-violet end of

83

the spectrum is necessary for normal, vigorous growth of plants. They also indicate that ultraviolet radiation is not necessary, although it may not be without influence."

MODERN CONCLUSIONS

A remarkably complete exposition on the influence of color will be found in a two-volume work edited by Benjamin M. Duggar, *Biological Effects of Radiation.* Length of exposure to light seems to be more significant to growth and development than light intensity. Complete darkness produces in a plant what is known as etiolation. The plant turns whitish or yellowish and has long internodes and undeveloped leaves. There is a lack of chlorophyll.

Just as too much exposure to intense light may be harmful to human beings, so also does it adversely affect the plant. Chlorophyll formation is usually greater when a plant is exposed to relatively low intensities for long periods than when it is exposed to high intensities for shorter periods. Hardy L. Shirley writes, "At low intensities the plant requires a very efficient photosynthetic apparatus. This is provided in large thin leaves, high in chlorophyll concentration and widely spaced on the stem. At high light intensities the plant with large thin leaves is at a disadvantage in meeting the excessive transpiration losses. In this case, the smaller, thicker, cutinized leaves are an advantage. Also a contraction in the volume occupied by the plant is advantageous." Shirley points out that, under high intensities, plant starch may rapidly accumulate and then disappear. The plant may become chlorotic and may slowly die.

LENGTH OF DAY

An excellent review of color and plant growth is given by Earl S. Johnston in the 1936 report of the Smithsonian Institution,

84

Sun Rays and Plant Life. Johnston mentions that under the action of light, carbon dioxide and water are united in the presence of chlorophyll to form simple sugars. These sugars are elaborated into starch, proteins, organic acids, fats, and other products. Most of these compounds are foods—for the plant as well as for the animals that come to feed upon them.

Further, the growth of the plant is vitally affected by the length of day, the intensity of light, and by color—even more so than by temperature and moisture (which also depend on light).

Of primary significance to plant growth is the length of day and duration of sunlight. At the equator there are approximately 12 hours of sun and 12 hours of night each full day. In the extremes reached at the poles, there may be 24 hours of sunlight in summer and 24 hours of darkness in winter. Intermediate latitudes have sunshine values between these two extremes. These factors may in part account for the wide range of vegetation in the world.

Johnston notes that some flowers belong to a short-day group and others to a long-day. The short-day plant matures early in spring or summer, while the autumn flower is a long-day plant. In one experiment with the Mammoth Maryland tobacco plant (a short-day plant) the discovery was made that it would not flower under long-day periods of summer light. A long day, in effect, delayed its seeding. However, under winter greenhouse cultivation it flowered naturally. And when sunlight was supplemented with electric light to lengthen the day this flowering could again be delayed.

To quote from an article by Victor A. Greulach (*Science Digest,* March, 1938), "Among the common short-day plants are asters, ragweeds, dahlias, cosmos, poinsettia, chrysanthemum, cypress vine, nasturtiums, soy beans, tobacco, and all the early spring flowers such as violets and bloodroots. Most garden vegetables and farm crops are long-day plants. Wheat grows rapidly under long days. By using electric light to increase the day-length three generations of wheat have been grown in one year. The extremely long summer days in Alaska are largely responsible for the large crops of hay, wheat, potatoes, and vegetables grown there. It is principally due to the longer days in the northern part of the central valley of California that oranges from that district are ripe and ready for the market several weeks earlier than those grown four hundred miles farther south.

"We usually think of everblooming or everbearing plants as being particular species of varieties, as of roses or strawberries, but many plants may be made into everbloomers by keeping the length-of-day within their natural flowering range. For most plants this range is quite narrow, so we have few everblooming plants in the temperate latitudes, where the day-lengths are constantly changing. In the tropics, where the day-lengths are at or near twelve hours all year everbloomers are the rule rather than the exception, just as you would expect."

W. W. Garner and H. A. Allard have reported a rather strange reaction in plant growth to light exposures of extremely short duration. This work is included in the Johnston report. Groups of plants were exposed to light each day for 12 hours, 1 hour, 30 minutes, 15 minutes, 5 minutes, 1 minute, 15 seconds, and 5 seconds. Result: there was a steady decrease in size, height, and weight for the groups exposed less than 12 hours and down to 1 minute. Then, for some inexplicable reason, the plants exposed for less than 1 minute showed marked improvement. The plant exposed for only 5 seconds grew to a height of the plant exposed for 1 hour—while the plants of all intermediate intervals (30 minutes, 15 minutes, 1 minute) were dwarfed. All intervals below 1 hour were unfavorable for flowering, however. Johnston comments: "These are exceedingly interesting growth responses to the duration of light and to date no satisfactory explanation has been given."

Dr. R. B. Withrow, by using artificial light to supplement daylight, has achieved results that seem out of proportion to the treatment applied. He experimented with Mazda light for night illumination and arranged intensities from 1 to 100 foot-candles. He discovered that very little difference was shown in the growth of an aster. In fact, the one exposed to a mere 3 foot-candles grew almost as well as one exposed to 100 foot-candles!

Evidently many plants grow best in light of moderate intensity. Thus a lot of the energy of the sun must be wasted.

THE EFFECT OF COLOR

Dr. Withrow also experimented with color and found that responses differed for short-day and long-day plants. In the long-day plants, such as the stock, greatest response occurred in the red region. The plant grew tallest under orange-red light. The next best growth was under red. Under yellow, green, and blue the plant did not grow tall nor did it flower, although the foliage was rather abundant. A plant treated under infrared did not flower, despite the fact that this radiation lies next to visible red and red-orange in the spectrum. With short-day plants (cosmos, salvia) supplementary red light hindered flowering.

What such control means commercially is well expressed by Dr. Withrow in the Johnston report previously mentioned. He states that supplementary light and color may be used to cause earlier and increased flowering for such plants as the aster, Shasta daisy, and pansy. Delayed flowering may be produced in the chrysanthemum. No significant response was noted in the rose or carnation.

In Holland, red neon light has been commercially applied to flowers and strawberries. Vapor lamps, similar to those found on highways, are used for 8 hours at night to force a growth that supplements the normal growth attained during the day.

Photosynthesis, necessary to plant life, derives its energy chiefly from visible light. What particular rays are utilized? W. H. Hoover of the Smithsonian Institution made extensive tests with wheat and measured the assimilation of carbon dioxide. Through the use of filters he separated narrow bands from the spectrum and let the hued light shine on glass tubes in which the wheat was grown. Temperature and atmospheric moisture were controlled. A special device measured the amount of carbon dioxide absorbed.

Three series of tests were undertaken: filtered Mazda light; filtered mercury-arc light; filtered natural sunlight. All rays were fairly monochromatic. Red rays proved to be the most productive. As the main regions of the spectrum were utilized, there was a falling off in plant growth with yellow and green rays and a pickup with blue rays which ranked second. Incidentally, "the infrared and ultraviolet contribute nothing to the assimilation of carbon dioxide in wheat."

In most plants, leaf stems turn toward the light source. In brief, the shaded side grows more rapidly than the illuminated side, causing the plant or sprout to "lean" toward the light. Johnston sought to determine what reaction might be found with different colors. "To obtain an answer a plant might be placed half-way between two equally intense lights . . . and the direction of bending noted. The plant's sensitivity to different colors could thus be determined in a general way." With oat seedlings Johnston found the region of greatest sensitivity to be in the blue. "That is, growth is retarded most by blue light. Orange and red light have no effect in retarding the growth of these oat seedlings."

Lewis H. Flint, in similar experiments, found that the short waves of light—violet, blue, green—inhibited the germination of lettuce seed. Long waves of red, orange, and yellow promoted germination. Another experimenter was able to increase the pigmentation of apples through the use of ultraviolet. Infrared in this instance caused the fruit to become wrinkled.

MITOGENETIC RAYS

There is one further curiosity to be noted—some plant life has an aura! In 1923 Alexander Gurwitsch wrote of the discovery of so-called "mitogenetic energy." An onion, for example, may emit rays in the shorter ultraviolet region of the spectrum, such energy passing through quartz but not through glass. Although of extremely low intensity, it has tangible and measurable existence. Though Gurwitsch's work was ignored for some years, it was later verified by subsequent investigators. Today the phenomenon is still shrouded in mystery, various scientists holding bitter and conflicting opinions. It may be that to some the idea of an onion emitting waves of radiant energy is too bizarre. Yet Gurwitsch is likely to have the last word after all despite the fact that he has been termed a "sensationalist" by some of his fellow biologists.

CHAPTER 8

Invertebrates and Vertebrates

THE LIVING THINGS of this earth have been conditioned to solar radiation through countless ages of survival. Had this energy been different, no doubt the world—and man—would have been different (had they existed at all). Because solar radiation is predominant in rays of light visible to the human eye, with added shorter waves in ultraviolet and added longer waves in infrared, it is obvious that these frequencies must be vital to animal life (and to plants) and must influence it accordingly.

Thus, as a prelude to the physical effects of color upon the human organism, this chapter is presented on lower forms of animal life. Here is a great field of inquiry, and devoted to it have been a large number of diligent investigators. Yet it is unfortunate that the work of such men has seldom been brought to-gether in one source. The student of animal biology may have only a cursory acquaintance with the findings of the student of animal psychology. Research efforts may overlap, and the subject of color may be encountered only in isolated instances.

The true difficulty lies in the fact that to tell a consistent story of color, it becomes necessary to review an almost endless array of references. Scientific men seldom write books on color alone. One must therefore do much literary foraging, making his way through a vast bulk of literature for an occasional find. Yet because the magic of color is unfolded time and again, because the researcher runs into it head on during the course of his pursuits, an impressive exhibit of curiosities and facts may be assembled and a fairly coherent essay written about them.

THE LOWLY AMOEBA

Most living things not only react to light but are strangely sensitive to it. The lowly amoeba, for example, "sees" with its entire organism, moving or contracting itself as the light stimulus changes. Taken out of darkness, the amoeba may grow quiet. After a while motion may be resumed until still another intensity strikes it. However, if the change of light is gradual rather than sudden, the amoeba may go about its simple business without much ado.

Certain species may have definite preferences for light intensity, moving about until a satisfactory brightness is found. Green hydras collect in relatively weak light; medusae collect in shaded regions; some polyps have a day-night rhythm. Maier and Schneirla write, "The place in which the animal finally settles is mainly determined by light, by the amount of oxygen in the water, and by the temperature. Except at extreme temperatures, or when the animal has been without food for some time, light is the most important factor."

On up the scale, such creatures as worms are made uncomfortable by light. Some marine forms will continue to move until darkness is reached. Light from one direction may drive them the opposite way. General light overhead may cause them to waver about aimlessly. The earthworm, of course, fears the light even more than it does the robin and will remain in nether regions until actually flooded out.

When the "eyes" (ocelli) of a starfish are severed, the animal will respond to light through its skin. A slug with one eye removed will keep circling toward the eyeless side. Likewise does the cockroach scamper away from the light and a moth flutter toward it.

INSECTS

Color vision is not apparent in the lowest forms of animal life. It exists, however, in insects, fishes, reptiles, and birds. It is found lacking in most mammals, and restored again by nature in apes and men.

However, the color vision of insects differs from that of men. Scientists are largely agreed that the eye of the insect responds to the yellow region of the spectrum (but not the red), being sensitive to green, blue, violet, and on up into the energy of ultraviolet. E. N. Grieswood, in experimenting with fruit flies, noted a reaction to wave lengths invisible to man, which in shortness of frequency approached X rays. Such radiation must have come as a surprise to the insect inasmuch as it is not found in solar radiation. In similar tests Bertholf found the range of sensitivity in bees to extend from about 550 millimicrons (yellow-green), through green, blue, violet and into waves as short as 250 millimicrons (ultraviolet). The human eye is sensitive to a region extending from about 700 millimicrons to 400.

Ants placed in a box that is illuminated by a complete spectrum of sunlight will carry their larvae (always kept in darkness) out of the ultraviolet and into the visible red. Von Frish has demonstrated that the bee can be made to see the difference between a blue and a gray of the same brightness. It can also differentiate blue from violet or purple, and yellow from any of these. This has been shown by training the bee to fly to certain colors in order to obtain food. With red the bee is hopelessly confused and sees no difference in it from neutral gray targets. With wasps, however, Molitor found that in entering a nest, a black entrance was preferred to a blue one, and blue to red.

Frank E. Lutz has assembled many interesting facts about the "invisible" colors of flowers and butterflies. Not only does the insect have a sense of vision that differs from man's, but the patterns on its wings may also appear different to insects than to human beings. Quite obviously the butterfly finds real significance in ultraviolet energy. A red zinnia, for example, does not reflect ultraviolet, while the red portulaca does. Hence the two flowers, while alike to men and probably to birds, appear dark and light respectively to the butterfly.

Lutz writes: "While not all yellow flowers . . . are ultraviolet, most of them seem to be. In this connection a yellow spider much given to hiding in yellow flowers is interesting. According to theory, the yellow color of the spider prevents flower-visiting insects from seeing it against the background of a yellow flower in time to avoid being caught. However, the spider is only slightly ultraviolet and, so, to an insect that can see ultraviolet the yellow spider must be rather conspicuous as it sits on a yellow-ultraviolet flower."

Similarly the patterns of moths and butterflies differ under natural and ultraviolet light. The creatures thus "look" different to themselves than to men.

INSECT REPELLENTS

Experimenting with night-flying insects, L. C. Porter and G. F. Prideaux have found that brightness is a dominant factor in attraction power. Next to this, the more a source of illumination approaches the blue end of the spectrum, the more insects it will gather; the more it approaches the red end, the fewer it will gather. "The substitution of yellow lamps for white lamps of equal candle power reduces the number of insects attracted by approximately 50 per cent." Consequently, blue is the preferred hue, while red and yellow the least noticed. Thus a yellow lamp of low wattage over the porch, with a blue lamp of high wattage placed at a distance, will effectively divert invasion on a summer night.

For daylight insect traps, however, using paints and not light bulbs, yellow seems to be most useful. Frederick G. Vosburg reports, "For some reason a yellow trap will catch more Japanese beetles than any other color."

The "likes" and "dislikes" of flies and mosquitoes have been carefully studied with practical ends in view. The results given below are obtained from notes assembled by Deane B. Judd and presented in *News Letter* 45 of the Inter-Society Color Council.

For houseflies, several investigations have led to contradictory results. E. Hardy, for example, found yellow to be avoided and white to be preferred. On the other hand, P. R. Awati considered yellow to have the greatest attraction, red and violet the least. O. C. Lodge found no preference at all. S. B. Freeborn and L. J.

94

Perry found the fly repelled by pale colors, while R. Newstead had reason to conclude that light colors were preferred to dark colors. Something must be wrong somewhere. Either the methods of research are unreliable, or the flies with haunts in different parts of the world have different ideas about the matter. Possibly, the safest conclusion is that flies are more attracted to lightness than to darkness, for the weight of evidence seems to indicate as much.

In Holland, at least, horse stables and cow stalls are frequently treated with blue to get rid of the pests. So in Holland the flies must dislike that hue.

Regarding mosquitoes, however, the authorities are in far better agreement. Here light colors are the repelling ones. G. H. F. Nuttall and A. E. Shipley found that the common European malaria-bearing mosquito alighted most on dark blue, red, and brown, and least on yellow, orange, and white. (Subsequent to this particular report, the U.S. Army withdrew its regulation shirts in malaria districts and substituted lighter colors.) During five years in South Africa, Shariff found that pink and yellow mosquito curtains did not harbor insects. When boxes were lined with navy blue, pink, gray, and yellow flannel, the interiors of the blue and gray boxes were thickly covered with mosquitoes, while but two or three were found in the pink or the yellow boxes. Hoodless also found that New Caledonia mosquitoes prefer blue and avoid yellow.

FISHES

One of the most exhaustive books ever written on the vision of animals is that of Gordon Lynn Walls, *The Vertebrate Eye*. It offers a comprehensive review of visual phenomena and is replete with data on color as an influencing factor in animal survival and behavior. Walls writes, "Color vision itself is a potent aid to visual acuity in its broad sense, and was certainly evolved for this application rather than for the aesthetic ones which it has come to have in human vision." That color may be tied in with the most primitive and mundane of life processes is not often acknowledged. Certainly color vision to a lower animal has nothing to do with sensuous delight. Nature had definite purposes in view and she endowed her creatures with a sense of color in order to equip them for the practical battle of life.

"No fish is known *not* to have color vision" (Walls). Yet color in the life of a fish is far less significant than brightness, form, and motion. Walls points out that because it is difficult to see under water, fishes are better able to get about, if blinded, than most other vertebrates.

Scientific work on the color vision of fishes is quite plentiful. Hess determined that green was seen as the lightest color, then blue, yellow, orange, with red the darkest color of all. "The intensity of any color needed to balance pure yellow was only half that required to balance green."

According to Walls, "Fishes generally seem either to shun red, or to prefer it decidedly." This may be due in part to the fact that red radiation is quickly absorbed as it passes through water and that red, therefore, is not a common experience to the fish. Cora Reeves in experiments with mud minnows found that respiration rate rose with increase in brightness. When ruby glass was placed across an artificial light source, the respiration rate increased even more. "In this experiment it was perfectly clear that the response was to redness as such, since the respiration rose with an increase of brightness, but rose still higher when that brightness was somewhat reduced by a filter which introduced hue" (Walls).

96

That color has much influence on the behavior of fishes has been well proved by experiments such as the above. S. O. Mast, working with flounders, painted the floors of tanks in various hues. Where a fish had been blue-adapted, it tended to choose this color as a resting place and to avoid other hues.

Fishes capable of color change depend upon visual processes and lack the ability when blinded. Here again there is a curious disregard of brightness alone. Except under extremely high or low illumination, the fish will not respond to gradual changes in the amount of light entering its eye. Yet the moment its substrate or background is modified in lightness or darkness, the skin of the fish will rapidly conform in "value" to it.

THE TURTLE

A turtle's ability to find water will perhaps always remain a mystery. Theories are many. One is that the turtle avoids shadow, knowing instinctively that clear reaches of sky are without overhanging verdure and therefore must have water underneath. Another theory is that blue is the attracting force. Certainly orientation to the sun is meaningless, for turtles will persistently move in any direction that is clear and unobstructed.

In turtles, as in other reptiles, color vision is well developed. While discrimination of brightness and intensity is poor, colors are readily distinguished from grays.

According to Walls, "The most important hues for the turtle appear to be orange, green, and violet. Yellow and yellow-green, when not accurately discriminated, were apparently most often seen as orange; but red was separated from the general orange category and seemed to be more akin to violet for the animal, which thus had a closed color circle." Wagner, in studies of lizards, noted discrimination of red, orange, yellow, yellow-green, ice blue, deep blue, and violet. Vision was keenest to red and blue and weakest to green.

Luminescence is one of the most startling of all color phenomena in nature. About thirty different kinds of luminous bacteria are known. Some grow on dead fish and were noted centuries ago by Aristotle. Another type has been known to invade butcher shops at seaside towns and to cause the meat to glow. Frequently small animals like the sand hopper will eat a meal of them and promptly be converted into the bright aspect of glowworms. Bacteria and worms may all die.

In less minute creatures, luminous colors shine with the intensity of lanterns. J. Arthur Thomson in *The Outline of Science* describes an expedition by the Marquis de Folin in which coral was dredged from a great depth. "There were many coral animals, shrub-like in form, which threw off flashes of light beside which the twenty torches used for working by were pale. Some of these corals were carried into the laboratory, where the lights were put out. There was a moment of magic, the most marvelous spectacle that was given to man to admire. Every point of the chief branches and twigs of the coral Isis threw out brilliant jets of fire, now paling, now reviving again, to pass from violet to purple, from red to orange, from bluish to different tones of green, and sometimes to the white of over-heated iron. The pervading color was greenish, the others appeared only in transient flashes, and melted into the green again. Minute by minute the glory lessened, as the animals died, and at the end of a quarter of an hour they were all like dead and withered branches. But while they were at their best one could read by their light the finest print of a newspaper at a distance of six yards."

In recent years much has been learned about the luminous colors of deep-sea creatures. Some of these have organs resembling eyes which throw forth light. In the pit of the ocean there is total darkness, tremendous pressure, and coldness that lingers at the freezing point. All is calm, silent, monotonous, and plantless. The creatures that haunt these forlorn places have been oddly equipped. Nearly all have a highly developed sense of touch. More vital, perhaps, nearly all are luminous after some fashion or other. Descriptions of some of them, written by such devout researchers as William Beebe, read like fantasy. One is dense black without scales. It has two rows of luminous spots along its sides. The upper row shows green, blue, and violet; the lower row, red and orange—like a double-deck steamer passing in the night. A smaller fish is velvety black and has about 1,500 luminous organs. Another eellike creature is luminous throughout its sleek length. A deep-sea cuttlefish has regular porthole lights. The melanocetus carries a lantern on the end of a stalk.

Luminescence does not occur in any creatures higher than the fish and insect. At times, however, the growth of bacteria may give phosphorescence to the wings of birds and to the fur of animals. Much of this colorful light is fairly intense. The emissions of a glowworm have been found to contain visible light only, of a cold nature and without wasted energy in infrared and ultraviolet radiation. The light will affect a photographic plate, produce fluorescence in many substances, cause plants to bend toward it, and stimulate the growth of chlorophyll.

What is the value of luminescence to the organism? In some instances it appears to have no purpose. The shrimp which feeds on a diet of luminous bacteria dies—both to its own destruction and to theirs. In deep-sea creatures the light unquestionably has utility. It may prove a lure to attract food. It may frighten intruders. It may serve as a lantern to help the fish get about. In a definite pattern it may help kin find kin. It may be a sex signal. The toadfish, for example, is luminous only at mating time.

Among fireflies and glowworms, the sexual attraction of light seems to have dominant importance. In one British species the female is wingless and creeps on grassy banks. She is far more luminous than the male. Her signal is more prolonged and she may call a whole circle of suitors about her.

Finally, what of these colors? In the glowworm one distinguishes a pale green. Green is also found in certain brittle stars. Blue is seen in the Italian firefly, red in some sea squirts. A purplish color is found in some coral. In general the most common hues are pale blue and pale green. The colors of deep-sea fish are likely to be brighter and more varied. They may have the full range of the spectrum. One cuttlefish with twenty luminous spots on its body was found to gleam with deep blue, rich red, pale blue, and silvery white.

PROTECTIVE COLORATION

Nature commonly gives her creatures a similar appearance if they grow in the same habitat. A moth, a toad, a bird, and a mammal may all be brownish like natural undergrowth. Green may be found among caterpillars, frogs, and snakes living in the same region. Desert animals are generally light, water birds soft and toned in hue. Jungle birds may be gaudy, mammals drab. Shore fishes may be brilliant with color; others, that swim in the mud, may be mottled and dark. In the open sea nearly all fishes are found to be colored alike.

By confusing the eye with weird patches of design and color, nature is able to defy a clear perception of butterflies and moths, birds, snakes, zebras, leopards, and tigers. The mallard duck with its patches of green, blue, purple, white, black is effectively lost amid rocks, weeds, marine flowers, and the like. As it moves about, it is seen in one appearance, then another—never being precise in form. The peacock, macaw, scarlet tanager, humming-bird, jay, kingfisher, and hundreds of others have bold coloration of this sort—beautiful, yes, but primarily self-protecting to the creature.

Where the creature is equipped with formidable weapons, nature may make it conspicuous rather than inconspicuous. Tree frogs, cobras, coral snakes, magpies, skunks have little to fear and flaunt their bizarre raiment to the world.

Most mammals are brownish, blackish, grayish, or white. Purer hues are rare but are to be seen in the faces and rumps of certain monkeys and baboons. Colors may change with change in season. The brown stoat becomes the white ermine in winter. The mountain hare dons white with the coming of snow.

In the course of their lives, caterpillars, butterflies, crabs may modify their hues as their environments change. Shrimps may adapt their colors to their hiding places. One species will change to a translucent blue at night and remain so until dawn.

Instantaneous color change is nature's most surprising legerdemain. Some crustaceans (lobsters, crabs, shrimps) will match their coloration to that of the surface on which they rest. The Coney has a repertoire of white, red, green, brown. Like other such protean creatures, its skin is covered with pigment cells or chromatophores. Stimulation comes through the eye, and the cells expand or contract to bring forth the numerous vestments—not only distinct hues, but even mixtures and degrees of brightness and hue.

Flatfishes—the plaice, sole, and flounder—shift in pattern as well as hue, resembling sandy or rocky ocean bottoms. The cuttlefish has like ability, plus an ink bag with which it throws a "smoke screen" about its enemies. Many tropical fishes have palettes as varied as the rainbow, six or more individual appearances being a natural talent. These colors will flash and shift intermittently and for no apparent reason. Authorities insist that there is not much biological significance to the guises. The fishes may be affected by fright, anger, distress. Most of them are too agile to need the protection of camouflage. But nature, practical always, may have in view "warning and immunity coloration, signal and recognition marks and sexual selection." Without doubt color serves some practical functions.

In the American chameleon (a lizard of the genus *Analis*), one finds a notable trouper in nature's show of magic. Expanding and contracting pigment cells are supplemented by refractive granules under the skin. Normally the animal is a brilliant emerald green. It is extremely sensitive to light and will undergo change even while at rest. As it moves about, its hues shift and melt one into another. The transformations seem to be regulated by direct-wire connections from the eye. When enraged, however, the creature will bluff its adversary with a black cloak and a great pink mouth opened wide.

In other families of lizards, color change may also be found. At times, however, the change in hue and pattern may be less regulated by environment than by light intensity, temperature, and emotional stimuli. Thus the normal color may be a gray-green, with numerous dark patches on the sides of the animal. Darkness may produce a cream color with irregular yellow patches. Full sunlight may produce black. High temperature without intense light may produce green; low temperature may produce gray. Excitement may bring paler shades with brown and yellow spots. Anger may cause darkening.

Response to color reaches a very high development in birds. Here the organ of sight is both intricate and versatile. Many birds, for example, have two foveal areas on their retinas enabling them to see sharply while feeding as well as in flight. The eyes of birds also contain colored droplets (red, orange, yellow). The predominating yellow droplets in most diurnal birds are a definite aid to vision. They cut out blue light, minimize glare and dazzle, and, according to Walls, let through, "unimpeded, most of nature's hues." Similarly the red droplets aid the bird during early morning feeding when the sun's rays, slanting through space, are reddish in tint. The kingfisher (also the turtle) has a predominance of red droplets which unquestionably aid vision through glaring water. Most birds, perhaps for the above reason, are partially blind to blue but see red colors with remarkable clarity.

Nocturnal birds, however, have few if any colored droplets. Walls mentions that F. L. Vanderplank found the tawny owl sensitive to infrared and apparently able to see its prey in "pitch" darkness by distinguishing the radiation of body heat. Infrared energy, which had no action on the pupil of the human eye, closed the owl's pupil and frightened the bird. In a subsequent study by Hecht and Pirenne, however, Vanderplank's findings were disputed if not refuted. These two researchers did not find the owl (of a different kind from Vanderplank's) very sensitive to infrared. It was their conclusion that the owl had an exceedingly low visual threshold—about ten times as sensitive as the human eye, and to the same part of the spectrum.

There seems to be a definite color preference among birds, associated no doubt with feeding habits. Hummingbirds favor red and will readily feed from a red container or vial. Arthur G. Abbott in his book *The Color of Life* points out the disinterest of birds in the color green. Poisons meant to destroy field mice and rodents may apparently be dyed green to protect bird life. (The rodent is color-blind.) "In one field the oats [poisoned] were dyed yellow and green. In a third they were left uncolored. In the uncolored area 28 birds were poisoned; in the yellow area, 9 birds; in the green area, no birds at all."

REACTIONS TO LIGHT AND COLOR

Bird migration has been partially explained in terms of length of day. As the summer comes to an end and the days grow shorter, a reaction may take place (possibly through the pituitary gland) which speeds the bird on its way to more favorable climates. Migration may even take place before crops and seeds are ripe and before nature's autumn banquet is completely set.

In a series of fascinating experiments with birds, Bissonnette and others have well proved that migration and sexual cycles are less dependent on temperature than on light. With the male starling, sexually quiescent during winter, testicle development occurred when the birds were given added light. This held true as well with color. To quote Bissonnette, "Birds subjected to red light and white light were stimulated to testis activity. . . . The order of decreasing amount of germ-cell activity is therefore red, white, control, green, with green inhibitory."

MAMMALS

Bissonnette found similar results with mammals. "Increased night-lighting induces cotton-tail rabbits to undergo sexual activity in winter." In experiments with weasels, ferrets, mink, he was

104

able to achieve winter fur coloration during the hot days of mid-summer. "It is, therefore, indicated that the assumption of white prime pelt by mink may be induced in summer in spite of relatively high temperatures or hastened in autumn by reducing the duration of the periods of light to which the animals are exposed daily."

With goats, like results were achieved. Though a cow will give milk the year around, goats are less generous. Because they may fail to breed between April and September, milk supply may be interrupted. Bissonnette has demonstrated that breeding—and milk supply—can be perfectly controlled. "Results indicate that breeding cycles in goats are controlled by daily periods of light in such a way that short days induce breeding while long days inhibit it."

Because most mammals are virtually color-blind, reaction to color becomes all the more interesting because it demonstrates the existence of forces to which the creature is visually indifferent. Yet color does startling things. Ludwig and von Ries found the same rate of growth in rats under blue light as under normal light. Under red light, however, weight substantially increased. "They also expressed the belief that the activity of a hormonal substance was increased by red light, destroyed by ultraviolet light, and could be activated again by red light" (B. D. Prescott).

A number of further references to the effects of visible light and color on animals will be given in later pages. Warm-blooded animals apparently have little need of a color sense. Walls writes, "In a survey of mammals, we can perceive no majestic progress in the evolution of color vision from an imperfect system in primitive groups to a complex one in the highly specialized orders." Cattle pay as much—or as little—attention to green as to red. Colored cloths hung on a line will arouse equal curiosity in a bull, regardless of their hue. Cats, however, may be more sensitive to short wave lengths than more diurnal animals.

With apes and men, however, full-color vision appears again as in fishes and birds, but with many added refinements. Monkeys readily distinguish different hues and can be taught to match colors. Yet as will soon be clarified, physical effects for color may take place independently of vision. Men and animals, like plants, may be variously influenced by color in their life processes, their health, sickness, and well-being, whether or not the color is actually seen by them.

CHAPTER 9

Diagnosis through Color

THE MODERN MEDICAL practitioner is inclined to look upon color as a distressing reminder of chicanery and quackery, a black art practiced by certain fakirs who confuse issues in a cloud of esoteric gibberish. The physician holds—and perhaps rightly—to an impersonal viewpoint. He relies upon clinical proof, on formal and unprejudiced investigation. He will admit the therapy of ultraviolet, for example, when he can look into a microscope and see germs destroyed. But who may claim with equal certainty that the *visible* colors of the spectrum are also potent in a physical way? The study of color, unfortunately, does not always lend itself to facts and proofs. Where it may be seen by the eye, it may have psychic components which are not likely to have much regularity.

107

The attitude of the recognized physician is well expressed by Richard Kovacs: "It has been claimed that by separating the visible white into its component parts, red, yellow, blue, etc., these colored bands can be utilized for specific therapeutic purposes, such as blue for sedation and red for stimulation. There is little evidence so far to substantiate these claims, chiefly because the filter arrangements for the production of such pure blue, red or other light, if effective physically, usually produce an inert radiation by keeping off the bulk of the electromagnetic wave energy. The different colors of light undoubtedly exert a certain amount of psychological effect irrespective of the amount of effective radiation." There is a general admission, however, that visible rays of light do mitigate the burn produced by ultraviolet by increasing the supply of lymph and blood and thereby "washing" away some of the product of tissue damage.

Perhaps the modern physician's attitude is too conservative, or perhaps the color healer is too quick to assign magic to the spectrum. No doubt color therapy is to some extent beneficial, just as exposure to light is beneficial. And perhaps the efficacy of invisible electromagnetic energy has in the past been falsely credited to red or yellow, green or blue. None the less, there are enigmas about color which still have to be answered before anyone may definitely accept or definitely reject color as a curative.

Americans in particular seem to disdain color phenomena as applied to healing. Yet much research has been done by recognized medical science which is neither to be slighted nor ignored. For example, there are electrical waves which originate in the human brain and which may be recorded and measured. Epilepsy and many psychotic disturbances may be diagnosed by means of these waves. They are studied for clues to personality and to certain mental processes and mental derangements. With an instrument having the lengthy name of the electroencephalograph, electrodes are clamped to the head, generally in the region of the ear, and brain patterns are recorded. These patterns take the form of jagged lines running horizontally and are analyzed not only for their frequency but also for the relation between slow and fast waves over a period of time.

BORDERLINE PRACTICE

Certain practitioners in the field of medicine have used color and still use it today, though more in Europe than in America. Red light has frequently been specified for erysipelas, urticaria, scarlet fever, measles, eczema. Küster has employed it favorably in cases of excessive functioning of the sex organs and uterine hemorrhages. It has been found to reduce pain in postoperative incisions, acute inflammation, and ultraviolet burn. Red produces heat in the tissues, dilates the blood vessels, and also perhaps brings about a reflex action that is soothing to the nerves. R. Douglas Howat refers to its value in the treatment of lumbago, myalgia, rheumatoid arthritis, sciatica, neuritis, and fractures.

Blue, on the other hand, has bactericidal properties. It is said to increase the output of carbon dioxide in certain cold-blooded creatures, whereas red exerts the most influence among birds and rodents. Moleschott has shown that light in general increases the elimination of carbonic acid in animals.

Blue has been prescribed to cure "thumping" headaches, high blood pressure of nervous origin, and intractable insomnia. Whether its action is direct or indirect (through the eye and emotions) matters little. Results, after all, are what count.

Yellow has been found by some qualified investigators to raise low blood pressure associated with anemia, neurasthenia, and general debility. Applied abdominally it seems to increase the flow of gastric juices—just as it may stimulate action in the bowels.

Green seems to be generally neutral.

In other experiments a definite antagonism has been found between red light and ultraviolet light. Substances activated by ultraviolet have been rendered inactive by red light. The activity of hormones has been increased by red and destroyed by ultraviolet. F. Ludwig and J. von Ries believe that various portions of the spectrum have a specific influence on the hormones of the body, and that endocrine problems may some day find their solution through more intensive photobiological studies.

The evidence is encouraging if not plentiful. Humanity may well hope that prejudices will one day be cast aside and that capable men will be more eager to prove the efficacy of color than to disprove it.

THE TOKENS OF DISEASE

However, if modern medicine hesitates to accept color for its direct therapy, it certainly makes common use of it in diagnosis. Here the physician finds a significance that ranks in importance with pulse and temperature.

Dr. John Benson in an article for the *American Journal of Clinical Medicine* (December, 1907) remarked that as a general rule a white tongue reveals a system in need of alkalies, while a person with a bright red tongue is likely to need acids. He points out that dark red is often a sign of infection or sepsis, a brownish tongue a sign of typhoid.

Pigmentation of the skin may be even more significant. Benson presented the following interesting list:

Thick, dirty, muddy complexion (also the ruddy face and bulbous nose) : Evidence of autotoxemia.

Yellow face: Hepatic condition.

Thin, clear transparent skin, with prominent blue veins: Impaired vitality, symptoms of tuberculosis.

Greenish, waxy skin and pallid lips: A sign of anemia.

Restricted spots of deepening red, often shading into purple: Pulmonary lesions of pneumonia.

Any good book of diagnosis is filled with descriptions of color as tokens of disease. Color symptoms are well known to doctors and are indicative of many ailments. Here are a few random notes gleaned from medical literature:

Apoplexy: An ashen gray complexion.

Chronic arthritis: Often irregular areas of yellow pigmentation.

Chlorosis: A peculiar sallow color which may be called "green sickness."

Syphilis: A peculiar sallow color sometimes termed *café au lait*.

Argyria: The skin becomes bluish gray or slate color.

Cancer: Color change may not be apparent in early stages. In late stages the skin may be yellowish, yellowish brown, or greenish brown.

Pernicious anemia: "The combination of pallor with good nutrition is striking. The skin, instead of presenting the white, deathlike appearance commonly seen in severe anemia, is usually a peculiar lemon-yellow tint."

Diabetes: Bronzing of the skin in a great many cases.

Pellagra: The skin becomes a deep red.

Tuberculous peritonitis: Bronzing of the skin, especially on the abdomen.

Osler's disease: Superficial blood vessels, capillaries, and veins look full, the skin being congested. In warm weather the face may be brick red or plum color.

Chronic alcoholism: The face is congested, causing a dusky redness. The nose is often large and red.

Carbon monoxide poisoning: The skin may turn a bright cherry hue.

Chloasma: The skin has yellowish, brownish, or blackish splotches.

Addison's disease: The skin is bronzed, at first the face and hands and then perhaps generally. The hue ranges from a light yellow to a deep brown or slate color.

Smallpox, measles, scarlet fever, scurvy: "Hemorrhages into the skin cause lesions of various sizes. These gradually change color and disappear."

Typhus fever: Rose spots turning to a purplish rash.

Leprosy: White patches.

Erysipelas: Bright red over bridge of nose, then creeping gradually outward.

Frostbite: Skin whiter than normal, then passing into dark red, reddish, or reddish-black color.

The color of blood (the relation of white to red corpuscles), the color of urine, of discharges from the nose, of the human stool, likewise are important. The retina of the eye may show patches of white, gray or black, bluish green, or grayish green. The membranes of the eyelids may appear reddish or bluish. There may be redness of the feet. The lips may be purple. A white circle about the baby's mouth may tell of gastric or intestinal irritation. The gums may be blue in lead poisoning, purplish or bluish in gum infections, blackish in bismuth poisoning. In chronic copper poisoning there may be a green line where teeth and gums meet.

Pallor and sallowness are associated with disease in general. In pregnancy the skin may become brownish and the areola of the breast much deeper in shade. Finally are the signs of death, recognized by Hippocrates: "A sharp nose, hollow eyes, collapsed temples, the ears cold, contracted, and their lobes turned out; the skin about the forehead being rough, distended and parched; the color of the whole face being brown, black, livid or lead-colored."

Arthur G. Abbott has given an excellent description of the protean aspects assumed by the human body. "The redness of blood is influenced by oxygen and carbon dioxide. The rosy cheeks of youth indicate a healthy blood condition, together with a delicate and healthy skin. A white man can appear all colors under certain conditions, so he might more appropriately be called 'colored,' whereas the Negro, whom we speak of as 'colored,' is black, which denotes an absence of color. A white man can appear nearly white from fright, loss of blood, etc.; grayish from pain; red from exertion, anger, etc.; greenish from biliousness and introduced poisons; yellow from jaundice; blue from cold, poor circulation, and lack of oxygen; brown from sun tan; purple from strangulation; and black from decay."

In a remarkable device known as an oxyhemograph, an electric eye is employed to record changes in blood color. Fastened to the ear, it will indicate fall in oxygen supply. The device reacts to the color of blood: bright red where there is enough oxygen, darker as the oxygen diminishes. One of the dangers of long operations, for example, is from cerebral anoxia, which may paralyze or kill a patient. In the past, surgeons have relied upon respiration and pulse. The oxyhemograph has proved vital in heart cases and "blue babies." Indeed, in this latter affliction the surgeon may know the success of his operation even before he sews up the incision.

To quote again from Abbott, this time with reference to an odd diagnosis of cancer: "From Germany comes a fish, called the *Elritze,* that provides a remarkable test for cancer. A sample of the suspected patient's blood is prepared and injected into the fish, which is normally a silver-brown color; if any cancer hormones are present in the injected fluid, the fish immediately turns red, remaining so for about 5 minutes, after which it returns to normal and can be used for another test."

COLORED VISION

In some diseases an afflicted person may experience colored vision, a sensation in which the field of view appears weakly or strongly tinted. In jaundice the world may appear predominantly yellowish. Red vision may follow retinal hemorrhage or snow blindness. Yellow vision may follow digitalis or quinine poisoning. Green vision may be caused by wounds of the cornea. Blue vision has been reported in cases of alcoholism. In tobacco scotoma the vision may be reddish or greenish.

In santonin poisoning the world may at first appear bluish. There may be a second stage of yellow vision of longer duration and a stage of violet sight before complete recovery. Following the extraction of a cataract, the patient may experience red vision, sometimes followed by blue vision. Green and yellow are rare.

Vision and the organ of sight have been subjects of extensive medical research. In color therapy, attempts have been made to relieve certain conditions of human distress by shining colors into the eye in an effort to stimulate or relax eye nerves and in turn to affect the body itself, possibly through a chain of interreactions. Blue and violet lights, shining into the eye, have been reported as favorable in cases of headaches. Red light is said to increase blood pressure and cope with some types of dizziness. Yellow, green, or blue light is said to relieve digestive ills; yellow light to be beneficial in certain cases of mental disorder.

Again, however, the evidence is none too convincing. Yet to return to diagnosis, the eye may be studied to detect a wide variety of ills. One authoritative book on the subject is that of I. S. Tassman, *The Eye Manifestations of Internal Diseases.* One is struck by the fact that so many human afflictions somehow make themselves known through the eye. The delicate membranes and tissues are quick to be affected and lesions may form. Such lesions may be traced to hereditary causes, to infections and diseases, to the degeneration of other organs in the body, or to mechanical causes. The eye, being sensitive, promptly reacts to the disturbance.

Congenital syphilis may be noted, or hereditary weaknesses and tendencies to disease may be manifest in the eye. Allergy may quickly be revealed in itchy eyelids, redness, and a burning sensation. Circulatory and metabolic diseases may interfere with blood supply and become obvious in the eye. In anemia the optic nerve head may appear white, and a "cherry-red spot" may show on the macular area of the retina.

WHAT THE EYE SHOWS

In scarlet fever, the lids of the eye may be swollen and may have a noticeable redness.

In whooping cough, the eyes may grow bloodshot. Although hemorrhages may interfere with vision, they may gradually disappear.

In typhoid fever, there may be ulcers of the cornea. Significant "spots of color" may appear on the retina.

In influenza the eyelids may be affected by abscess. Pus may appear about the lids. The eyeball may become reddish and may show signs of congestion.

In pneumonia, ocular lesions may form during or after the course of the disease. The eyeballs may grow pale from lack of blood.

In diphtheria, the eyelids may be red and swollen and vision itself may become highly sensitive to light.

Erysipelas of the face may be considered in part a disease of the eyelids and is rather hazardous to vision. It is generally accompanied by superficial abscesses and redness.

In gonorrhea, inflammation is noted, the lids growing swollen and red. The cornea may become hazy or cloudy.

Leprosy in many instances is accompanied by blindness. A dull gray layer may form over the eye. Heavy pigmentation may appear in the iris.

In undulant fever, there may be a grayish clouding of the iris.

Tularemia, a disease transmitted by rabbits, mice, and other rodents, has been mentioned by Duke-Elder as "the only widespread disease of the human body discovered through the agency of ophthalmology." It usually affects one eye. The lids may be red and swollen, and yellowish ulcers may spread over the eyeball: "yellowish polka dots on a piece of red calico."

In syphilis, blindness frequently occurs. According to Tassman, "It has been estimated that about 2 per cent of all eye diseases are caused by syphilis." Lesions may occur in the eye, accompanied by paralysis of the iris, lens, and eye muscles.

In tuberculosis there may be a growth of granulation tissue resembling a "cockscomb," also lesions of the lids and eyeball.

116

Before the general practice of vaccination, about 35 per cent of blindness was due to smallpox. In the disease, pustules may form and the eyes may be sensitive to light. Smallpox has always been a "red" disease, credulously treated in the old days with red trappings.

Though mumps rarely involves the eyes, in measles vision may be seriously attacked. Spots may appear on the eyeball, accompanied by puffiness and redness of the lids.

In malaria, ulcers may appear on the cornea. The retina may be unduly red, and "bluish-gray stripes" may create a network about the macular region.

Similarly, dental infections, tonsils, nose and sinus infections may all show up in the eye. "Ordinary recurrent 'head colds' which usually indicate the presence of an infection in the sinuses may be accompanied by ocular manifestations."

In alcohol poisoning, vision may be fogged. "A sensation of fluttering and spots before the eyes and colored after-images may also be complained of" (Tassman). Methyl alcohol may cause complete blindness.

VITAMIN DEFICIENCIES

Deficiency in vitamin A, which leads to night-blindness, will be discussed in a later chapter. Where the body is not properly fed and where there may be vitamin deficiency, the eyes once again may tell a significant story.

Where the human system may lack vitamin B_1 (thiamine), diseases such as beriberi may cause dilation of the pupil of the eye, poor vision, burning of the lids, redness of the eyeball. In vitamin B_2 (riboflavin) deficiency the skin may grow rough and red and be cracked. This vitamin, which is readily destroyed by visible and ultraviolet light, may through its deficiency in the body cause dimness of vision, burning sensations, and roughness of the eyelids.

Vitamin C deficiency, associated with scurvy, causes extreme redness of the eyes. Vitamin D deficiency, like that of vitamin A, is related to night blindness and may produce opacities in the lens.

Finally, the larvae and maggots of flies have been known to infect the eyes in an affliction known as myiasis. They must be destroyed with a narcotic and then removed through surgery.

MENTAL DISORDERS

In epilepsy, visual auras are often found, "blurred vision," "half vision," "flashes of light," and hallucinations in which objects and colors are seen. In many psychotic conditions the pupil of the eye may not react to brightness.

In hysteria and neurasthenia, the patient may suffer with complexes and be fearful of blindness. Cases are on record of "hysterical blindness," the strange result of a sensitive and distorted mind. Therapy here requires the application of psychological and psychiatric methods and dramatically shows how the visual process may be as neural as it is optical. Good eyes require good brains and good health.

It is known that the condition of the body may affect the "visual form fields" of the retina. Prolonged eye abuse and disease may cause a degeneration in the nerves on the outer boundaries of the retina. Through perimetry these fields of sensitivity may be measured.

In an article for the *American Journal of Ophthalmology,* James E. Reeder, Jr., writes of a possible diagnosis of insanity through a study of the form and color fields of the retina. Normally, the smallest area of sensitivity to color is for green, then red, then blue, with the peripheral areas of the eye sensitive only to black and white. "In the abnormal field there is a marked decrease in the size of the form as well as the color. The fields are irregular in shape also, but the most decided change is that of the position of the colors. Instead of being from without in, the colors are interlaced or they may even be inverted. It may so happen that the colors extend outside of the form limits."

Reeder makes no great claims for his observations, which he admits are in need of more objective proof. However, through a study of "psychogenic" color fields he has discovered neurotic tendencies which were previously unsuspected. He speaks of the perimetry test as one that cannot be faked, "therefore malingerers cannot make use of it." In other words, where sensitivity to color is abnormally distributed over the retina, human beings are likely to be mentally abnormal.

In another intriguing study, H. W. Brosin and E. O. Fromm noted color "shock" among neurotic color-blind persons who had been shown the Rorschach test cards. (Rorschach Research Exchange, April, 1940.) In general, neurotic individuals show color shock, while normal ones do not; that is, the sight of colors in the "ink blots" may, in mentally disturbed patients, cause distress, shyness, delayed response, rejection, and the like. "Thus we come to the conclusion that the most important factor in causing a reaction may be the *physiological (brain) effect of the physical stimulus.*" The color-blind person "may lack the phenomenal color experience from the physical stimulus, but there seems to be no reason to doubt that he experiences the same physiological (brain) effects." In other words, color may cause things to happen in the human brain even though they may not be clearly perceived.

CHAPTER 10

The Effects of Visible Light

THE EFFECTS OF visible light are
treated in this book from three different viewpoints. First are the
direct biological effects discussed in this chapter. Here the action
of visible light is considered as it exists apart from vision. In many
respects this is *color therapy,* for it deals with the influence of
radiant energy on the human organism, and whether or not the
individual "sees" it.

The second viewpoint is the emotional one, the effects of color
as they are evident in sensory reaction. Here one encounters the
so-called "psychology of color" and is made aware of the many
strange responses that may follow the visualization of hue.

The third viewpoint has to do with the organ of sight and the
mechanism of vision itself. In this study attention is paid to

the adverse effects of eye fatigue, eyestrain, and abuse of the eyes.

All three viewpoints, of course, relate to human welfare, because all have direct or indirect bearing on the life process, on physical and mental health, on man's survival.

THE MEDICAL PROFESSION

It is unfortunate that in America the medical profession by and large disdains the general subject of color therapy. There is a tendency to deny any and all such therapeutic phenomena. This attitude is traditional with American science, for in this country basic and theoretical science have never been greeted as enthusiastically as applied science. American medical men are presumably not interested in color. Indeed most research here has been conducted in an all too obvious effort to disprove the work of others across the Atlantic. While some tolerance has been shown toward the psychiatrist and toward the psychotherapeutic aspects of color, direct color therapy as such has mostly been attended by an inexorable skepticism and by raised eyebrows.

What few references one finds in American medical literature (entirely excluding the assumptions of mystics and chromopaths) are nearly always negative in character. Some years ago, for example, Sidney L. Pressey wrote an article, The Influence of Color upon Mental and Motor Efficiency. This exposition set quite a pattern and has been widely quoted ever since. After conducting a series of experiments, Pressey found that the more optimistic views of the color exponent were to be seriously questioned. "It would seem reasonable to conclude that if color *does* have any fundamental physiological effect, such as would influence mental and motor efficiency, the connection must be of a very general and elementary nature; brightness may stimulate, or red irritate and distract, but more specific effects are hardly to be expected."

Another American, Herman Vollmer, similarly took the color therapists to task. He repeated a number of experiments performed abroad on plants, guppies, ants, flies, rats, and human beings, gaining negative results all along the line. "Nowhere can one find a common biologic denominator for the various experimental data. Neither the non-specific 'irritation theory' . . . seems to be generally applicable, nor is there sufficient experimental basis for the biologic specificity of certain wavelengths."

However, despite so contrary an attitude in America, it is largely meaningless and futile to deny the reality of color therapy. Visible light *does* affect the human organism. Anyone who insists otherwise is merely bespeaking prejudice and closing his mind to a great mass of reliable and competent evidence.

As often happens, color therapy has become another subject caught in a sort of Aristotelean trap. Two schools of thought— mystics and skeptics—are at loggerheads with each other, one making exaggerated and preposterous claims and the other shouting denunciations of the entire business. In consequence, a reasonable and fair attitude is overwhelmed. And color therapy, humbly enough, must sit quietly by in the hope that the tempers of men will one day grow sufficiently sober and calm to enable them to pursue the study of color on a rational and impartial basis. Surely mankind would profit.

PHOTOBIOLOGY

Photobiology embraces the study of the action of light on living organisms. In the endeavor of this chapter to explain the physical effects of color and to speak in behalf of color therapy, the writer will do his best to proceed from a discussion of simple phenomena to more highly complex manifestations of the action of visible light.

In all fairness, however, it should be understood that normal sunlight is generally beneficial to life. It perhaps has no pronounced action other than that under which the world and all its living things have come to flourish. In other words, if sunlight is the normal condition of life, effects for color must be shown over and above it, or at least aside from it. Thus Ellinger has written: "In view of what has been said about the frequently antagonistic effects of individual spectral colors, it will be easily understood why *white daylight* usually does not show any biological action."

What happens, then, when nature's balance is changed and when the energy of individual colors is separately applied?

The action of light is essentially photochemical. It was once supposed that such action was due chiefly to ultraviolet radiation, or at least that this region of the sun's spectrum was most active. Photobiological processes, however, cover the entire range of visible light and color. The absorption of light by any living organism will naturally vary. Yet because ultraviolet radiation has little power of penetration, its effects are more or less superficial. Blum writes, "The region of greatest penetration lies, in general, in the visible."

THE DISCOVERY OF RAAB

In 1900 Oscar Raab of Munich published a number of important findings on the toxicity of dyes. Experimenting with different dye solutions, he discovered that the time required to destroy microscopic organisms was related both to the intensity of light in his laboratory and to the density of his dyestuffs. Organisms exposed to sunlight might survive over long periods. However, when dye was introduced the organism could be made sensitive to light and promptly killed.

Raab's work led to much subsequent research. Dyes and pigments could be used to sensitize a wide variety of living organisms. While the dye itself might be chemically inert, it stained the microbe, caused light to be absorbed, and resulted in death.

With reference to this phenomenon, substances which are fluorescent in solution are likely to have the most intense action. What happens is that the dye causes different (and perhaps unfavorable) wave lengths to be absorbed. Although absorption of ultraviolet is harmful, so also is absorption of visible light, for investigations have shown that such metabolic effects can be achieved with visible light alone.

LIGHT SENSITIVITY

Any number of dyes and substances can be used to make an organism (or human skin) sensitive to light. Eosin, a red dye, has been added to milk to treat rachitic children on the principle that ultraviolet radiation will be more readily absorbed. Rose bengal and methylene blue will cause particular sensitivity to green and yellow light.

Strange skin eruptions may follow the use of cosmetics, ointments, perfumes, after-shave lotions. Frequently associated with poisoning, such "diseases" are often to be attributed to the fact that the substances make the skin light-sensitive and, in effect, aggravate "sunburn."

The red blood cells of mammals, suspended in salt solution, will withstand sunlight for several hours without appreciable change if exceedingly short wave lengths are excluded. However, where a fluorescent dye may be added, an almost immediate damage to the cell structure will be noted.

The introduction of dyes will also inactivate a long list of toxins, antitoxins, viruses, and venoms. Hormones may likewise be destroyed. "Human skin may be locally sensitized by photodynamic dyes, . . . and in this case intense itching occurs when the sensitized part is exposed to light" (Blum).

Hence there is a form of color therapy in which inert dyes are injected into the blood stream and the animal (or human patient) is then exposed to light. In experiments with white mice, Hausmann showed that large quantities of dye and intense light destroyed the animal within a short period. Weaker solutions and reduced light intensity also produced comas, weakness, and skin eruptions. With animals such as rabbits and dogs, light sensitization causes a general circulatory collapse. The addition of dyes into an aquarium may similarly affect fishes, causing them to gulp air at the surface, to lose their scales, and eventually to die.

It may well be that certain forms of "hives," such as "strawberry rash," represent instances in which the eating of certain foods makes the skin light-sensitive. As a case in point, a great amount of study has been given to the effect of buckwheat in the diet of animals. In fact, many diseases of animals may be traced to light sensitivity brought about by eating certain foods. Both in Arabia and Australia sheep have been painted—with good success—on the theory that dark animals seem to be less troubled with certain afflictions than light ones. In practically all cases of sensitivity to light, animals with the least pigmented skin are most affected.

There are also many instances in which contact with certain substances may cause eruptions. The chlorophyll of ordinary grass, crushed onto the skin, may produce lesions if the person rolls over and exposes the area of skin to sunlight. The handling of parsnips and figs may produce dermatitis. Coal-tar products may represent an occupational hazard to some individuals. Many workers handling coal-tar products find themselves extremely sensitive to light.

On this relation between pigmentation and reaction to light, L. Roule has presented an unusual theory regarding the migration of salmon. At the end of the second year, the young fish begins to lose pigment from its skin. This results in an irritating effect as strong sunlight penetrates shallow water, and drives the salmon downstream and into the sea. "Very probably this is not the only factor in bringing about the movement. However, it appears significant that the trout, a close relative which loses much less pigment than does the salmon, remains in fresh water" (Maier and Schneirla).

URTICARIA SOLARE

There is a strange and rare condition of photosensitivity in human beings known as urticaria solare. It offers striking evidence of the biological effect of visible light, for in urticaria solare visible blue and violet light are the undoubted cause of the ailment.

The amount of sunlight necessary to produce this skin affliction (called "triple response" by Blum) is very small. In one case an exposure of three minutes produced a definite discoloration and swelling. "It is safe to say that this response occurs in skins which are otherwise apparently normal, because of the presence of a photoactive substance which absorbs in the blue and violet regions of the spectrum. This substance is probably not present in normal skins, although it may be present but not active under normal circumstances." In experiments conducted by Blum and others, blue and violet light, which had been isolated with the aid of color and temperature filters, still produced the erythema of urticaria solare. All too clearly this minor affliction is one that is aggravated by visible blue and violet light, not by heat rays or ultraviolet rays. Though it may be exceedingly rare to medical science, it should admonish the skeptic and remind him that visible light and color are not without action on the human body.

THERAPEUTIC STUDIES

In 1940 a number of intriguing studies were made in Japan and reported in recognized medical journals throughout the world.

In experiments with guinea pigs, the young of those irradiated with red light attained rapid growth. Those irradiated with blue light showed signs of undernourishment. When the heads and mammary glands of the animals were irradiated with red light, milk secretion was accelerated. Blue light retarded milk secretion. Dr. Kotaro Menju thus wrote, "I am convinced that these effects of the visible light upon the milk secretive function are induced through the vegetative nervous system and the function of the endocrine glands."

With rabbits, red irradiation caused no immediate response but later was followed by a drop in blood pressure. "No matter whether the red ray radiation was applied to the whole body or abdomen, it affects to lower blood pressure."

Under blue light, blood pressure dropped immediately but was followed by a pronounced rise.

These reactions have been noted by other researchers. In general, red causes an immediate increase in blood pressure. It acts like a stimulant and is later followed by depression. On the other hand, blue causes a drop in blood pressure which may in time be trailed by an accelerated reaction.

Dr. M. Natume and Dr. S. Mizutani found a clear relation between color and the healing of wounds. Their work has been reported with that of Dr. Menju. Using blue dye (to absorb red light) healing was quickened. Red dye (which absorbed blue light) retarded healing. "As for the effects of the visible light upon tumor tissue . . . red rays affect to prevent the growth and blue rays affect, though slightly, to accelerate it."

THE EFFECT OF RED COLORS

Red light devoid of heat has no great action upon the skin. However, red radiation has great power of penetration and probably affects the blood. According to Ellinger, therapeutic applications exist for red light in the activation of sex hormones. Irradiation of the heads of four- and five-month-old blind ducklings has resulted in a better development of the testes than in non-irradiated controls. (An effect such as this has previously been mentioned in connection with the work of Bissonnette.) "In regard to enzymes, increased glycolysis has been observed in guinea pig blood."

In the much-quoted work of Ludwig and von Ries, rats grown under blue light had the same growth as normal rats. Under red light, however, weight developed far more rapidly. Vollmer in making the same test reported, "The blue and daylight animals showed no noteworthy difference in the course of their weights. The red rats seem to be a little retarded in their growth up to maturity, but later they exceeded the daylight animals definitely and continuously." Yet Vollmer was skeptical of these reactions and gave origin to a story which has since become something of an American classic: "The superiority in weight of the red animals at the end of the experiment is partly explained by pregnancy of one of these animals."

Nonetheless, red light unquestionably does affect the living organism. The experiments of Ludwig and von Ries with rats are hardly to be doubted in their verity. Red light may promote rapid growth and weight, but as Ellinger points out, "Following exclusion irradiation with red light, young mice eventually die, apparently due to a vitamin deficiency."

The use of red light to counteract inflammation has also been reported, though its therapeutic benefits have not been conclusively proved.

THE EFFECT OF BLUE COLORS

To some extent blue light is antagonistic to red. It is said to promote oxidation in the tissues and to retard hormonal activity. It has little effect upon the skin but is slightly germicidal. It would seem only logical that antiseptics meant to be applied to the skin should be blue, not red or brown, in order to assure the absorption of red radiation.

With reference to blue, Ellinger writes: "Most interesting of all are probably the effects upon the respiratory enzyme. According to O. Warburg, light influences the respiration of a yeast suspension in a carbon monoxide–oxygen mixture in such a manner that blue light is about three times as effective as green or yellow light, while red light is ineffective. . . . This is of clinical interest in that it supports the report of Koza on the favorable effects upon carbon monoxide poisoning that appear to be produced by quartz lamp irradiation. In view of the slight penetrating powers of ultraviolet rays, an effect by them upon the respiratory enzyme is unlikely. It is important to remember, however, that this light source is also rich in [visible] blue light, which has a sufficiently high penetrating power to exercise an effect in keeping with Warburg's observations."

As to the biological effects of other colors, the yellow-green region of the spectrum seems to be generally neutral. This fact will again be referred to in connection with other research.

REACTIONS THROUGH THE EYE

In practically all of the notes given above, biological effects for color have been described in which vision itself was inoperative.

It seems evident that color tends to stimulate the pituitary gland and, in fact, the glandular system of the body in general. B. D. Prescott writes: "Veil found that catfish from which the pituitary had been removed became almost white after twenty-four hours, even on a black background. After an injection of pituitary extract they temporarily turned dark again, only to resume their pale appearance after the effect of the injection wore off. It was also observed that during sleep some fish turn lighter, since metabolic functions are naturally retarded in the dormant state. It was further noted that they turned dark when they were excited, due to increased hormonal activity."

It would thus appear that reactions to color in man follow a similar pattern, that color influences the endocrine system, and that the chain of events taking place sweeps throughout the body.

In 1910 Stein called attention to a general light tonus in the muscular reactions of the human body. The word "tonus" refers to the condition of steady activity maintained by the body. Conditions of muscular tension and muscular relaxation, for example, are tonus changes. They are to some extent noticeable and measurable and are a good clue to the action of color. Feré discovered that red increased muscular tension from a normal 23 units to 42. Orange increased the units to 35, yellow to 30, green to 28 and blue to 24—all above normal. In the main, however, the warm hues are stimulating, while the cool hues are relaxing.

Through optic excitation A. Metzger observed that when light was thrown on one eye of many animals and humans, a tonus condition could be produced in the corresponding half of the body. Metzger's work has been mentioned by Felix Deutsch. Accompanying these tonus changes were changes in "the superficial and deep-seated sensation, both showing a regular dependence upon optical stimuli." He concluded that the influence of light not only acted on the muscles but was effective in producing changes over the entire organism.

As to experimental methods, Metzger had his subject stretch out his arms horizontally in front of his body. When light was thrown on one eye there would be a tonus increase on the same side of the body. The arm on the side of the light would raise itself and deviate toward the side of the illuminated eye.

When colors were employed, red light would cause the arms to spread away from each other. Green light would cause them to approach each other in a series of jerky motions. In cases of torticollis (twisting of the neck) exposure to red light increased restlessness, while green light decreased it.

Even more striking perhaps are the experiments of H. Ehrenwald, mentioned by both Felix Deutsch and Friedrich Ellinger. Ehrenwald demonstrated that when the face and neck are illuminated from the side, the outstretched arms will deviate toward the light if red and away from it if blue. To quote Deutsch, "This reaction takes place quite independently of the visual apparatus. It occurs also when the eyes are tightly sealed to exclude light and is said to have been observed in blind individuals." The same phenomenon has been dealt with by Kurt Goldstein and will be mentioned again in the next chapter. Blum remarks that the reaction "appears to point to a rudimentary form of radiation sensory centers in the human skin," a view that will please the liberal of mind and perhaps rouse the ire of the skeptic.

THE HUMAN ORGANISM

Like Ehrenwald, Hoffman is also of the opinion that the body has a radiation sense. The skin must contain cells having close association with the nervous system and a sense perception of radiant energy. Tonus reflex seems to be in two directions. Yellow-green is the neutral point, where no specific reaction takes place. Toward orange and red there is an attraction to the stimulus. Toward green and blue there is a withdrawal from it. Even infrared and ultraviolet, both invisible, will cause reflex actions, lending further evidence to the fact that the body does react to color without seeing it. Pincussen has written of a substantial increase in blood sugar under the action of red light. He believes that ultraviolet acts on the superficial layers of the skin, the region from blue to red acts on the blood, while the radiation of red and infrared affects the deeper layers of the flesh.

Some years ago Daitsch and Kogan, in another series of experiments, concluded that yellow and purple light had the best effect upon human metabolism. Red tended to weaken it considerably and green slightly. The influence of color, weak or strong, also depends upon whether it is seen as brilliant or dim. The pulse is generally slower in darkness than in bright illumination—regardless of the colors involved. Thus the application of "color therapy" must contemplate not only hue but illumination intensity. This suggests that warm hues, being aggressive and stimulating, have most potency in brilliant light, while cool hues, more passive and subduing, lend themselves to suppressed light.

This, then, is a brief review of color therapy and the physiological action of visible light. As expressed by M. Luckiesh in *The*

Science of Seeing: "One should not be surprised if it is revealed some time in the future when we know more about the human being, that all wavelengths of radiant energy from the sun are intricately entwined in the life and health processes of human beings."

Unquestionably color does have a physical effect upon the human organism. Brightness and warmth of color stimulate the autonomic nervous system. Blood pressure and pulse rate actually do increase. Whether a person likes the idea or not, the flesh will become warmer and the temperature will rise. Conversely, dimness and coolness of color release the stimulation of the autonomic nervous system. Blood pressure and pulse decrease and the flesh becomes relatively cooler.

Part 3

THE PSYCHOLOGICAL ASPECTS

CHAPTER 11

Emotional Reactions

Though MEDICAL SCIENCE may
eschew the idea of color therapy for any direct biological action
upon the human body, it does admit actions and influences in the
realm of the psychic. Thus while "color therapy" is not a vener-
ated term in medical literature, references to *psycho*therapy are
becoming quite common. One would indeed be an iconoclast to
reject color entirely. Its role in all forms of life is too evident to
be either denied or ignored.

Many researchers in the field of psychiatry have pointed out
certain interesting and basic facts about human likes and dislikes
for color. In the well-known Rorschach test, for example, an
emotionally responsive person will react quite freely to color in
general. An emotionally inhibited person may be shocked or

embarrassed by the intrusion of color into his inner life. The rigid, emotionally indifferent type may remain unaffected.

In the main, it may be said that normal persons who are or attempt to be well adjusted to the world, and hence "outwardly integrated," like color in general and warm colors in particular. "Inwardly integrated" persons may favor cool colors and be none too enthusiastic about them—or about any other colors, for that matter.

The following remarks by Dr. Maria Rickers-Ovsiankina may be read to good profit by those seeking an understanding of the emotional significance of color. "Finally Jaensch, quite independently, again reached the same dichotomy of red yellow versus blue green. He finds that all people can be grouped in a way similar to red-green color blind subjects, namely into those more sensitive to the warm end of the spectrum and those more sensitive to the cold end. The warm color dominant subjects are characterized by an intimate relation to the visually perceptible world. They are receptive and open to outside influences. They seem to submerge themselves rather readily in their social environment. Their emotional life is characterized by warm feelings, suggestibility, and strong affects. All mental functions are rapid and highly integrated with each other. In the subject-object relationship, the emphasis is on the object.

"The cold color dominant subjects in the Jaensch experiments have a detached 'split-off' attitude to the outside world. They find it difficult to adapt themselves to new circumstances and to express themselves freely. Emotionally they are cold and reserved. In the subject-object relationship, the emphasis is on the subject. In short, the warm color dominant subject is Jaensch's outwardly integrated type, the cold color dominant his inwardly integrated type."

As to the so-called psychology of color there is much to be said. J. P. Guilford writes, "I think that it is more than a figure of speech to say that living tissue, particularly brain tissue, generates colors and pleasantness or unpleasantness just as other collections of matter generate the phenomenon of heat, or magnetism, or electricity." Light striking the eye sets up reactions which spread throughout the organism. There may be excitation or depression, a quickening of nervous response or an effect of tranquillity. Impressions of pleasure or displeasure may be less associated with spiritual and æsthetic qualities than with the reaction of the brain and, indeed, the entire organism.

It is well known today that inhibitions and repressions may lead to afflictions and may actually cause adverse pathological conditions within the body. Mental conflicts may impair certain physical functions and lead to specific illness.

Stomach ulcers are a case in point. In the first state the digestive process may be impaired. If this continues long enough, an ulcer may develop. David Dietz writes, "Thus the bridge between a mental cause and a physical result has been crossed. Under the old point of view, the physician had only the stomach ulcer to deal with. But psychosomatic medicine teaches that he must deal with the emotions as well."

The person who struggles against odds to maintain an equable disposition may develop high blood pressure. Other mental sufferings may bring on colitis or asthma. Even patients with broken bones may have become accident-prone through a disturbed frame of mind. One doctor has attributed over half of all human ills to unhappiness. There is no doubt that mental and physical health are closely related.

However, the reader should be skeptical of sensational stories. One may hear of a person attempting suicide because the colors on his or her living-room walls were ugly, of divorces and broken homes caused by inharmonious surroundings. Most of such "lore" is mere fabrication. When tracked down, the incident invariably turns out to be one that has happened to someone else.

Many notions about the effect of color on the human mind are mere absurdities. There are persons obsessed by the belief that red is a furious and deadly color. One author writes: "Lady Duff-Gordon has an antipathy—which, I confess, I share—to red, the most powerful color we have, and the one which drives people mad quicker than any other. She reminded me of that prison in which color is used as a torture; a man placed where he can see nothing but red goes mad in twenty-four hours and dies. It takes purple half as long again to produce the same result."

All this is fiction, of course, and the red torture chamber referred to is a mere invention of some febrile imagination. When people dislike a certain hue they often vent their rage in this way. The painter Wassily Kandinsky showed a similar disgust for yellow: "Yellow is the typically earthly color. It can never have profound meaning. An intermixture of blue makes it a sickly color. It may be paralleled in human nature with madness, not with melancholy or hypochondriacal mania, but rather with violent, raving lunacy."

REACTIONS IN GENERAL

To give the reader a "feeling" of color—to check against his own psychological reactions—here are a few general notes.

140

In the main, the colors of the spectrum are to be associated with two moods, the warm, active, and exciting qualities of red and its analogous hues, and the cool, passive, and calming qualities of blue, violet, and green. Areas of these hues tend to enliven the mood or to quiet it. Likewise light colors are active, while deep colors are likely to be passive. Beyond the feeling of warmth or coolness, brightness or dimness, the exact choice of a hue or tone is a fairly optional matter, and its power to arouse pleasure or displeasure may depend on individual predilections.

Pure colors, however, are likely to be severe. Too much "harping" on any one color may prove distressing.

Even more pronounced in "moods" are chromatic lights, greens and blues that turn the lips black and give the flesh a cadaverous aspect. Here the mere sight of a person's face may be revolting. Green light has been thrown on criminals in a mirrored room to help force a confession.

A few psychologists have carried out research to determine the moods which people associate with the colors of the spectrum. N. A. Wells found that deep orange has the most exciting influence, then scarlet and yellow-orange. The most tranquilizing color is yellow-green, then green. Violet has the most subduing influence, purple next.

Dr. Robert R. Ross of Stanford University has endeavored to ally colors with dramatic intensity and emotion. Gray, blue, and purple are best associated with tragedy; red, orange, and yellow with comedy. William A. Wellmann of California has likewise worked out a "theatrical" palette, red being the color of vigor, yellow the color of warmth and joy, green of abundance and health, blue of spirituality and thought, brown of melancholy, gray of old age, white of zest and awareness, and black of gloom.

Not many writers on the subject, however, seem to be aware of the fact that a color may have contradictory qualities, depending on the particular viewpoint of the observer. Green is an excellent case in point. As seen objectively, it is cool, fresh, clear, and altogether pleasing. But green illumination shining on the human flesh causes a subjective viewpoint that instantly makes the color repulsive. Thus no list of color associations is adequate unless it takes into consideration these subjective as well as objective aspects. For reactions will differ as a person associates color with the outside world or with himself.

While warm colors are not greatly different objectively and subjectively, cool hues may be antithetical. Red, however, may seem far more intense as applied to one's self than it does as applied to external objects. Blues and greens which appear peaceful in one aspect may be terrifying in another.

Thus the moods conveyed by a color may be rather diverse. A number of modern associations are presented in a separate tabulation. Here the major colors are described in their general appearance, their mental associations, direct associations, objective and subjective impressions.

RESEARCH IN COLOR PSYCHOLOGY

Research on the psychological aspects of color is difficult for the mere reason that human emotions are none too stable and the psychic make-up of human beings varies from person to person. However, there are a number of general and universal reactions to color which seem to be noted in most persons. Gilbert Brighouse in measuring human reactions under colored lights, tested muscular responses among several hundred college stu-

MODERN AMERICAN COLOR ASSOCIATIONS

Color	General appearance	Mental associations	Direct associations	Objective impressions	Subjective impressions
Red	Brilliant, intense, opaque, dry	Hot, fire, heat, blood	Danger, Christmas, Fourth of July, St. Valentine's, Mother's Day, flag	Passionate, exciting, fervid, active	Intensity, rage, rapacity, fierceness
Orange	Bright, luminous, glowing	Warm, metallic, autumnal	Halloween, Thanksgiving	Jovial, lively, energetic, forceful	Hilarity, exuberance, satiety
Yellow	Sunny, incandescent, radiant	Sunlight	Caution	Cheerful, inspiring, vital, celestial	High spirit, health
Green	Clear, moist	Cool, nature, water	Clear, St. Patrick's Day	Quieting, refreshing, peaceful, nascent	Ghastliness, disease, terror, guilt
Blue	Transparent, wet	Cold, sky, water, ice	Service, flag	Subduing, melancholy, contemplative, sober	Gloom, fearfulness, furtiveness
Purple	Deep, soft, atmospheric	Cool, mist, darkness, shadow	Mourning, Easter	Dignified, pompous, mournful, mystic	Loneliness, desperation
White	Spatial—light	Cool, snow	Cleanliness, Mother's Day, flag	Pure, clean, frank, youthful	Brightness of spirit, normality
Black	Spatial—darkness	Neutral, night, emptiness	Mourning	Funereal, ominous, deadly, depressing	Negation of spirit, death

143

dents. He found that reactions were 12 per cent quicker than normal under red light, while green light retarded the response.

It is perhaps even more true that the human organism is likely to be quickened under bright light than under dim light. The amount of illumination appears to be more significant than hue.

D. B. Harmon has observed that most living things tend to orient themselves toward light or toward brightness. Also, as the energy of stimulation goes up, response tendency goes with it. In his opinion, therefore, bright environments will condition the organism for what he calls avoidant (big-muscle) activity. On the other hand, brilliance may hinder more sedentary tasks (mental activity). This would suggest a number of conclusions. Activities of a muscular nature are better performed in bright light and amid bright surroundings. Exacting mental and visual tasks are better performed with softer and deeper colors in the environment (though with ample illumination over the task).

THE WORK OF KURT GOLDSTEIN

One of the most stimulating and prolific of writers on the psychological aspects of color is Kurt Goldstein. "Life is a condition alternating between excitation, destruction, and unbalance, *and* reorganization, equilibrium, and rest. In the course of life colors play their role. Each color has a special importance and all colors together help to guarantee normal life."

Goldstein is a recognized authority on psychoneurology, and his writings and observations are well regarded in the medical field. His book, *The Organism,* and his contributions to American medical journals, contain not only a rich fund of clinical research but a keen sense of logic and human understanding.

Goldstein writes, "It is probably not a false statement if we say that a *specific color stimulation is accompanied by a specific*

144

response pattern of the entire organism." Confirming the work of Metzger and Ehrenwald mentioned in the last chapter, organic response may be noted when the stimulation of color is carefully introduced and its action observed. This would mean that response to color is deep-set, that it is entwined in the life process.

"The influence of color is increased in neurotics and psychotics." Goldstein writes of a woman with a cerebellar disease who had a tendency to fall unexpectedly and to walk with an unsteady gait. When she wore a red dress such symptoms were more pronounced. Green and blue clothing had an opposite effect and restored her equilibrium almost to normal.

Thus color may affect the ability of the body to maintain its position. As already stated, red light causes the outstretched arms to spread away from each other; green light causes them to move toward each other. In a patient with a left-sided lesion of the brain, the arm on the affected side deviates far more than normal. "Because this deviation under certain conditions is definite in amount and is changed definitely by different color stimulations, this phenomenon can be used as an indicator in studying the influence of colors on performance."

The equilibrium of the human organism is disturbed far more by red than it is by green. Goldstein thus comes to a conclusion that offers an important answer to those concerned with the "psychology of color." He states, "The stronger deviation of the arms in red stimulation corresponds to the experience of being disrupted, thrown out, abnormally attracted to the outerworld. It is only another expression of the patient's feeling of obtrusion, aggression, excitation, by red. The diminution of the deviation [to green stimulation] corresponds to the withdrawal from the outerworld and retreat to his own quietness, his center. The inner experiences represent the psychological aspect of the reactions of the organism. We are faced in the observable phenomena with the physical aspect."

Therapeutically, many persons suffering from tremors and twitching may find such disturbances relieved if green glasses are worn. This has the action of screening out red light rays and having a quieting effect. "How color therapy, based on experimental research about the influence of colors on the function of the organism, may be helpful in treatment of neuroses and psychoses the future will reveal."

TIME, LENGTH, AND WEIGHT ESTIMATIONS

Mental judgments of common tasks may also be influenced by color. According to Goldstein, under the influence of red light time is likely to be overestimated. Conversely, under the influence of green or blue light, time is likely to be underestimated. In the functional application of color, cool hues would thus seem best where routine and monotonous tasks are performed, such as in offices and factories. Warm hues would be suitable for living rooms, restaurants, and cocktail lounges—where time in apparent "slow motion" might be more pleasurable.

Similarly, "Estimation of the length of sticks based on visual touch stimulation is much less correct in red light. The threshold is lower in green and enlarged in red stimulation." In other words, things are likely to seem longer and bigger under warm light, and shorter and smaller under cool light.

Results of the same nature are encountered in estimations of weights. Under red light, weights will be judged as heavier; under green light they will be judged as lighter. Again, functional applications for color would suggest the use of light, cool colors on boxes and containers which must be carried about in workaday activities.

146

It should be noted that in most tests of color, hued rays of light rather than a painted environment are usually employed. There is a good reason for this. In the process of seeing, the eye is conscious of two things—the illumination that fills space and the appearance of objects that are localized within the space. Where a person may be exposed to a large area of red, for example, and where the illumination may be normal, his vision will not be thoroughly "saturated" by hue. But where the illumination may be red, the effect of the color will be more pronounced. This means that colored lights can be made to have a more intense action than colored surfaces.

COLOR AND OTHER HUMAN SENSES

It has long been known that the stimulation of color will produce reactions throughout the human organism and that the activity of one sense organ will influence another. Sherrington has written, "All parts of the nervous system are connected together and no part of it is probably ever capable of reaction without affecting and being affected by various other parts, and it is a system certainly never absolutely at rest." There may be suppression of sensation or activation of it. Popcorn may not have much taste if eaten while riding on a roller coaster. An effort to hear at night in the woods will seem to sharpen the sense of sight as well as the sense of hearing.

In the early part of this century, investigators noted a definite relation between sound and color. Rod vision (black and white) is presumably reduced during sound stimulation of the ear. Cone vision (color) may be enlarged, particularly for green light, under the same conditions.

In 1931 Karl Zietz reported an unusual phenomenon relating to color and sound. This work is mentioned by Heinz Werner in his *Comparative Psychology of Mental Development.* While tones of high pitch or low pitch were sounded, small areas of color were exposed to the eye for a fraction of a second. Sounds of low pitch tended to shift the appearance of colors toward an adjacent deeper hue. Sounds of high pitch tended to shift them toward adjacent lighter hues. Thus low pitch tones had the effect of making red appear deeper or more bluish; orange became reddish; yellow became brownish and sometimes reddish; green became bluer; blue became more like violet. High pitch tones gave red an apparent yellowish or orange cast; orange shifted toward yellow; yellow became paler; green became yellowish; blue seemed lighter and greener.

Similar effects were observed in studying the influence of tone on the appearance of afterimages. High pitches tended to sharpen the contours of afterimages, whereas low pitches tended to blur them. In view of more evidence to be presented later in Chapter 17 relating to accelerated dark adaptation in the human eye, it perhaps may be said that sounds of high pitch tend to aid acuity and to sharpen perception, even though slightly.

In 1935 a Russian scientist, S. V. Kravkov, published a further series of intriguing data and conclusions on the effect of sound upon the color sensibility of the eye. Kravkov's observers were seated in a dark room before a spectroscope. Sounds were transmitted to their ears by means of telephone receivers. After the eye of an observer had been adapted to the light and after a check had been made on his particular sensibility to the hues of the spectrum, sounds were poured into his ears. Another check was then made. Kravkov reports, "The cone sensibility to the rays of the green-blue parts of the spectrum *rises* under the action of a simultaneous sound, whereas the sensibility to the yellow-orange-red parts of the spectrum *decreases.*"

1. Sound decreases the rod sensitivity of the eye. That is, the general character of illumination as seen on the outer boundaries of the retina grows dim.

2. Sound increases the sensibility of the cones of the eye to green (maximum) and to blue.

3. Sound decreases the sensibility of the cones of the eye to red (maximum) and to orange.

4. No decrease or increase is experienced in the yellow-green region.

These reactions are quite pronounced. In general, when the ears are thudded with sound vibrations the eyes have a hazier perception of colors of long wave length, while sensibility is increased for hues of short wave length. Kravkov writes, "The reduction of the color sensibility to red under the influence of sound renders it necessary to revise some standards relating to the visibility of red signals."

In studying the effect of electric currents on the retina, Kravkov similarly found that an ascendent current increased cone sensitivity to green-blue and diminished it to red-orange. A descendent current had the reverse effect, decreasing sensitivity to green-blue and increasing it to red-orange. Yellow was the neutral point in the spectrum.

OTHER RESEARCH

The work of Kravkov has been repeated and extended by Frank Allen and Manuel Schwartz of Canada. These two men have confirmed the same findings and have also studied the effect of the stimulation of taste and smell upon color perception.

Although, as with Kravkov, sound lowered the apparent intensity of red colors and enhanced the apparent intensity of green colors, "When a rest interval of 3 minutes was taken, . . . a complete reversal of sensitivity of the red and green . . . occurred, the red color now appearing brighter and the green dimmer than normal."

To state a principle, it seems that the immediate action of any color stimulation is followed in time by a reverse effect. Red increases blood pressure, which later becomes more than normally depressed. Green and blue decrease blood pressure and later cause it to rise. From this evidence it would appear that therapeutic applications of color should be organized in terms of color sequence, not single colors alone. The stimulation of red may be far more dramatic and pronounced if followed by a subsequent stimulation of green or blue.

According to Allen and Schwartz, stimulation of the sense of taste likewise affects the color sensibility of the eye. Using an aqueous solution of sulfate of quinine, which has a bitter taste, red sensation was depressed and green sensation was increased. Sugar had no apparent visual effect.

As to the sense of smell, "With the odor of oil of geranium as the stimulating substance, the red and violet sensations . . . were depressed in sensitivity and the green enhanced." Again, after a prolonged rest period, a reversal occurred.

The significance of these tests and reactions may perhaps be well reviewed in a statement by Kurt Goldstein. If the reader seeks a generalization that might enable him to apply the so-called psychology of color, here may be his opportunity. "One could say *red is inciting to activity and favorable for emotionally-determined actions; green creates the condition of meditation and exact fulfillment of the task. Red may be suited to produce the emotional background out of which ideas and action will emerge; in green these ideas will be developed and the actions executed.*" (The italics are Goldstein's.)

150

CHAPTER 12

Neurotics and Psychotics

PERSONS TROUBLED WITH nervous (neurotic) and mental (psychotic) disturbances are greatly affected by color and are responsive to it. Because these sensitive and frequently unbalanced individuals are likely to conduct themselves without much rational deliberation, the meaning of color to them is highly significant.

Light itself, including infrared and ultraviolet, affects the metabolism of the body, the ferments and antibodies, the skin, the pigment formation, and so on. Out in the sun the human organism glows with warmth and its skin tans. Thus light and color in general are salutary.

Recent work by psychologists and psychiatrists has thrown significant light on the human mind. A mechanistic approach to psychology, for example, is giving way to an organic approach. One new understanding is that mental traits may not follow a straight line from ignorance to intellectualism or from the primitive to the highly developed intelligence. The best of all men may live a life on all mental levels. As Heinz Werner makes clear, the troubled or neurotic individual can hardly be likened to a primitive. Mental ailments are not a matter of retrogression but of collapse. The truth of this is shown by Werner: "The primitive man lives in a world to which he is admirably adjusted; the pathological individual tries to adjust himself by means of primitive behavior to a world for him inadequate and non-primitive."

THE WORK OF DEUTSCH

One notable investigator in the psychiatric meaning of light and color is Felix Deutsch, a physician. His work is both authoritative and convincing and represents one of the best analyses of color that have yet come to the author's attention. His research is unprejudiced, and his findings throw important light not only on color in medicine but on the whole psychology of color.

Deutsch writes, "Every action of light has in its influence physical as well as psychic components." Simply, light energy affects the body directly and also through the eye and brain. He points out, for example, that in treatment of pulmonary diseases such as tuberculosis with light there is a true biological effect. Beyond this, however, the patient shows a cheerful response to the pleasing qualities of fresh air and sunshine. He experiences "sensations and psychic excitations, which, through the vegetative nervous system, boost all life functions: increase the appetite, stimulate circulation, etc., and through these manifestations the physical influence of light upon the disease process is in turn enhanced."

152

Thus Deutsch speaks of a light influence and a light impression. The one is physical, the other emotional. Each is individually therapeutic, and both together comprise a highly efficacious "remedy" in a great many instances.

It is a matter of common observation that the moods of men are changed by environment, by ugliness and beauty, by sunny weather and rainy weather. Reactions to color are likewise depressing or inspiring. Placed in a bright, harmonious setting, most people will find their dispositions improved. And with a better spirit the vascular system, pulse, blood pressure, nervous and muscular tension, may be affected. These responses to hue are subtle and do not follow any universal laws, according to Deutsch. "In estimating these reactions which one could also call emotional and which only secondarily show their manifestations organically, one has to rely almost exclusively upon the statements made by the individuals tested, statements whose validity is not always easy to determine."

This brings one close indeed to a better understanding of the psychology of color. The hues of the spectrum may not be different tonics each of which is to be used for a limited number of specific ailments. The strategy is perhaps not a matter of prescribing red over blue, or green over yellow at all, but of applying *any color* that will call forth a favorable reaction from the patient! The magic of color becomes the magic of the rainbow itself. Color is beneficial when it appeals.

THE INFLUENCE OF ENVIRONMENT

Deutsch in his practice has found that color influences a change in blood pressure. This takes place in an indirect way. The patient sees the hue, likes it, and thereupon finds that his whole system is relaxed. His viewpoint changes. He becomes more

153

optimistic. There is a physical result from a purely visual and mental impression.

Deutsch writes: "The influence of mood, psychic disturbance, fear, happiness, sadness, and impressions from the outer world make themselves readily noticeable in both subjective and objective changes referable to the vascular system. Changes in pulse frequency and rhythm as well as fluctuations in blood pressure are objective expressions of the psychically influencing factors which have taken place." Thus in the use of color he has treated patients whose conditions were of nervous origin or who had disturbances in heart rhythm. "During the period of investigation all other therapeutic measures which might have affected the vascular system were abandoned."

A room was chosen overlooking a garden. The glass panes of the windows were arranged to accommodate different hues, and colored artificial light was employed in the interior. Two main colors were enlisted, a warm red and a cool green.

The subject was asked to look quietly out the window. He was left alone for a quarter or half an hour. After this he was questioned regarding his general feeling and about his impression of the illumination. Finally he was asked to build free associations and to recall anything that might come to his mind.

CASE HISTORIES

The general influence of color on his patients may be described by reviewing two of the many case histories quoted by Deutsch. One patient troubled with anginal fear complained of shortness of breath, air hunger, and palpitation of the heart. She feared the return of a spasm which years ago had caused her to lose consciousness. An examination of her heart revealed a fairly normal condition. She had a slight thyroid enlargement. Her

154

pulse rate at the time of her examination was 112, her blood pressure 115/70.

This patient was placed in a red environment. (Green as a color was decidedly unpleasant to her.)

First session: pulse 112; after treatment pulse was 80.

Second session: pulse 92; after treatment pulse was 76.

Third session: pulse 92; after treatment pulse was 80.

Fourth session: pulse 84; after treatment pulse was 74.

During following sessions her pulse was always 74. The patient experienced a comforting sensation of warmth. Her insomnia disappeared and she felt restored calmness.

In another case, the patient complained of attacks of weakness, shortness of breath, and pressure sensations over the chest which led to fear of choking. When she was admitted, her blood pressure was 245/125. Medical therapy did not produce any changes in this reading, nor did it lessen the patient's subjective complaints.

When she was placed in a green room for short periods, however, the following reduction in blood pressure took place:

First session: 250/130; later 210/125.

Second session: 245/130; later 205/120.

Third session: 240/125; later 205/120.

Fourth session: 220/120; later 195/110.

Fifth session: 210/115; later 210/110.

Sixth session: 200/110; later 180.

Seventh session: 195; later 180.

"In the course of other sessions the blood pressure fell to 180 mm. Hg and was attended by subjective, relative feelings of well being."

Deutsch assumes that biological actions take place following the use of color. There is a certain reaction of the whole organ-

155

ism, plus "the participation of the psychic apparatus." It will be noted that his application of color is usually for a calming effect. The influence of hue to stimulate and excite the organism will be discussed later.

The value of color in dealing with neurotic and psychotic maladies thus becomes evident. To summarize his conclusions, Deutsch makes four points.

1. Color brings about a reflex action upon the vascular system, if only through the feelings and emotions.

2. The effect achieved is not specific for any one or any certain hues. Warm colors may calm one person and excite another. Cool colors may likewise be stimulating to one person and passive to another.

3. Irradiation with red or green light may produce an elevation of blood pressure and a quickening of pulse rate. Or the opposite may take place, depending on the particular psychic make-up of the individual.

4. "An organic, non-optical color sense has not been proved so far." However, the response that follows exposure to color may have an organic effect.

What happens? "The emotional excitements which are recognized through changes in blood pressure, pulse-frequency and rhythm, are brought forth through association." Green may recall nature, mountains, lakes. Red may recall the sunset, the fireplace. "These superficial associations lead to deeper lying memories, which explain the affective emphasis of the attitudes toward the colors."

Thus the therapy of color is successful as it affects the emotions. The patient is relieved of anxiety. He finds himself "transferred

156

to a world which is more pleasing and presents fewer conflicts, the reaction upon the organism cannot fail to appear." Even where he rejects a color as being repellent, with this rejection goes much of his ill feeling. He responds eagerly to the color he prefers. As Deutsch states, "The psychic process which is brought into play here is easily stated: the colored light changes the environment. Through the changed appearance of the environment the individual is lifted out of reality." He is on the road to recovery, helped along by his own mental processes.

AURORATONE FILMS

In the treatment of depressed psychotic patients, results similar to those of Deutsch have been achieved with abstract sound motion pictures developed by Cecil Stokes of California. These unusual films combine music with a flow of mobile color effects, featuring orchestral and organ music and the singing of Bing Crosby.

The Auroratone films of Stokes have been studied in their psychological and therapeutic aspects by Herbert E. Rubin and Elias Katz in an army general hospital. "During a period of preliminary observations, it was noted that manic-depressives in the depressed state had catharsis experiences and appeared to benefit from exposure to the films."

As explained by Rubin and Katz, a badly injured or crippled patient may become depressed. He may think of suicide and may stubbornly resist all medical aid. As his depression grows worse, he may become seriously ill.

The tremendous value of color in such cases is that it makes the patient more "accessible." A flood of emotion passes over him. The abstract color, the music, help to relieve mental and emotional tension. The patient may weep. "In this state of accessibility it was possible for the psychiatrist to establish rapport with individual members of the group."

"Patient E. This 26-year-old patient was admitted . . . on 5 June 1945 for further treatment of multiple second and third degree burns of the body. . . . He did not show any mental symptoms until 16 August 1945 when he wrote on American Red Cross stationery, 'Please get some poison to kill me.' The patient is disfigured as a result of severe burns of the face involving the ears as well as both hands. He is restless, agitated, depressed, retarded and self-absorbed. He ruminates a great deal about having lost his grip on life. . . . He frequently expresses a desire to die as a means of solving his emotional problem."

If color and music did not cure Patient E, they rendered invaluable aid. Rubin and Katz write: "21 September 1945. Prior to the showing the patient appeared somewhat depressed. He sat with his head down and fumbled with his shoes. Throughout the showing, he seemed completely absorbed with the music and the color. . . . At the close of the showing, he sat up and looked about the room. His countenance was no longer despondent. During the group discussion afterward, he cooperated with the psychiatrist, answering questions freely. As he left the room he did not drag his feet." Obviously, there was hope now for Patient E.

MENTAL DISORDERS

A generation or more ago many experiments were made with color, and mental hospitals throughout the world employed it both to afford relief and to effect cures. In 1875 a European doctor by the name of Ponza fitted several rooms with colored glass windows, colored walls, and colored furnishings. Red and blue were the colors principally used. Regarding red he wrote, "After passing three hours in a red room a man afflicted with taciturn delirium became gay and cheerful; on getting up the day after his entry into the room, another madman who had refused all food whatever asked for breakfast, and ate with surprising avidity." As to blue, "A violent case who had to be kept in a strait jacket was shut in the room with the blue window; less than an hour afterwards he had become calmer."

Today, however, the red and blue rooms of the asylum are no more. While colors may influence the mood, their action affords relief but not cure. Through the application of such therapies as insulin shock and artificial fever, modern medicine is achieving far more potent results.

Yet color is needed in hospitals, and further research is still being undertaken. In 1938 the Worcester State Hospital in Massachusetts carried out a series of tests and issued a report in the July, 1938, *Bulletin of the Massachusetts Association for Occupational Therapy.* The experiments were made in a small mental ward in which a nurse and attendant were in charge. Colored lights were used and careful notes kept on the reactions of the patients.

"Magenta used with disturbed patients had a quieting effect for several weeks with a diminution of efficiency after the initial period. There was an associated stimulating effect which contributed somewhat to a feeling of tension. However, when magenta was replaced by white light after a month, the patients became quite excited.

"Blue had a striking and prolonged quieting effect. Patients and attendants commented on its soothing effect. This color was the most effective of those used.

"Yellow was used with depressed, melancholy patients and had a very slight stimulating effect. Red used with the same group of patients produced more stimulation than the yellow. The reaction of the depressed patients to color was short and less obvious than that of the disturbed patients."

The author is advised that the Worcester experiments are no longer being conducted. The conditions under which they were attempted were perhaps far from ideal. Color for the sake of color is not enough. The exclusion of daylight, the lack of proper attention to a color scheme or color effect that is "artistic" as well as "scientific," may lead to invalid results. Human beings, as Deutsch has shown, are sensitive not alone to color but to the appeal of the environment under which it is displayed. Psychotherapy with hue also demands orderliness, harmony, and beauty.

THE SIGNIFICANCE OF COLOR

The relationship of color to insanity is a subtle one. The patient may accept or reject certain hues depending on his particular psychosis.

In the well-known Rorschach test, which involves an interpretation of abstract ink blots, color is significant. Marguerite Emery writes, "The psychoanalysts have shown that frequently a death wish lies buried in the unconscious of people suffering from these [depressed] disorders—a desire to kill someone and to shed blood. A choice of red, therefore, is not unnatural."

Feeble-minded individuals, when asked to use colors, will apply red freely. As to other hues, "Green was also the choice in a few cases of psycho-sexual infantilism, and of one feeble minded girl. . . . Patients almost without exception who had regressed to, or had failed to progress beyond a markedly infantile level chose yellow. This was particularly true of the schizophrenic group."

Dr. Eric P. Mosse points out that insane people consider themselves constantly exposed to danger. "The difference between mental health and mental disease consists at last in nothing else

160

but how this predicament is handled. The normally balanced individuum will face, brave and adapt himself to his problems, whereas mental disease is the manifestation of different depths of escape. With this fact in mind, we automatically understand why in achromatopsia of the hysterical the order in which the colors disappear is violet, green, blue and finally red. Aside and above this experience we generally found in hysterical patients, especially in psychoneuroses with anxiety states, a predilection for green as symbolizing the mentioned escape mechanism. The emotional attack of the outside is repressed, the 'red' impulses of hatred, aggression and sex denied. . . . For the same reason we will not be surprised that *red* is the color of choice of the manic and hypomanic patient giving the tumult of his emotions their 'burning' and 'bloody' expression. And we don't wonder that melancholia and depression reveal themselves through a complete 'black out.' Finally we see yellow as the color of schizophrenia. . . . This yellow is the proper and intrinsic color of the morbid mind. Whenever we observe its accumulative appearance we may be sure that we are dealing with a deep lying psychotic disturbance."

CHAPTER 13

Associations and Analogies

COLOR ASSOCIATIONS exist by the score. Man finds in the hues of the spectrum emotional analogies with sounds, shapes and forms, odors, tastes. Color expressions work their way into language, symbolism, tradition, and superstition. The reason is probably that the sensation of color is of a primitive order. Reaction to it, appreciation of it, requires little effort of intellect or imagination. Color conveys moods which attach themselves quite automatically to human feeling. It is part and parcel with the psychic make-up of human beings.

COLORS AND SOUNDS

In a psychological phenomenon known as synesthesia (to be further discussed in Chapter 15) many persons are found who innately and subconsciously "see" colors in sounds. The two arts —color and music—have freely exchanged terms. Tone, pitch, intensity, volume, color, chromatic are all a part of the nomenclature of art and musical composition. Christopher Ward suggested a number of emotional associations when he wrote: "From the faintest murmur of pearl-gray, through the fluttering of blue, the oboe note of violet, the cool, clear wood-wind of green, the mellow piping of yellow, the bass of brown, the bugle-call of scarlet, the sounding brass of orange, the colors are music."

In the seventeenth century Newton related colors to the notes of the diatonic scale: red for C, orange for D, yellow for E, green for F, blue for G, indigo for A, violet for B. Subsequent colorists and musicians have devised other scales. In his *Prometheus,* Alexander Scriabin developed a part for a color organ which he called "Luce." The composition was to be played in darkness, with colored lights thrown upon a screen.

Among other composers, Liszt is credited with several pet phrases: "More pink here." "This is too black." "I want it all azure." Beethoven called B minor the black key. Schubert likened E minor "unto a maiden robed in white and with a rose-red bow on her breast." To Rimsky-Korsakoff sunlight was C major, and F sharp was strawberry red.

MODERN RESEARCH

Color "hearing" has been extensively treated in a monograph written by Theodore F. Karwoski and Henry S. Odbert. In a study of 148 college students, at least 60 per cent experienced some kind of color response when music was heard, 39 per cent were able to "see" a color or colors, 53 per cent were able to "associate" a color, and 31 per cent "felt" a color response. "It

163

seems safe to say that a good majority of the population in one way or another relates colors to music."

Karwoski and Odbert found that slow music was generally associated with blue, fast music with red, high notes with light colors, deep notes with dark colors, and that patterns as well as hues were involved. Most significant, "The horizontal dimension might be related to the development of music in time; the vertical dimension to changes in pitch. A third dimension of depth may eventually be available to denote volume or intensity." Surely most people who have given thought to correlation of music, form, and color will be in sympathetic agreement with this conclusion. Music moves along quickly or slowly depending on its tempo. It jumps into tints for high notes or drops down into shades for low notes. When it is fortissimo, the colors are near, intense, heavy, and bulky. When it is pianissimo, the colors are filmy, grayish, and far away.

Color hearing is common among children and probably exists extensively among primitive people. It is also discovered among psychotic persons, especially schizophrenic types. It may be induced by drugs such as mescalin. To quote Werner: "A subject under the influence of mescalin experiences color simultaneously with tone. High tones evoke vivid, garish colors, and deep tones engender duller colors. If there is a steady knocking on the wall, let us say, the subject will see optical images dancing before his eyes in a rhythm that synchronizes with the measured beat of the knocking. One subject described his sensations in this manner: 'I think that I hear noises and see faces, and yet everything is one and the same. I cannot tell whether I am seeing or hearing. I feel, taste, and smell the sound. It's all one. I, myself, am the tone.'" This confusion of the senses may be experienced in dreams or during extreme illness.

Men such as Thomas Wilfred and Tom Douglas Jones have endeavored to develop an art of color that is independent of music. In many respects, color is more fundamentally emotional than music and requires even less mental effort to enjoy. Such an art has been conceived by the great physicist Albert A. Michelson. In his *Light Waves and Their Uses* he writes: "Indeed, so strongly do these color phenomena appeal to me that I venture to predict that in the not very distant future there may be a color art analogous to the art of sound—a *color music,* in which the performer, seated before a literally chromatic scale, can play the colors of the spectrum in any succession or combination, flashing on a screen all possible gradations of color, simultaneously or in any desired succession, producing at will the most delicate and subtle modulations of light and color, or the most gorgeous and startling contrasts and color chords! It seems to me that we have here at least as great a possibility of rendering all the fancies, moods, and emotions of the human mind as in the older art."

An art of mobile color holds many possibilities. For example, the Chromaton of Tom Douglas Jones represents an advanced phase in the perfection of color organs. This particular instrument, still under development, has definite application to art teaching and art expression. However, its chief value (still to be properly capitalized) is in the study of human personality. A method such as the Rorschach test could be given added features of color, motion, time. All this should help provide even better and more revealing clues to neurotic and psychotic disturbances. Free-flowing or abrupt rhythms, mellow or hard forms, subdued or brilliant color could all be brought into play by the Jones Chromaton. If it served a useful purpose in diagnosis, it might also serve an appealing and pleasing purpose in some well-directed form of psychotherapy.

Although associations between colors and odors are less obvious, they none the less enter into the experience of many persons. The most preferred odors are rose, lilac, pine, lily of the valley, violet, coffee, balsam, cedar, wintergreen, chocolate, carnation, orange, vanilla. The least liked odors are lard, rubber, olive oil, kerosene, fish, turpentine, vinegar, onion, gasoline, garlic, human perspiration.

In a simple way, pink, lavender, pale yellow, and green are perhaps the best "smelling" colors. Poor examples would be found in gray, brown, black, and deep shades in general. Odors resemble film colors and lack comparison with things structural.

Sensory relationships have been investigated by science. Attributes seem to be coordinated. The phrase "unity of the senses" expresses the concept that colors, sounds, odors, tastes, tactile experiences, all may be "heavy," or "light," or have "volume" and dozens of other psychological similarities. Edwin G. Boring writes, "Von Hornbostel in 1931, having regard to the fact that colors have brightness and that brightness is one of the vigorous candidates for attributehood with tones, undertook to equate the brightness of a gray to the brightness of an odor, and then the brightness of a tone to the same olfactory brightness. He found that things equal to the same thing equal each other, that the brightness of the gray and tone appear equal when both equal the brightness of the odor."

COLORS AND FOODS

Practically everyone is sensitive to the colors of foods. Appetite will be quickened or dismayed in almost direct relation to the observer's reaction to color. Among pure hues a spectrum red (vermilion) seems to be most appealing. This is the rich color of the apple, the cherry, the rare cut of beef. Toward orange the appeal is still high. At yellow it begins to fall off decidedly, and at yellow-green it finds a low point. There is a pickup at clear green, the hue of freshness in nature. However, blue, despite its beauty in an esthetic light, is none too appealing in most foods. A similar attitude seems to be held for violet or purple. It will be noted that the greatest drops occur in small intervals of the spectrum—between yellow-orange and yellow-green, and between red and red-violet.

Tints are neither as upsetting nor as savory as pure hues. Although pure red is succulent, pink is by no means so. The best tint seems to be orange. A yellow tint is slightly better than a pure yellow. A green tint is also agreeable. Tints of blue and violet are not as "inedible" as pure hues or shades of the same colors.

Among shades, orange stands dominant. Here is the rich hue of brown associated with well-cooked meats, with breads, and wholesome cereals. Red shades tend to be purplish and thus lose out. A shade of yellow-green somewhat resembles a pure, clear green and picks up in appeal. But shades of blue and violet are by no means good food colors.

However, foods which might have a good taste with the eyes blindfolded (such as a black fig) may even take on a good appearance if the palate properly converts the eye. Yet where the association is well established, liberties cannot be taken with color. A Western baker who once tried to market bread in pastel tints such as blue and green found the venture a dismal failure.

For the most part, peach, red, orange, brown, buff, warm yellow, clear green, are the true appetite colors. Pink and tints of blue and violet are decidedly "sweet" and not for the entree or filling part of a meal.

Although blue is none too appetizing, its universal appeal comes to its rescue. If it is not in itself a suitable hue for things to eat, it is excellent as a background and will display foods harmoniously and pleasingly.

In associations with the sense of touch, colors will appear warm or cool, dry or wet. This reaction is inherent in the psychological make-up of most human beings. Perhaps it is built upon the association of warm things—the sun, fire—with red and orange colors, and of cool things—water, sky—with blue and green.

Yet despite the overwhelming evidence of the senses, attempts have been made to prove that the qualities of warmth and coolness in color were illusory. The *Lighting Handbook* of the Illuminating Engineering Society states, "This appears to have no foundation in fact." Tests in the psychological realm are all too frequently invalidated when the observer is made self-conscious of the test method and procedure. Appetite itself may be lost if an investigator deals soberly with it and perhaps goes about strapping electrodes to human tongues to measure flow of saliva.

In the *Bulletin of the American Physical Society* (February 5, 1940), S. M. Newhall writes, "Unless the test situation is sufficiently similar to the actual situation, the test results can have no practical value in application to the actual situation." In his study, Newhall exhibited 50 color samples to 297 observers. They were asked which colors appeared warmest and which appeared coolest. "The 'warmest' judgments show a minor mode in the violet . . . but a strikingly major mode in the red-orange region. . . . The 'coolest' judgments exhibit no such marked mode, but range irregularly all the way from yellow through green and blue to purple." In other words, a color such as red-orange is perceived as unquestionably "warm" by most persons. A greater latitude is shown toward "cool" hues, for green may express the quality to some, blue to others, and violet to still others. "The relatively great hue-range covered by such perceptually cool objects provides opportunity for the psychological association of coolness with a relatively great range of hues."

As pointed out in the last paragraph of Chapter 10, colors may be warm or cool, active or passive on a purely physical and physiological basis. Red will stimulate the autonomic nervous system, while blue will tend to relax it. The equilibrium of the body, pulse rate, heart action, respiration, nervous tension, even digestion will all be affected.

If there is no warmth or coolness in color, as the editorial staff of the Illuminating Engineering Society and other skeptics insist, then there is no such thing as hunger. A child comes to dinner, drools at the sight of his food, and cries, "Gee, am I hungry!" Hunger is a feeling backed up by a flow of gastric juices. Yet when his father yells, "Sit up! Why are your hands dirty? Where the devil are your table manners!" the drooling ends, the juices stop flowing, and the hunger is gone. Indeed, there are few sensations in life which cannot be destroyed as above. Color must be approached in a human way, an organic way. To use it otherwise is to foster spurious and invalid research and to neglect the fact that the mental and psychic life of man is in every way as real (and as functional) as his physical life.

LANGUAGE

Man's emotional attitude toward color is well expressed in his language, his slang, his metaphors, his colloquial expressions.

To him red is an ardent and passionate color, assigned to saints and sinners, patriots and anarchists, love and hatred, compassion

169

and war. He paints the town red, sees red when angry. When his business is without profit he is in the red—indeed, his book-keeper uses red ink to indicate the loss. Politicians draw red herrings across the line and shout of reds and radicals. There are red-letter days, redheads, redcaps, and vagrants without a red cent to their names.

Yellow is a despised hue. Though it once referred to the heathen, it now marks the scoundrel or the coward. Yellow journalism (sensationalism) sprang up in 1895 when a New York paper ran the cartoon of a child—the Yellow Kid—as an experiment in printing.

Green is the color of jealousy. Greeners are inexperienced workers, and greenhorns are rustics from the country.

Blue has a meaning all its own as expressed in "feeling blue," or "blue music." The color once referred to the insane, then to mental depression in general. There are blue laws, blue gloom, blue Monday, blue-bloods. Man yells blue murder and curses the air blue. Things happen in life once in a blue moon or suddenly like a bolt from the blue.

In 1832 Dickens wrote in *Pickwick Papers,* "He'll come out done so exceeding' brown that his friends won't know him." Black connotes despair and an evil conscience. There are terms such as blackball, blackmail and black list. "White" expresses the vanity of the Caucasian race. To say that a man is white is an Americanism dating back to 1877, when it was supposed to cast aspersion on red men and black men. The white-haired boy, however, is Irish and the pride of someone.

COLOR AND FORM

In an abstract sense, colors are to be related to forms. Red, for example, suggests the square or cube. It is hot, dry, and opaque in quality. Being advancing in character, it holds strong attraction and appears solid and substantial. Because it is sharply focused by the eye, it lends itself to structural planes and sharp angles.

Orange suggests the form of the rectangle. It is less earthly than red and more tinged with incandescence. Optically it produces a sharp image, is clearly focused by the eye, and lends itself to fine angles and details.

Yellow is abstractly related to the inverted triangle or pyramid. It is the color of highest visibility in the spectrum and therefore pointed and sharp. However, it is more celestial than worldly and it lacks substance and weight.

Green suggests the form of the hexagon or icosahedron. It is cool, fresh, soft. Because it is not sharply focused by the eye, it does not lend itself to much angularity.

Blue suggests the form of the circle or sphere. It is cold, wet, transparent, celestial. It is retiring in quality and creates a blurred image on the retina. Blue objects seen at a distance are never sharp to the eye.

Purple suggests the form of the oval. It is soft, flowing, and cannot be clearly focused. Unlike blue, however, it seems to cling more closely to the earth.

COLOR AND PERSONALITY

If the speculations of this present chapter are to be forgiven, a few more fanciful notes may be presented on the color relationships suggested by human personality. It has been said that athletic people prefer red, intellectuals blue, egotists yellow, while the convivial favor orange. Such "character analysis" may not be as meaningless as the reader might suppose. Color preference is something of a clue to personality.

When a number of people are questioned as to their predilections for color, it will be found that extroverts are inclined to favor red, while introverts are inclined to favor blue. Goldstein and others have stated that red stimulates the organism to action, while green and blue lead to meditation. Thus impulsive persons and conservative ones naturally express different color preferences. The same colors are not compatible with all people.

Purple is frequently popular among artists, if not by innate choice then at least by training, for purple has subtle qualities not found with most other hues. Yellow may be preferred by persons with a strong spiritual or metaphysical bent. Where the choice may be for an intermediate color such as blue-green, a finical nature may be exposed. Logic would indicate that average people like simple colors; when the preference is at all fastidious, the person is one who may not get along well with others.

SYMBOLISM

A symbolism for color, in every way psychological, has been built upon many centuries of history, religion, tradition, and superstition. This deserves brief mention simply because it represents an expression of man's feelings and associations as developed in the course of his civilization.

In the Roman Catholic rite, for example, the color of the vestments has a definite significance:

White is the symbol of light and signifies innocence and purity, joy and glory.

Red, the symbol of fire and blood, signifies charity and generous sacrifice.

Green, the symbol of nature, signifies the hope of eternal life.

Purple, the gloomy cast of the mortified, represents affliction and melancholy.

Black is symbolic of the sorrow of death and the somberness of the tomb.

Another old survival of tradition is found in the symbolism of heraldry:

Here red ("gules") means courage and zeal.

Blue ("azure") signifies piety and sincerity.

Yellow or gold ("or"), stands for honor and loyalty.

Green ("vert") means growth and hope.

White, or silver ("argent"), represents faith and purity.

Black ("sable") signifies grief and penitence.

Orange ("tenné") means strength and endurance.

Purple ("murrey") represents royalty or rank.

In America (since 1893) the universities and colleges have recognized a code of color to identify their major faculties. Scarlet represents theology, blue is for philosophy, white is for arts and letters, green is for medicine, purple is for law, golden yellow is for science, orange is for engineering, pink is for music.

"The body of man is red, his mind is yellow, and his spirit is blue." The fact that man has given color so important a role in his life since the dawn of history is in itself of psychological interest. For in many respects the emotions and attributes encountered in the historic symbolism of color meet with verification in the scientific research of a modern age. Only now the knowledge is more complete and the control more enlightened.

CHAPTER 14

The Anatomy of Beauty

ALTHOUGH A PERSON may feel that his particular likes and dislikes for color are personal to him —a part of his spiritual make-up—an astonishing similarity of preferences is noted when thousands of opinions are analyzed. Even the elusive qualities of beauty seem to follow universal laws.

Because of extensive research in æsthetics, it becomes possible to discuss the artistic side of color and color harmony on a scientific basis—not alone to define those colors and color arrangements having most appeal, but to explain a number of emotional reactions in physiological terms. This viewpoint is rather new to the literature of color and has seldom been presented. It naturally holds an important place in this book because it contributes still more factual data on the enigmas of color. Indeed, it may well be that predilections for color may be in a person's glands as much as in his soul.

At least fifty authoritative tests have been made of human color preferences. The literature is so complete and the results are so uniform that one is hardly able to question the conclusions reached.

To give some order to this matter of color choice, consider first the reaction of babies. In the first months of life it is difficult enough to learn to see, to fix both eyes on the same object, and to make sense out of visual experience. Some authorities declare that touch and form are dominant in infants, and that a real love for color does not become evident until well after the second year. Then color perception begins to rival form perception. R. Staples exposed disks to infants and measured the duration of visual concentration. The babies looked longer at bright colors than they did at dull tones. Their favorites, judged by certain eye fixations and reaching efforts, were red and yellow. Apparently the infant is most attracted to brightness and richness of hue.

C. W. Valentine likewise exposed colored skeins two at a time to three-month-old babies and measured the length of time each skein was given attention. The babies stared longest at yellow, then white, pink, red. Least attention was paid to black, green, blue, and violet.

At six months a baby may be able to distinguish the primary colors. As he grows, he will continue to be intrigued by color and will be more sensitive to it than to form. David Katz has reported a very unusual experiment on color-form abstraction among children from three to five years of age. They were given a number of red triangles and green disks and asked to select those which were the "same" as a *red disk*. Curiously, the children did not hesitate to group the red triangles with the red disk and to consider "sameness" a matter of color, not form. With older children and adults, the same test was too ambiguous and too confusing, no doubt because of a more advanced appreciation of shape and form.

In larger children, a liking for yellow begins to drop away— and to keep dropping with the years. Now the preference is for red and blue, the two universal favorites, which maintain their fascination throughout life. The order in childhood, therefore, is red, blue, green, violet, orange, yellow.

With maturity comes a greater liking for hues of shorter wave length (blue, green) than for hues of longer wave length (red, orange, yellow). The order now becomes blue, red, green, violet, orange, yellow. And it remains thus, the eternal and international ranking.

That color preferences are almost identical in human beings of both sexes and in persons of all nationalities and creeds is substantiated on every side.

T. R. Garth found that American Indians preferred red, then blue, violet, green, orange, yellow.

Among Filipinos, the order was red, green, blue, violet, orange, yellow.

Among Negroes the order was blue, red, green, violet, orange, yellow—the same as for practically everybody else.

Even among insane subjects, S. E. Katz found almost the same rankings—blue, green, red, violet, yellow, orange. Green was best liked by male inmates, and red by female. Warm hues seemed to appeal to morbid patients, and cool hues to the more hysterical ones.

To summarize the whole picture, H. J. Eysenck tabulated a

mass of research involving some 21,060 individual judgments. Blue ranked first, then red, green, violet, orange, and yellow. In a similar recapitulation of sex differences, the order was the same, except that while men put orange in fifth place and yellow in sixth, women put yellow in fifth place and orange in sixth.

A great deal of research has also been devoted to color combinations. In working with children, M. Imada found that color preference was not haphazard, even though good discrimination was not highly developed. Given black crayons, the youngsters were inclined to draw inanimate things, vehicles, buildings. When the same children were given colored crayons, their fancies were more inspired to attempt human beings, animals, and plants. Red with yellow and red with blue were favored combinations.

In similar experiments, Ann Van Nice Gale found yellow popular in combination with red-violet or blue. The combination of blue and green also was liked. Contrast, naturally, was more exciting than analogy or subtlety.

In testing adults, using colored lights thrown upon a screen, William E. Walton and Beulah M. Morrison found the combination of red and blue highest in ranking, then blue and green, red and green, clear and blue, amber and blue, amber and green, red and amber, with clear and amber last.

THE WORK OF GUILFORD

Among the ablest investigators in this field is J. P. Guilford, who has conducted numerous tests with colors and color combinations. As to harmonious arrangements, he writes, "There is some evidence that either very small or very large differences in hue give more pleasing results than do medium differences. This tendency is much stronger for women than for men." Thus a person is likely to see harmony either in colors that are closely related, or in those which are antithetical and opposite—not in other relationships. To visualize a color circle, yellow, for example, will seem harmoniously combined with yellow-orange and yellow-green; with blue, blue-violet or violet. It will not be particularly well liked in combination with orange, with green, or even with red.

Guilford has likewise determined through research that where the choice is between grayish tones and pure hues, the pure forms will be preferred. Where the choice is between dark tones and light tones, the light tones will be preferred.

NATURAL LAWS OF HARMONY

According to Guilford, people like color combinations based on (1) closely related colors and (2) complementary colors.

With single colors other facts are noted. Those variations are best which represent clear-cut expressions of color. That is, pure hues should be rich and intense; pastel tints should have a light, delicate quality; shaded colors should be deep and autumnal. Where a color may lie on a borderline, compromising the above "forms," ugliness may result. Thus a little white added to red may weaken its appeal. However, if enough white is added to shift the sensation from that of a full color to that of a pastel tint (pink), appeal may be restored. A red with a touch of black in it may seem nondescript and "dirty." When enough black is added to shift the form to a deep shade of maroon, beauty may again be evident.

I. H. Godlove has noted a "natural order" for color combinations. When light and dark variations of different hues are combined, the appearance is best when the light variation is derived

178

from a full color that is normally light, and the dark variation derived from a full color that is normally dark. Thus pale green looks better with dark blue than pale blue looks with dark green. As full colors, blue is deeper than green.

Orange buff looks better with deep violet than lavender looks with brown (which is a deep shade of orange).

Pink looks better with dark blue or purple than lavender looks with maroon.

Pale yellow looks better with brown or blue or violet than any pale greens, blues or lavenders would look, for instance, with olive green (which is a deep shade of yellow).

In harmonizing modified colors, natural sequences also hold most appeal. Thus pure hues combine beautifully with tinted colors and white. They all have elements in common. Pure hues combine well with dark shades and black. Grayish tones are the most neutral of all color forms. Because they contain pure hue, white, *and* black in their make-up, they naturally blend well with other types of colors.

SCIENTIFIC THEORIES

It has already been mentioned in the last chapter that extroverts prefer red and introverts prefer blue. This also seems to apply to brunets and blonds, the former preferring red and the latter blue. In explanation E. R. Jaensch, in his book *Eidetic Imagery,* mentions the difference between a predominance of "sunlight" in the more tropical regions of the world, and of "skylight" in the more polar regions. As one travels from cold to hot climates sunlight increases and skylight decreases. Intense light requires sun adaptation, or "red-sightedness," and this may be accompanied by a strong pigmentation on the foveal area of the retina.

Red-sighted persons are typical brunets, such as the Latins. They are likely to have dark eyes, hair, and complexion. Their natural preference is for red and all warm hues, a predilection which may be far from spiritual in origin and probably due to a physiological process of accommodation to long waves of light.

Blonds, on the other hand, are green-sighted and may have a different pigmentation on the retinas of their eyes. They are the Nordic and Scandinavian types, with bluish eyes, light hair, and light complexion. Their preference is for the blue and green.

To support Jaensch's theory, it is an observable fact that the deciding factor in color preference seems to be sunlight (or lack of it). Where sunlight is abundant, people are likely to show a preference for warm, vivid hues. Where there is relatively less sunlight, preference for cooler colors and softer tones will be found. The influence of length of day on plant growth and on the sex cycles of animals, already mentioned, suggests that man's feelings and reactions to color may similarly have a biological basis. One authority has posed the hypothesis that there may be a connection between the more active functioning of the endocrine glands in the spring of the year (when length of day increases) and the rise in preference for light, clear tints which most persons exhibit at this particular season.

The fact that a preference for blue increases as a person grows older has also inspired explanation. The fluids in the human eye grow yellowish with age. The lens of the eye of a child will absorb about 10 per cent of blue light; that of an old man, 85 per cent. It therefore might be assumed that another sort of accommodation takes place. Human eyes may grow "thirsty" for blue as the lens proceeds to filter more of it out.

One authority who prefers not to be quoted has noted a relation between diet and color discrimination. Working with Mexican school children, he observed a preference for simple colors such as red, yellow, green, blue to exist where there was calcium deficiency. When diets were corrected, color preferences appeared to change in the direction of finer discrimination and appreciation for more subtlety in color.

THE ELEMENTS OF SENSATION

In human vision there is a marked tendency to simplify all experiences and sensations. Because this process is in the brain, it is highly psychological. How many colors are there? Estimates by some authorities have ranged into the millions. Yet in a broad sense there are surprisingly few colors.

To speak of "all the colors of the rainbow" is to deal with finite numbers. Selig Hecht writes, "The normal eye can separate the visible spectrum with complete certainty into about 180 patches of hues which cannot be made to look like one another by varying their intensities." Spectral colors, of course, are pure ones and do not include variations in which white, gray, and black are a part.

Indeed, in looking at the spectrum (or the rainbow), human vision tends to "bunch" things together. Although the eye may be stimulated by innumerable wave lengths of light, a person sees a red area which blends into an orange area, then into yellow, green, blue, violet. Although red and violet represent extreme opposites in wave length, they appear psychologically related and may be brought into sequence through purple. Purple, which is not a spectral hue and has no wave length of its own (it is a blend of red with violet or blue), thus makes the color circle possible.

In the psychology of vision there are four primary or primitive color sensations: red, yellow, green, blue (and also black and white). Though yellow in light mixtures may be formed by com-

181

bining red with green, the sensation of yellow is unique and certainly shows no hint of red or green in it. Red, yellow, green, blue are the simplest of colors and cannot be formed through *visual* mixtures of other hues. Further, while orange may look something like red and like yellow, both red and yellow do not resemble orange.

This type of psychological simplification is also observed when white, black, and gray are introduced into color mixtures. The reader's own experience will probably check with the following notes. The natural form of color is a triangle, with pure hues (any and all) on one angle, white on the second and black on the third. White and black are unique as sensations; they differ from each other and differ from pure hue.

Whitish colors, which may be called tints, follow mixtures of pure hue with white. Blackish colors, which may be called shades, follow mixtures of pure hues with black. The combination of white and black forms gray. When all three are combined —pure color with white and black—a grayish tone is exhibited.

In the main, all color sensations fall into these seven classifications: pure hue, white, black, whitish tints, blackish shades, gray, and grayish tones. Thus do the human eye and brain find common denominators for multitudinous color sensations.

If the eye can distinguish a million colors, as some authorities aver, they are observable only under the most ideal conditions of illumination and background. When colors are examined in average or dim light, viewed from a distance and held slightly apart, fine differences are tremendously reduced.

Language itself gives further evidence of this human tendency to see few rather than many colors. Within a reasonable length of time the average person can mention only about thirty distinct color names. And most of these will be synonyms (scarlet, red, crimson) or borrowings from other things, such as orange and violet. If language is an expression of man's interest in his environment, then fine differences in color are of no great concern to him, for his dictionary has very few words for color.

It is conceivable that a patch of blue sky, a piece of blue paper, and a bottle of blue liquid could all be made to "match" in the physical sense. All could have the same wave lengths and brightness. Yet the visual impression of each would be unique from the psychological standpoint.

Ostwald, Katz, and others have pointed out a difference between "related" and "unrelated" colors. This distinction, a highly important one to the psychologist, has not been fully appreciated until modern times. Indeed, as great a physicist as Helmholtz was apparently unaware of it.

Unrelated colors are the hues of light. They are celestial in quality, uninfluenced by environment, and usually contain no black. They are *film* colors and in human perception have the quality of seeming to fill space.

Related colors are *surface* or *object* colors. They are usually seen in relation to an environment and are the colors which distinguish paints, textiles, and other material substances. They are definitely localized by the eye, are structural and palpable, and generally have black in their makeup. Surface colors may be changed to the appearance of film colors by viewing them through an aperture screen—a card with a hole in it.

A third type of color (Katz) may be called a *volume* color. This has a three-dimensional quality; it occupies a definite position within space. For example, fog is a film color until objects are seen through it. Then it is perceived as a volume color.

The chief difference between related and unrelated colors is observed in the phenomenon of black. To the psychologist all visual sensations involve color. Because black is perceived in vision and is as unique as any hue, it is, of course, a color. Peddie writes, "Physiologically *black* implies the absence of stimulation: psychologically the recognition that illumination is absent is itself a positive perception." Helmholtz also understood this: "Black is a real sensation, even if it is produced by entire absence of light. The sensation of black is distinctly different from the lack of all sensation."

Black is a color that is in every way as definite and unique as red or blue or white. It mixes in with other colors to change their appearance. An orange light (unrelated) in a dark room will maintain its same general appearance whether the intensity of the light is strong or weak. It will merely be a bright or a dim orange. But when the intensity of an orange paint is lowered by adding black to it, the mixture will change to brown which is not very much like orange. In light rays black seldom plays much of a role. There is no such thing as brown or maroon in a rainbow or a sunset. Yet in life, black is found everywhere, an integral part of other full hues, modifying their aspect and forever making itself apparent in vision. Southall says, "To argue that because a black body apparently does not deliver a specific physical stimulus to the retina, therefore black is a mere negation or complete lack of sensation, is not only to beg the question from the start but to deny the evidence of our senses."

PHYSICS AND PSYCHOLOGY

The study of color is essentially a psychological one. Southall writes: "From the standpoint of psychology, colors are the properties neither of luminous objects nor of luminous radiations but are contents of consciousness, definite qualities of vision." In discussing the psychological aspects of vision, it is of interest to point out a few phenomena in which color as energy differs from color as sensation. It should be appreciated that human beings do not respond to light stimulation in a matter-of-fact way. The eye is far from a mere light-responding medium.

First of all there is no close, orderly, or measurable relationship between light energy and the sensation of color. It is impossible to seize upon certain wave lengths or intensities and to establish them as fixed stimuli, forever the same to the eye. What, for example, is the difference between black and white or between gray and white? This cannot be answered satisfactorily with spectrometers or in terms of brightness or reflectance alone. White is not synonymous with bright light or black with feeble light— or even with no light at all.

With the eyes tightly closed in a dark room one does not see black but a deep "subjective" gray that seems to fill space—the so-called "retinal chaos." This gray has not the depth or solidity of a black surface. Again, black will appear blacker the stronger it is illuminated. No average surface absorbs all light; what the eye sees as black may reflect 5 per cent or more of the light shining upon it. Yet a surface like this looks increasingly blacker when more light strikes it—and when, in truth, more light is reflected into the eye.

More curious than this phenomenon is the transformation of a white surface into the appearance of a gray surface without changing in any way the volume of light reflected by it. In a classical experiment devised by the great psychologist Ewald Hering, a piece of white cardboard is placed upon a window sill with the observer facing the light. Now a second white card is held on a horizontal plane over it. In the center of this latter

185

card is a square hole through which the lower card can be seen. If both pieces are exactly horizontal, and if the upper piece does not cast a shadow over the lower, they both will appear white.

Now, however, if the upper card is tilted away and down on its horizontal axis toward the window sill, it will immediately reflect more light. Result—the card seen through the hole will appear gray or even black. By changing the conditions of the experiment the lower card can be made to shift from white to gray—yet the amount of light it reflects will not be modified in the least! Color as radiant energy and color as sensation are different.

OTHER PSYCHOLOGICAL PHENOMENA

There are further peculiarities of vision not to be answered in terms of light energy alone. The human eye cannot distinguish and separate the component elements of a dominant hue. When several notes are struck at once on the piano, the trained ear can easily identify each one. But when light rays are mixed, the eye sees one result only.

This means that the eye pays little heed to the physical composition of colors. Polarized light looks the same as ordinary light. Colors which owe their existence to the absorption and reflectance of pigments are not greatly different from opalescent and iridescent colors which may owe their existence to diffraction, interference, the scattering of light rays. Grays mixed through a combination of white and black may not be visually different from grays formed with red and green, or orange and blue.

Again, a yellow surface will appear brighter on a black background than it will on white. Highlights appear opaque to the eye; shadows appear transparent. Conjoined shadows seem to melt into an object and to become part of it. Cast shadows seem to cover a surface like a transparent membrane.

186

Finally, there are a number of subjective illusions which do not have much relationship to electromagnetic energy as such. Pressure on the eyeball will produce sensations of hue. The visualization of an area of red may bring out a response to its opposite, green. Lustrous surfaces such as silks involve other visual phenomena. The eye sees a difference between white cotton and white silk; one has gloss or luster, the other does not. Cottons will still look like cotton in brilliant light, and silk will look like silk in shadow. Amount of light reflected is of minor consequence.

Certain sensitive persons are able to hold a mental picture of a red area in their minds and then actually see a green afterimage. Likewise color appearances are affected by mind and imagination. It is human to see blue eyes as bluer and red hair as redder than they actually are. Always the sense of color struggles actively within the body of man, working itself outward to influence the things he sees.

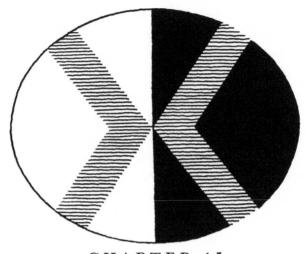

CHAPTER 15

This Illusory World

SEEING IS AS MUCH in the brain as it is in the organ of sight. Perception is often a matter of interpretation rather than a simple reaction to stimuli. While there are innumerable curiosities associated with human vision, one of the most interesting is that centering around the more or less stable appearance of the world under varying conditions of illumination.

As a rule a person is not greatly conscious of the fact that natural daylight changes considerably from dawn to dusk, both in intensity and hue. Dawn may be yellowish; reflected light from the sky may be bluish; sunset may be a rich pink. There may be 10,000 foot-candles of light in the open at midday, 1,000 under the shade of a tree, and less than 100 in twilight. Yet for all these

188

differences (which would be marked indeed if measured with a photometer) human vision operates with remarkable uniformity, giving the world a normal appearance at all times and simplifying and coordinating a complex array of optical stimuli.

There is something highly mysterious about the interrelations existing between illumination and color. David Katz writes, "Seeing is not a matter of looking at light waves as such, but of looking at external things mediated by these waves; the eye has to instruct us, not about the intensity or quality of light coming from external objects at any one time, but about these objects themselves." Light itself is rarely seen. Its presence is made known by the appearance of surfaces upon which it shines. The eye may recognize the existence of dim light, for example, by the appearance of objects in its field of view; it does not have to examine or analyze the light source itself. Conversely, impressions of bright illumination may be gained from the general appearance of areas and surfaces being perceived. Obviously, high surface brightness is associated with intense light, and low surface brightness with dim light.

Regardless of light intensity, however, colors tend to maintain a "genuine" appearance at all times. Here is the phenomenon of color constancy, one of the most remarkable of all facilities of vision. Technically speaking, a white surface is one that effects a total (or almost total) reflection of light. Such a surface if viewed under isolated conditions can be made to appear gray, as demonstrated in Hering's experiment (described in the last chapter). However, if the white surface is viewed under conditions of general illumination over the field of view, it will remain white whether the light be strong or weak! White surfaces set at different angles in relation to a common light source (and reflecting different amounts of light) will all tend to appear white to the eye. Similarly, white pieces of paper near a window or away from it will have the same aspect as to color. This phenomenon of vision defies reproduction by a camera.

THE MAGIC OF COLOR CONSTANCY

Because of color constancy, there is no such thing as underexposure or overexposure (within reasonable limits) in human vision. From brilliant July sunlight to the dim recesses of a basement, a white object will persist in appearing white. A gray hen standing in the sunlight and a white hen standing in the shadow of a barn will look respectively gray and white—even though the gray feathers may actually reflect a greater amount of light into the eye. Color constancy is even maintained under chromatic light. When a large area or interior is showered with red light, for example, the eye senses the quality of the illumination and still persists in seeing white objects as white—despite the great distortion produced by the illumination and despite the fact that the light reflected by the white area is in reality red.

However, in very dim light all colors (except possibly white and black) undergo odd changes. When a body, such as a piece of iron, is heated to incandescence, it begins to emit light at the red end of the spectrum. As the substance grows still hotter colors of shorter wave length are seen, ranging through orange, yellow, into a whitish blue.

In a fashion similar to this the colors of the world fade out of vision as illumination is decreased. The phenomenon is known as the Purkinje effect. While yellow and yellow-green occupy the point of highest visibility in the spectrum under daylight conditions, the laurels pass over to blue-green under dim light. The brightness quality seems to shift over toward the shorter waves of blue and violet. In consequence dim light appears to increase the values of the cool colors and to decrease the values of the warm. Orange and red may have high values in daylight, but in dim light they may appear darker than either green or blue.

These illusions are common experiences of everyone. In twilight the red hues of nature will appear black, while blues and greens may seem fairly light (but not pronounced in hue). The explanation usually made is that the task of seeing is taken over by the rods of the eye when illumination is decreased—the rods being more sensitive to blue and violet radiation than to red. In dark-adaptation, however, the rods are largely insensitive to wave-length differences and do not convey specific chromatic impressions to the brain.

The role played by illumination in the perception of colors has been treated in many of its strange aspects by Harry Helson. Studying the effect of colored illuminants upon gray materials he found that three things happened:

1. When the gray samples illuminated were high in brightness they took on the hue of the light source.

2. When the samples were intermediate in brightness they apparently remained grayish (through the strange influence of color constancy).

3. When the samples were low in brightness they took on the hue of the afterimage or complement of the light source.

He found that change in background seriously affected the appearance of all samples. Yet change in illumination, as regards either intensity or hue, produced little change.

Experimenting with hued samples, Helson found that they tended to remain more normal in appearance than neutral grays when viewed under chromatic light. However, they seemed to lose saturation or purity and to be more filmy.

Chapter 13 has told of persons who "see" colors in sounds. The varieties of this phenomenon, known as color synesthesia, are many. The hues of the spectrum may be associated with lines, forms, figures, letters, numbers, words. They may relate to tastes, odors, or sounds. Even cutaneous and organic sensations have by some persons been said to resemble colors.

Over fifty years ago Francis Galton wrote his *Inquiries Into Human Faculty* and established himself as the first serious investigator of the phenomenon. Galton noted that his "color-thinkers" held no common agreement. Yet they insisted that the color associations experienced were quite innate and were for the most part not to be explained. Further research also led to the belief that synesthesia was hereditary and that it followed the laws of heredity.

Many of Galton's reports are entertaining and will serve to illustrate a few typical experiences. One of his correspondents wrote: "I do not know how it is with others, but to me the colors of vowels are so strongly marked, that I hardly understand their appearing of a different color, or what is nearly as bad colorless to anyone. To me they are and always have been, as long as I have known them, of the following tints:

"A, pure white, and like china in texture.

"E, red, not transparent; vermilion with china white would represent it.

"I, light bright yellow; gamboge.

"O, black, but transparent; the color of deep water seen through thick clear ice.

"U, purple.

"Y, a dingier color than I.

"The shorter sounds of the vowels are less vivid and pure in color. Consonants are almost or quite colorless to me, though there is some blackness about M. . . .

"Of my two daughters, one sees the colors quite differently from this (A, blue; E, white; I, black; O, whity-brownish; U, opaque brown). The other is only heterodox on the A and O; A being with her black, and O white. My sister and I never agreed about these colors, and I doubt whether my two brothers feel the chromatic force of the vowels at all."

Another correspondent, the head teacher in a school for girls, wrote: "The vowels of the English language always appear to me, when I think of them, as possessing certain colors. . . . Consonants, when thought of by themselves, are of a purplish black; but when I think of a whole word, the color of the consonants tends towards the color of the vowels. For example, in the word 'Tuesday,' when I think of each letter separately, the consonants are purplish black, u is a light dove color, e is a pale emerald green, and a is yellow; but when I think of the whole word together, the first part is a light gray-green, and the latter part yellow. Each word is a distinct whole. I have always associated the same colors with the letters, and no effort will change the color of one letter, transferring it to another. Thus the word 'red' assumes a light green tint, while the word 'yellow' is light green at the beginning and red at the end. Occasionally, when uncertain how a word should be spelt, I have considered what color it ought to be, and have decided in that way. I believe this has often been a great help to me in spelling, both in English and foreign languages. The color of the letters is never smeared or blurred in any way. I cannot recall to mind anything that should have first caused me to associate colors with letters, nor can my mother remember any alphabet or reading book colored in the way I have described which I might have used as a child. I do not associate any idea of color with musical notes at all, or with any of the other senses."

Galton also wrote of a man who associated colors with numerals in this fashion: 1 was black, 2 was yellow, 3 was a pale brick red, 4 was brown, 5 was blackish gray, 6 was reddish brown, 7 was green, 8 was bluish, and 9 was reddish brown. "These colors appear very distinct when I think of these figures separately; in compound figures they become less apparent. But the most remarkable manifestation of these colors appears in my recollections of chronology. When I think of the events of a given century they invariably appear to me on a background colored like the principal figure in the dates of that century; thus events of the eighteenth century invariably appear to me on a greenish ground, from the color of the figure 7."

Galton presents several charts in which these color associations are illustrated. He shows the appearance of words like "London," "argue," "agree," "grind," "grand," "range," "sweet" in which hues express the particular letters or vowel and consonant sounds as experienced by one individual.

Synesthesia is inborn. Almost always these curious associations are discovered in early years and will persist, without change, during the entire course of a person's life. It is difficult to attribute them to childhood memories or to any definite experiences which might have provided a basis for them.

THE FLIGHT OF COLORS

There are many subjective effects to be noted in the study of color. Two thousand years ago Aristotle mentioned a "flight of colors" upon looking into the sun. He wrote, "If after having looked at the sun or some other bright object, we close the eyes, then, if we watch carefully, it appears on a right line with the direction of vision, at first with its own color, then it changes to crimson, next to purple, until it becomes black and disappears."

Goethe saw the sequence as brightness first, then yellow, purple, blue. Sun gazing is a dangerous pastime. With less risk a person may gaze at a frosted electric-light bulb or a strongly illuminated piece of white paper. If the stimulus is of high intensity, the sequence may begin at green and proceed through yellow, orange, red and purple, then to blue, fading out in green and black. If the stimulus is weaker, the sequence may begin at purple and proceed through blue, green, into black. Though these hues have no external existence they are quite real to the senses and will move with the eyes, have form, and be localized.

THE WORK OF JAENSCH

In recent years the psychologist has studied mental imagery in general and has discovered numerous and astonishing phenomena. A notable investigator in this field has been E. R. Jaensch. The images experienced by human beings fall into three types— memory images, afterimages, eidetic images. The first of these is the product of mind and imagination, having the quality of an idea or thought. The afterimage is more literal. It is actually seen and may have shape, design, dimension, precise hue. Its size will vary as the eye gazes at near or far distances. Generally it is a complementary image, white being seen where black was originally, red being replaced by green, and so on.

The third type, the eidetic image, is the most remarkable of all. Jaensch writes: "Eidetic images are phenomena that take up an intermediate position between sensations and images. Like ordinary physiological afterimages, they are always *seen* in the literal sense. They have this property of necessity under all conditions and share it with sensations."

Eidetic imagery seems to be the gift of childhood and youth. While somewhat akin to the supernatural, it is none the less a sensory reality. The child playing with his toys may be able to project living pictures of them in his mind. These may not be mere products of the imagination. They may be far more tangible, with dimension, color, movement in their make-up. They are "lantern slides" of the eye and brain, projected into definite, localized space. They are images as real as projected lantern slides.

The phenomenon for the most part was given little attention up to recent years. Because it vanishes with age and is likely to disappear at puberty, the adult mind, capable of dealing with it, relegates it to the fervid period of childhood. Nevertheless images are seen. Pictures stand before the eyes and details are distinguished in them which may be counted and identified in hue. According to Jaensch, eidetic images are subject to the same laws as other sensations and perceptions. They are, "in truth, merely the most obvious sign of the structure of personality normal to youth." And they make for fascinating study.

THE EIDETIC FACULTY

For most persons there is an admitted gap between sensation and imagery. However, Jaensch says, "Some people have peculiar 'intermediate experiences' between sensations and images." They are true eidetics whose responses are quite frank and spontaneous. To them sensation and imagination may go hand in hand and be closely united in some literal and graphic visual experience.

To discover this eidetic personality Jaensch has outlined three test procedures. Although he is aware of the faculty in small children, he prefers youngsters of ten years or more, because they are better able to comprehend what the psychologist is trying to find out and to express themselves coherently.

First, the individual (or group of individuals) is cautioned that literal images and not memory pictures are to be recorded. To reveal the character of the true eidetic image simple experiments are made with afterimages. A square of red paper is concentrated upon for 20 seconds against a gray background. The individual then sees a green area of similar size. He is told that this is a real experience and has a physiological basis.

Repeating the experiment, but shortening the exposition time of the color sample, individuals are found who continue to see afterimages of prolonged duration. To a few, the afterimage will no longer be complementary (a green afterimage for red), but an image that is the *same* hue as the sample. Here the eidetic faculty is of relatively high degree.

Second, the eidetics, now detected, are shown a fairly complicated silhouette picture having numerous details and being slightly larger than a postcard. This is fixated for 15 seconds. The average person will see a somewhat blurred image, having bright and dark areas that are complementary to the original (and more like a normal afterimage). The eidetic, however, will see the whole picture or a greater part of it, and in colors that correspond to the original!

Third, the above experiments are continued with other pictures having an interest to attract the child. The fixation period is shortened still more. The true eidetic is revealed, and the pictures continue to live for him, projected before his eyes as literal things and experiences!

Eidetic images are filmy like afterimages. Although the original objects which prompt them may be of textured hues, the eidetic image is more like light. It is, as mentioned, a positive rather than a negative "picture." In some instances it may be tridimensional. Jaensch reports that the eidetic image is easier to recall than the memory image and will, of course, be more "real" when it is recalled.

He also found that treatments with calcium caused the eidetic disposition to be weaker. The image seen under this circumstance was likely to be complementary in hue and brightness to the original. Conversely, treatments with potassium occasionally made a latent type active and considerably heightened the eidetic disposition, giving it greater intensity.

PSYCHOLOGY AND PSYCHIATRY

The phenomenon of eidetic imagery has much of the fascination of extrasensory perception. In a more practical light, however, it may serve useful ends. Jaensch writes, "The eidetic investigators have already shown that the closest resemblance to the mind of the child is not the mental structure of the logician, but that of the artist." In education, the forcing of an adult viewpoint, mind, and manner upon the child may suppress the eidetic personality and consequently may stand in the way of creative and natural expression. Heinrich Klüver, an American investigator, writes: "For example, an eidetic child may, without special effort, reproduce symbols taken from the Phoenician alphabet, Hebrew words, etc. Or a person with a strong eidetic imagery may look at a number of printed words for a while and then go to the dark room and revive the text eidetically. It is possible to photograph the eye-movements occurring during the reading of the eidetic text."

The eidetic faculty is known to exist among primitive people and is unquestionably experienced by human beings under the influence of drugs. The curious hallucinations of the insane, the "miraculous" statues that move, speak, bleed, the "visions" of religious ascetics, may be traced in part to the phenomenon. Werner writes, "It is furthermore probable that the so-called naturalistic art of primitive hunters (Eskimos, Bushmen, etc.) is based on eidetic images which are actually seen as projected on the surface of the material on which the picture is to be drawn or painted."

Some authorities have striven to relate eidetic imagery to personality. Introverts are said to show a tendency to see meaningful, interrelated wholes. Extroverts tend to have reactions that are more objective and analytical in character. In psychiatry the eidetic image has been termed an "undertone of psychosis." No doubt the subject has psychiatric importance. It may, for example, have bearing on theories of hallucinations. It may also throw new light on the mysteries of human perception and on the dynamics of life in general.

PSYCHIC PHENOMENA

Explanations of psychological and psychic phenomena are not always easy—and indeed unnecessary. There are in man many strange and inexplicable mysteries regarding color. Thus to end this chapter, here are quotations from an article written by John J. O'Neill for the *New York Herald Tribune*.

"A telepathic antagonism to the color red has been revealed by experiments in extra-sensory perception conducted by Professor Gardner Murphy and Ernest Taves, of the Department of Psychology, Columbia University, as part of the research program of the American Society for Psychical Research. . . .

"In many of the experiments the choice was limited to two possibilities—yes-no, heads-tails, black-white. Other tests employed the ordinary extra-sensory-perception cards and a deck called 'Rook cards,' fifty-six cards made up of four suits, each suit numbered from one to fourteen and each suit in a different color. . . .

"When the readings of the Rook cards were tabulated and analyzed, it was found that the group as a whole had a slightly above-average record. When the results were subdivided by the color of the cards it was found that when calls were made of the suit in which the figures were printed in red on a white background the scoring dropped significantly lower than in any other test. . . .

"This effect involving red was considered so interesting that Professor Murphy communicated with several professors of psychology in universities throughout the country asking that the test be repeated by them. He made more extensive tests with the red cards among the American Society for Psychical Research group, running the total readings up to 6,975. Again the antagonism to red was found. . . .

"Despite the fact that the subjects were not informed when they were working with red cards, they became aware of it. Somewhere below the level of consciousness they sensed that involved was some faculty which prevented them from making a record as good as usual in identifying the cards by telepathy. This faculty had the same effect on the telepathic process as a red traffic light or a red danger sign. . . .

"The Columbia scientists, in commenting on the unusually low record on the red cards, declare: 'We have tentatively adopted a hypothesis, but further research is necessary before much can be said about it. It would appear, at least, that there may be something about the red-white situation which arouses negativism. This may be because of obscure effective factors— the symbolic values of red and white are deeply ingrained in our culture, at least, and this general effective tone of the material used may have something to do with the type of results obtained.' "

Part 4

THE VISUAL ASPECTS

CHAPTER 16

The Anomalies of Seeing

THE EFFECT OF illumination, brightness, and color on the eye directly—and upon the human organism indirectly—is a field of inquiry in itself. It has occupied the attention of science in recent years and has led to a number of remarkable findings. Out of this effort have come a science of seeing, a science of brightness engineering, a science of functional color. Because the author has taken an active part in such research and has devoted much time to practical applications of color in industrial plants, offices, schools, hospitals, he has gained firsthand knowledge of the benefits to be derived from the intelligent application of good technical practice.

It is known today that adverse seeing conditions may lower human efficiency, promote fatigue, and make men accident-

205

prone. The factors involved may have little if any relation to appearance or esthetics but may be traced quite directly to unfavorable reactions of the mechanism of vision. Where color may be used to relieve so-called "eyestrain," new techniques and scientific methods may be put to work which have received little mention so far in the pages of this book but which, in truth, constitute a separate and unique aspect of color study.

PRIMITIVE VISION

To understand the magic of human vision it is perhaps of interest to review a few notes on the eyes of lower animals. Response to light is vital to the survival of most living things. The humble amoeba moves in and out of light, "seeing" with its entire organism. A more advanced cousin, the euglena, has a few light-sensitive cells at the base of its "feeler." Some earthworms have receptor cells scattered along the walls of their bodies. In many snails the cells are at the ends of tentacles. The scallop has eye spots on the edge of its mantle, the clam on the inner region of its syphon. In the nautilus the "eye" lies at the bottom of a spherical cavity, and light reaches it through a small opening. Because light strikes the creature's retina from different angles, the nautilus perhaps has some sense of direction.

Such "eyes," however, do not "see" much of form, detail, or color—probably nothing at all. In the newt and salamander are cuplike growths of the brain covered with a lens of thickened skin. If the lens is cut off it will grow back again. If an optic cup is grafted on the newt's tail, a lens will promptly form over it.

It is likely that the ability to focus upon objects finds its evolutionary beginnings in such animals as fishes, frogs, cuttlefish. The lens, however, is hardened and is accommodated to distance by being moved back and forth like the lens of a camera. The self-

206

focusing lens develops in the snake and turtle, also the eyelid, the foveal area on the retina, and the beginning of a sense of color.

In birds there is a highly developed color sense. Few mammals, however, see color—apes and men excepted. Nocturnal creatures are likely to be most sensitive to short-wave radiation (blue). Diurnal animals are likely to be most sensitive to long-wave radiation (red). The eyes of night animals may also be equipped with a reflecting layer behind the retina (the tapetum) which makes them "shine in the dark." Day animals may have colored eye droplets or a strongly tinted yellowish lens to reduce the blinding intensity of brilliant sunlight and to aid acuity.

One must understand that the vision of animals lacks the more rational brain connection of man. The eye mechanism may be good, but the "gray matter" back of it is not. Yet the animal may be well adjusted to its life and environment. Visual reactions are more automatic, more instinctive. Existence is dynamic in quality. As a matter of fact, a frog may die of starvation if its food does not move. Werner writes, "Buytendijk, in certain experiments of crucial importance, demonstrated that a dog which, sitting at rest, was unable to discriminate between a circle and a triangle could perform the feat when allowed to run freely to and fro." The dynamics of seeing, so to speak, may some day revolutionize the science of illumination and, indeed, the science of functional color in schools, offices, industries, and the like. It may well be that carefully controlled changes in light intensity and changes in color will prove more normal and therefore superior to the static values recognized today.

THE OPTICS OF SEEING

The optical system of the human eye is perhaps none too good. Indeed the lens system is such that colors and forms may appear blurred under certain conditions. "Fortunately," says W. D. Wright, "the more serious effects of these aberrations are compensated in some way, either in the retina or the brain, to an extent sufficient to make us quite unaware of their existence in normal observations."

As most persons know, the human eye functions somewhat like a camera. Over the eyeball is the cornea, a transparent outer covering shaped like a watch crystal. Behind this is the iris, a ringlike structure which forms the pupil of the eye. Behind the pupil is the lens which accommodates for near or far objects. The iris, in front of the lens, expands or contracts to regulate the size of the pupillary opening—wide in dim light, narrow in brilliant light. Behind all this is the retina, a network of sensitive nerve endings. Here is where the light is focused and it is from here that impulses are transmitted to the brain.

To all indications the human eye has been designed by nature to see with good efficiency under widely different conditions of illumination. While man cannot see as well in darkness as can a cat or an owl, he can see better in daylight than they. While he cannot tolerate full sunlight as well as a prairie dog or an eagle, he does not have to retire when the sun goes down. Thus while man may not have the best daylight eye or the best nighttime eye, he does have vision which surpasses that of any other creature for all conditions of life.

The amount of light entering the eye is regulated by the iris. While the pupillary opening is round in man, it is slit vertically in cats and tigers, horizontally in goats and horses. This all suits the needs of the animal, enabling it to see well in leaping down from trees or rocks or in "keeping an eye" over the horizon.

Practically all mammals, including man, have blue eyes at birth. In this condition, the iris is without pigmentation and the blue seen is the result of scattered light in the dioptrical media of the eye. In some birds, the color of the iris may change over a period of time, generally becoming darker. The male bird may have a different colored iris from the female. In the common box turtle, the male may have a red iris and the female a yellowish or brownish one. In one species of penguin, the iris as well as the beak will change in hue from red to yellow and back again with the seasons. G. L. Walls writes: "One change is as meaningless as the other, though both are doubtless expressions of the ebb and flow of sex hormones in the blood stream."

THE RETINA

Vision, however, answers not to simple laws of optics. Indeed, if the optical system of the human eye may be said to be far from perfect, nature has performed miracles in the design of the retina and the cortical system of vision. One of the great books in this field is that of Stephen L. Polyak, *The Retina,* and may be consulted to real advantage.

"Structurally, the retina may be regarded as a light-sensitive expansion of the brain" (W. D. Wright). It is the photosensitive lining at the back of the eyeball within which physical light elicits nervous impulses that are forwarded to the brain. In the human retina there are two types of photoreceptor cells, the rods (about 130,000,000 in each eye) distributed rather uniformly over the entire expanse, and the cones (about 7,000,000) especially numerous and refined in the central area and fovea.

Although the exact process of vision is still a mystery on many counts, science is generally agreed that the so-called "duplicity theory" first stated by Max Schultze in 1866 has sense and veracity to it. In this theory, low intensity vision is a function of the rods of the retina; high intensity vision is a function of the cones.

The rods, it is believed, react chiefly to brightness and motion in subdued light. The cones, quite numerous in the very center of the eye, react to brightness and motion, but also see colors. In the central fovea and in the territory next to it, accordingly, most of the action of seeing takes place, for only in this locality does the eye see fine detail and color. Foveal vision is essentially cone vision and day vision; peripheral vision is rod vision, especially useful at night.

The foveal area of the retina is permeated by a yellowish pigment (the so-called "macula lutea" or yellow spot). Although this tiny area measures less than $\frac{1}{16}$ inch in diameter, it is crowded with tens of thousands of photoreceptors, especially the cones, *each* of which is said to have its own connection to the brain. Hence there is good reason for the fovea to be remarkably sensitive to fine detail. In the periphery, however, nerve connections both to the cones and to the rods are arranged in groups. Thus Wright observes, "This in turn implies that the peripheral retina is quite incapable of resolving fine detail in an image, although at the same time it enables the responses from weak stimuli to be summated and gives the periphery an advantage over the fovea in the detection of faint images."

THE CORTICAL RETINA

The cortical region of the human brain responsible for sight has areas corresponding to the fovea and periphery of the eye, with one interesting difference: the area devoted to peripheral vision is relatively small; the area devoted to foveal vision is relatively large. This means, in effect, that while the fovea is little more than a dot on the retina, its function in responding to fine detail and color is extremely vital and requires a sizable bit of "gray matter." Conversely, while the extrafoveal periphery of the retina is relatively large, its simpler response to brightness, motion, and crude form needs less area within the brain.

The fact that the right side of the brain controls the left side of the body (and the converse) applies also in a rather strange way to vision. In the case of human vision, the arrangement is as follows. The corresponding halves of both retinas connect with their own side of the brain. Thus the right half of the right retina and the right half of the left retina, which together see the left side of the world, send their fibers to the right cerebral hemisphere. Conversely, the left halves of the right and left eyes, which see the right side of the world, send their fibers to the left cerebral hemisphere. Some authorities believe, however, that the foveal cones connect with both sides of the brain. Wright comments, "It is still a matter of doubt whether the fibres from the whole fovea of each eye are duplicated in the two optic tracts or whether each half-fovea sends fibres along only one optic tract, in analogy with the rest of the retina. The evidence on the whole appears to support the latter arrangement."

That vision is as much in the brain as it is in the eye is well demonstrated by referring to a few more oddities. Human eyes see better than the eyes of lower animals simply because human brains are superior. Stimuli received by any eye, in fact, have no particular meaning until the brain interprets them. A rudimentary eye bud can be taken from a hen's egg and made to grow in a salt solution. It will actually develop and form a lens. Without a brain connection, however, it certainly does not "see."

Southall writes, "If the eye has had no previous experience to guide it in some particular instance, it may be difficult for the brain to interpret the visual phenomenon correctly. If therefore the chain of communication between the central part of the organ of sight and the adjacent optical memory tract is impaired or entirely broken in one of its links, the external object may indeed be visible to the eye but it cannot be comprehended by the brain. Under such circumstances the spectator will see it *per se* and indeed may perhaps even be able to draw a sketch of its outlines, but he cannot call it by name or make out what it signifies, unless he can also touch it and reinforce his sense of sight by the aid of other senses." In short, seeing is not a matter of recording external stimuli alone, but of bringing forth mental recollections and experiences. The brain and the eye are one.

Another such phenomenon has been described by Walls. When the right or left optic tract is severed between the eye and the brain, a person becomes blind to the left or right half of his visual field. Despite this, however, he may still experience contrast effects and afterimages. After looking at a bright area he may experience a sensation of brightness in the blind half of his vision. Concentration upon a specific color may likewise produce a complementary afterimage in the blind field. Walls concludes, "Only an interaction of the two sides of the cortex could account for such phenomena."

VISUAL PURPLE

Not much is known about the complexities of human vision after that point where light strikes the retina. LeGrand H. Hardy writes, "What happens when light acts upon a photoreceptor is in essentials unknown." It is likely, however, that electrical currents are produced in the optic nerve and conveyed to the brain.

Flooding the retina is a substance known as visual purple. Its color is normally a magenta red. It is bleached under the action of light and resynthesized in darkness. According to A. C. Krause, "The color of visual purple upon exposure to light at room temperature changes rapidly to yellow but in the cold it slowly turns into orange and then yellow. In both cases it becomes colorless in time."

Science has recently shown that vital connections exist between the eye, vitamin A, and the general health of the body. Krause writes, "The synthesis of visual purple is dependent upon the availability of vitamin A and the metabolic activity in the retina." Retinal vitamin A deficiency may, of course, be caused by abuse of the eyes, by extreme glare, or by prolonged exposure to high brightness. However, it may also be caused by certain diseases.

Highly significant is a recent observation by George Wald. He points out that "as vitamin A is liberated during light adaptation the retinal capacity to hold it is exceeded, and most of it diffuses out into contiguous tissues and the circulation. . . . This is an important phenomenon, for it connects the otherwise closed retinal cycle with the general circulation and metabolism of vitamin A throughout the organism." This may mean that the eye is not only an organ of sight but an organ for the distribution of vitamin A throughout the human body. Not only may vitamin A deficiency reduce the power of the eye to see clearly (especially in dim light), but some authorities believe that undue exposure of the eye to glare and extreme brightness may destroy vitamin A needlessly, interfere with its circulation throughout the body, and hence lead to general debility.

THE HUMAN EQUATION

Southall writes: "Good and reliable eyesight is a faculty that is acquired only by a long process of training, practice and experience. Adult vision is the result of an accumulation of observations and associations of ideas of all sorts and is therefore quite different from the untutored vision of an infant who has not yet learned to focus and adjust his eyes and to interpret correctly what he sees. Much of our young lives is unconsciously spent in obtaining and coordinating a vast amount of data about our environment, and each of us has to learn to use his eyes to see just as he has to learn to use his legs to walk and his tongue to talk."

An insect seeing through a compound eye will respond to a crude mosaic of brightness patterns. Birds and fishes, with eyes on the sides of their heads, may not be able to focus upon one object with the degree of clarity known to man. In fact, such creatures probably see two conflicting worlds at one and the same time, concentrating either upon one or the other through some process of "blanking out" right or left.

In the binocular vision of man, the foveal areas of the retina will simultaneously focus form, brightness, color, detail, assuring a clear image and a perfect sense of size, shape, distance, and the like. The peripheral areas will, at the same time, respond to brightness change or motion on the outer boundaries of the field of view. Thus the baseball player, with his fovea on the ball, will use his periphery to guide the arc of his bat. The prize fighter, with his "eye" on his opponent's chin, will be well protected from "haymakers" swinging in from the sides.

SPEED OF VISION

The human equation operates as well in the discrimination of detail. Ralph M. Evans writes, "A telephone wire may be seen at a distance greater than a quarter of a mile." While an image so small could hardly be recorded by a glass lens and photographic plate under the best of conditions, the human eye (and brain) is able to construct a remarkably accurate image. Apparently the retina requires but a few hints of the existence of the wire, whereupon the brain pieces it together.

In speed of seeing, the brain will record a fairly clear image of a scene or an object, even though the exposure may be a mere fraction of a second. Flashes of light will produce a higher subjective brightness than light that is shone continuously. When two lights are flashed simultaneously, one striking the fovea and the other the periphery of the retina, the light seen foveally will appear to flash ahead of the other. Similarly, blue lights require a slower blinking rate than red lights, if such blinking is to be seen. Walls states, "A Swedish railroad recently found that certain red signals, which had to be seen as blinking, could be so seen if they flashed 75 times per minute. Blue ones could be allowed to flash only 20 times per minute, else there was danger of fusion by the dark-adapted eye of the engineer."

THE BLIND SPOT

Near the fovea of the retina is a "blind spot" where the optic nerve of the eye connects. Located slightly inward toward the nose near the center of the retina, it points out obliquely into the world. This "dead spot" was discovered toward the end of the seventeenth century by Friar Mariotte, a French student of optics. E. W. Scripture wrote (1895): "Although man and his animal ancestors have always had blind spots as long as they have had eyes, these spots were not discovered until about two hundred years ago, when Mariotte caused a great sensation by showing people at the English court how to make royalty entirely disappear."

At close distance the blind spot covers a relatively small area in the field of view. At seven feet, this area measures eight inches across and increases its spread into the distance. Looking into the sky it covers a region about eleven times the size of the moon. Though the eye sees nothing at this point a person is never conscious of emptiness or blackness. The brain "fills in" with whatever happens to be in the environment. The blind spot surrounded by type matter will seem to be filled in by type matter. Looking at hues the same will be true—the eye will "think" it sees red in its blind spot if the surrounding area is red.

AFTERIMAGES

In viewing objects and hues there is a certain amount of retinal lag. Vision is not an instantaneous retinal process. When the eye scans space it does not do so in a continuous sweep but it skips and . hops. The stimulation received at any one moment holds over to the next. (Moving pictures are thus made possible.) Visual impressions remain lucid and are not blurred.

But more than this takes place. In viewing any hue there is a tendency on the part of the eye to bring up a strong response to its opposite. So pronounced is this reaction that it actually brings afterimages to view. Upon staring at an area of red and then gazing at a neutral surface, the sensation of green will be experienced. The afterimage of yellow will be blue. The phenomenon has much influence over color effects, giving intensity to strong contrasts and mellowness to analogous hue arrangements.

Recent scientific experiments would indicate that afterimage effects take place in the brain rather than in the eye itself. This also appears to be true of illusions associated with brightness contrast (the fact that colors look relatively light on dark backgrounds and relatively dark on light backgrounds). With reference to afterimages, hypnotized subjects have been asked to concentrate upon color stimuli which had no literal existence. Though their eyes actually saw nothing, color experiences were noted. The subjects "saw" complementary afterimages despite the fact that the retinas of their eyes had not been excited. Most

216

amazing of all, "these were persons who, in the waking state, did not know that there is such a thing as an afterimage—let alone, that it should be expected to be complementary to the stimulus!" (Walls).

THE DYNAMICS OF SEEING

In lower forms of animal life the nerves of eyes have "direct wire" connections to the muscles of the body. Reactions to light are often involuntary. To a rather surprising degree this same condition exists in man. Sudden brightness or motion on the outer boundaries of his vision may cause his head to dodge and his muscles to grow taut—even before he has a chance to think. His emotional response to a sunny day or a rainy day may be traceable to the reaction of his autonomic nervous system. Under the influence of drugs such as hashish or mescalin objects seen may change in size, form, position. That which is static may become dynamic.

The truth, of course, is that human vision has a flow to it that rises and ebbs with the whole physiological process of the body, with the moods of the mind, and with the extreme phases of nature. Illness may affect acuity and color vision. Extreme fear may impair sight in whole or in part. Bright days will, through vision, effect a different attitude and even a different perception from that noted on dismal days.

In brief, man sees best when he feels best physically and mentally. And to a large extent the cheerful environment is conducive to soundness of body and mind. The application of color to life—in the home, in industry, in schools—thus has a real significance that serves humble purposes as well as lofty ones, and that is as vital to the physical side of being as it is to the spiritual.

217

CHAPTER 17

Color Blindness and Night Blindness

I N ITS SENSITIVITY to color, the human eye responds to a relatively small region of the complete electromagnetic spectrum. Vision perhaps had its evolution in water, for the visible spectrum of light is in general the transmission spectrum of water. According to Walls, "The rod spectrum is closely fitted to water, the cone spectrum a little better fitted to air." Such development is perhaps natural enough.

Though color vision may connote things spiritual, emotional, and æsthetic to man, nature has been less interested in beauty than in visibility. The color sense aids perception. It has a functional basis. It was evolved by nature, not to make men happy but to assure better adaptation to environment. Light and color have biological significance. And from the direct effects of light

218

and color upon the eye and upon the body arise the more complex psychological reactions of the brain. These reactions, in turn, influence seeing. Just as nature imposes herself upon man through his sense of vision, so does man interpret nature as his brain directs. In brief, seeing works two ways: physical stimuli from an outside world enter the eye and send impulses to the brain; the brain thereupon adds experience, judgment, and perception to what it sees and "looks" wisely back at the world.

COLOR VISION THEORY

At best, science has been at a loss to explain the mysteries of color vision. In consequence, a goodly number of theories have been propounded over the years. Ewald Hering, for example, a psychologist, has proposed a system in which three reversible processes or substances are said to exist in the visual mechanism. There are a white-black process, a blue-yellow process, and a red-green process. Where a "breaking down" occurs under the action of light, white, blue, and red are experienced. Where a "building up" occurs, the sensations are of black, yellow, and green. The Hering Theory neatly explains complementaries and afterimages. Yet it falls short of conviction—as do all theories of color vision—when many other phenomena are considered.

In the Ladd-Franklin Theory, evolution of the color sense is supposed to have begun with a light-sensitive substance which enabled the eye to distinguish light from dark. Next came a yellow-sensitive and blue-sensitive substance. Finally, the yellow component was further divided to permit the eye to see red and green. While these postulations may be used to explain some forms of color blindness, and while they pay tribute to the red-green-blue primaries of the physicist and to the red-yellow-green-blue primaries of the psychologist, there is little evidence that the nerve fibers of the retina act in any such way.

In the Müller Theory, stoutly championed by many scientists, photochemical processes are assumed in an initial stage, followed by added processes giving rise to sensations of black, white, yellow, blue, green, and red. The optic nerves are stimulated by various parts of the spectrum. Chemical processes take place in the retina and transmit impulses to the brain. Color blindness is explained where there are defects in the optic nerves and where, in consequence, certain impulses are not transmitted. Deane B. Judd writes, "A frequent criticism of the Müller Theory is that because of its elaboration it explains everything but predicts nothing."

THE YOUNG-HELMHOLTZ THEORY

"A common assumption in theories of color vision is that there exists in retinal cones of the normal human eye a set of three spectrally selective substances capable of being decomposed independently by the action of radiant energy" (Judd). In the Young-Helmholtz Theory, three different types of cones are supposed to exist on the retina, one with maximum sensitivity in the red end of the spectrum, one with maximum sensitivity in the green, and the third in the blue. Various sensations of color are thus to be accounted for by the stimulation of these receptors. For example, stimulation of the red and green type cones supposedly gives rise to yellow; stimulation of all three receptors gives rise to white.

Although there has not been conclusive evidence that the retina contains cones of different type, supporters of the theory have not been discouraged. Recently, Polyak has mentioned three types of neural connections to the cones, and Granit has similarly obtained evidence of different spectral sensitivities.

In any event, work in the field of color vision and color blindness today generally proceeds on the assumption that the human eye has a trireceptor mechanism. With three lights (red, green, blue) all the hues of the spectrum are to be formed. "The evidence is, therefore, consistent in its indication that color of a uniform element in the visual field of a normal observer requires at least three independent variables for its specification" (Judd). Color blindness may be analyzed on a three-color basis. Colorimetry and spectrophotometry may likewise be carried out with three hues and utilized to measure and specify colors.

COLOR BLINDNESS

Although color blindness is fairly common to humanity, little attention was apparently paid to it until the latter part of the eighteenth century. The first intelligent description of it was attempted by John Dalton, an English chemist, in 1798. During his early years he had attributed errors in judgment to an ignorance of color terms. He discovered later that he saw no difference between a laurel leaf and a stick or red sealing wax. Dalton compared the color of a scarlet gown to that of the trees and once attended a Quaker meeting attired in drab coat and flaming red stockings. So famous was his report that "Daltonism" became the common synonym for color blindness.

Color blindness may be congenital or it may be acquired. Where a person is so born, there is generally no loss in his ability to see brightness, form, detail, and the like. The defect is far more common among men than among women, and is generally transmitted through the distaff side of the family. Normal mothers may transmit the defect of their sons. Color blindness among men has a frequency of about 8 per cent; among women its frequency is less than ½ per cent.

Acquired color blindness may occur in diseases of the eye, optic tract, or cortex. It may accompany pernicious anemia, vitamin B_1 deficiency, exposure to certain poisons such as carbon disulfide, lead, or thallium. Cases of acquired color blindness, however, usually involve a general deficiency of vision. Hence a study of them is seldom of much value to an understanding of what healthy color-blind persons see.

NORMAL COLOR VISION

Terminology in the field of color blindness is replete with multi-syllabic words such as protanopia, deuteranopia, trichromatism, dichromatism. In the reader's interest, however, an attempt will be made to describe the phenomenon in simpler terms. In normal color vision, the spectrum is seen to comprise red, orange, yellow, green, blue, violet. The region of highest brightness is in the yellow and yellow-green. All these spectral colors may be formed by mixtures of three lights, a red, a green, and a blue. To quote Judd: "It is convenient to classify the discriminations of a normal observer as light-dark, yellow-blue, and red-green; that is, a normal observer can tell light colors from dark ones, yellowish colors from blue ones, and greenish colors from red ones."

TRICHROMATS AND DICHROMATS

In a first group of color-blind individuals, three colored lights (as in a normal person) may be required to form all other spectrum hues, but the proportions needed to effect certain matches will differ radically from the normal. In some persons there may be an abnormal green function; in others, an abnormal red function. Such people may be thought to have a fairly good color sense and may, with effort, name a lot of hues. In many instances, however, experience may be a guiding factor, the individual knowing that the sky is blue, grass green, butter yellow, and so on. Where fine distinctions may be set up or where the colors may be grayish in tone, the so-called "anomalous trichromats" may find themselves hopelessly confused.

In a second group, only two colored lights are found necessary for the afflicted individual to match all spectrum hues. Practically always such a person (the dichromat) has visual discrimination for light-dark and for yellow-blue, but not for red-green. He will generally agree with any color match set up by a normal observer, but when he does his own matching he may do strange things. To quote Wright, "For instance, a grey surface may sometimes be described as grey and at other times be referred to as blue-green or purple by one type of colour defective. Or, on the other hand, a red surface, a dark yellow surface or a green surface may all be described as brown." Hues of short wave length are likely to appear bluish (not greenish), and hues of long wave length are likely to appear yellowish (not red or orange).

Most confusion among color-blind individuals is to red and green. Among the 8 per cent of men who are color-blind such red-green blindness is predominant in some form or other. A few rare individuals are deficient in yellow-blue discrimination, and a few others are totally blind to spectrum hues.

Although much experimental work has been done, no known cures for congenital color blindness have been found. Frequently, however, quackery is promoted in the form of drugs, psychotherapy, special training, special diet. Reporting for the U.S. Navy, Dean Farnsworth writes, "The best informed and most experienced specialists in the field of color vision are emphatically of the belief that congenital color deficiency cannot be remedied by the use of diet, medicine, training, or other treatment now known to science." Yet during the Second World War the public was exploited in advertising, over the radio, and in correspondence courses with such cure-alls as injections of iodine or cobra venom, electrical stimulation of the eyeball, dosage with vitamins, exercises in the viewing of colored lights, the wearing of colored goggles, etc.

LACK OF OXYGEN

The nervous system of the human body is highly sensitive to a lowering of the oxygen tension of the blood. Lack of oxygen affects vision and reduces its ability to see clearly. So-called "anoxia" (oxygen shortage) may occur at normal air pressures where the concentration of oxygen in the atmosphere is weak, or it may follow exposure to the "thin" air of high altitudes. There may be lowered visual acuity, less sensitivity to brightness and color, and partial or complete disappearance of afterimages. Voluntary eye movements may be disturbed and tasks such as reading made difficult. Perhaps to compensate for all this, the pupil of the eye tends to dilate and to admit more light to the retina.

Temporary loss of vision (without loss of consciousness) may take place when sudden high speeds or pressures are encountered such as in dive bombing. However, if suction is maintained over the eyeball, the occurrence of "blackout" may be prevented.

NIGHT VISION

To use a metaphor, the process of human vision does not rise as from the bottom of a well. That is, the ability to see does not follow a straight progression from darkness to brightness, nor is the reaction of vision in direct proportion to stimulus. Vision has its beginning, so to speak, in the middle of the well, for it has a mechanism adapted to seeing in dim light and a mechanism adapted to seeing in bright light. The two tend to function separately. In particular, cone vision fades out as light grows dim, while rod vision is enhanced. Strangely enough, a given stimulus of low intensity may actually appear to *increase in brightness* as general illumination is diminished. This would mean that rod vision grows better and better as less and less light enters the eye!

In Chapter 15, mention was made of the fact that the eye sees yellow-green as the brightest region of the spectrum under daylight adaptation, while the region of highest brightness to the dark-adapted eye is in the blue-green. As seeing shifts from the cones to the rods, there is a reduced sensitivity to red colors and an increased sensitivity to blue colors. This phenomenon, known as the Purkinje effect, adds further mystery and fascination to the study of vision. A red and a blue, for example, if equal in brightness under normal light, may fail to match under dim light; the red may appear dark and the blue light in tone.

It should be understood, of course, that color is seen only under normal light and then only in the center of the eye. To determine this a person may experiment with bits of colored paper drawn around from behind his head. Although he will be able to "see" the papers far to the side of his head, he will not be able to distinguish their precise hue until they are well in front of him. During such tests the fixation of the eyes should be straight ahead.

The fact that the eyes are color-blind during dark adaptation may as well be determined by remaining in dim illumination for a period of at least thirty minutes and then attempting to distinguish unidentified samples of hue. This is a good pastime for sleepless nights. A further experiment is to cup one eye with the palm of the hand, and then expose the other eye to a lighted lamp. In darkness again, vision will be quite acute in the dark-adapted eye and quite blind in the eye that had been exposed to light.

Charles Sheard writes in an article for the *Journal of the Optical Society of America* (August, 1944), "The most striking thing about the change of visual threshold, as one enters and remains in a dark room, is its range; it can easily cover a gamut from 100,000 units of light intensity at the beginning to 1 unit at the end of dark adaptation." As vision shifts from the cones to the rods, discrimination of color and brightness will be reduced. For example, the steps of a gray scale will remain distinct under normal or bright light. Under very dim light, however, medium and deep colors all tend to "melt together" in brightness and to resemble black. Night vision thus tends to be colorless, filmy, lacking in detail, and the silhouettes of objects appear flat and vague and very difficult to focus.

In near darkness the center or fovea of the eye is more or less blind. Hence dim objects are better seen when looked at "askance." In fact, small objects of low brightness may disappear if looked at directly.

Negroes are said to see better in extremely dim light than persons of other races. Those with dark brown eyes may also have lower thresholds than persons with blue eyes. Because vitamin A is essential to good vision in dim light and because it accumulates during dark adaptation, any deficiency of it will reduce the seeing ability of the eye. (Lack of vitamin A in the human system may be attended by other troubles such as dermatitis.) Tassman reports that 50 per cent of pregnant women have night blindness which can be improved when substantial amounts if vitamin A are administered. Night blindness is the poor man's ailment, for it usually attends inadequate diet. It is extremely common among entire colonies of people having improper or insufficient food.

During the Second World War, good night vision held great importance to the armed forces. The aviator, the lookout on a submarine or surface vessel, the reconnaissance scout, needed the best of vision at night and during the twilight hours of dusk and dawn. Diets were supervised and supplemented by extra quantities of vitamin A.

Both in England and in America, extensive work was carried out to unlock the mysteries of night blindness and night vision and to develop methods and means whereby the best possible visibility could be achieved. Where it was impractical to keep the eye in total darkness in order to aid dark adaptation, what color or colors would be most effective? Again, where objects such as instruments and dials had to be seen and where the observer at the same time had to peer out into the night, what hues would cause the least disturbance to sharpness of vision?

As has been mentioned, when the human eye is dark-adapted, sensitivity to red is relatively less than sensitivity to blue. In other words, a red color or light is seen distinctly only in the very center (fovea) of the eye; it is less distinct, if not invisible, on the outer boundaries of the eye (periphery). Because night vision is essentially rod vision, red light therefore was found to have great usefulness.

First of all, red illumination is frequently employed as a general light source where the eyes of men are being dark-adapted or where night vision must be maintained. Red goggles are similarly used for the same purpose. An aviator about to go on a night mission, or a sailor about to go on night watch, will have his vision fairly well adjusted if he has been exposed to red light of low intensity. (He will not to have to stay in darkness preparatory to his assignment.) Secondly, red light is used as a local illuminant over instruments and dials and will not disrupt dark-adapted vision.

Thus the rods of the human eye, accumulated mostly outside the central fovea of the retina, are practically insensitive to red light of low intensity. In fact, through the wearing of red goggles it is sometimes possible to condition the eye to dark adaptation while going about in daylight. The red filters will permit the cones of the eye to function but will leave the rods inactive and therefore waiting and ready to see in darkness.

It may be that the visual purple contained in the rods of the eye does not absorb much of the red light and hence is not bleached or chemically affected. Under red light, central vision is fairly clear and sharp, but peripheral vision is poor. Conversely, under blue light, central vision is blurred but peripheral vision operates fairly well. Instruments and dials thus are more sharply focused at night if illuminated by red light. However, a blue flashlight would enable a person to get about more safely at night, for the light it threw would be seen over a far wider range.

ACCELERATED DARK ADAPTATION

Under normal conditions and for most persons, dark adaptation requires 30 or more minutes to be complete. Is there any way of hastening the process? Aviators report that night vision may be kept acute by glancing occasionally at illuminated instruments. Apparently total darkness does not promote adaptation as well as an environment in which some feeble stimulus is present. No doubt there is a vast difference between putting the eye "asleep" and alerting it to darkness. Rapid breathing will aid vision at night, although the effect will not last. Lack of oxygen, as previously mentioned, handicaps the eye. However, alcohol and benzedrine are said to increase the power of the eye to see in darkness.

A series of unusual experiments, designed to force the rods of the eye to adjust more quickly to darkness, have been reported out of Russia. These are similar in nature to the studies of Kravkov described in Chapter 11 and indicate that stimulation of any sense organ will affect visual perception. It is evident that the nervous system of the body is closely tied in with the visual sense. The ability to see clearly is influenced by pulse rate, blood pressure, and respiration.

Investigation has shown, for example, that a feeble stimulation will improve night vision. Obviously, if a person becomes drowsy, his vision (as well as his hearing) will grow less sensitive. As the Russians have shown, stimulation in general acts upon the visual centers in the brain and in turn "sharpens" the eyes.

The effects of stimulation of taste, the application of cold water to the face, muscular activity, all seem to aid dark adaptation. According to K. Kekcheev, "Since the autonomic nervous system controls the synthesis of rhodopsin [visual purple] in the retina, experiments were conducted to hasten the onset of dark adaptation by stimulating the sympathetic nervous system. . . . By applying taste, cold, and proprioceptive stimuli [physical effort], the dark adaptation period was reduced to 5–6 minutes."

Once again, the fact is impressed that vision is a complex sense, that the brain and entire organism are involved in the seeing process. In studies of dark adaptation it is observed that the production of visual purple reaches a maximum beyond which the eye has no further need for it. Yet even at this point the eye can be made to see even better if other senses are stimulated. All too clearly, "A further increase in sensitivity of the dark adapted eye due to stimulation of other receptors should then be attributed to an immediate action of the sympathetic nervous system upon the visual center in the cerebrum" (Kekcheev). Not only does man find his vision reacting to the stimulation of his other senses, but mental effort, a will to see clearly, will in itself improve the acuity of his eyes.

CHAPTER 18

Problems of Eyestrain

IT IS GENERALLY understood these days that abuse of human eyes has many baneful consequences. Problems of eyestrain, glare, illumination, brightness, and color have become so acute that applied sciences known as "brightness engineering" and "color conditioning" have been developed within the past decade to cope with them. Here is a new field of utility for color, based on a functional approach and proved through measurable facts, technical research, and reliable engineering methods.

Where the eye is unduly fatigued, a long chain of reactions takes place within the body. The purpose of this chapter is to state the major causes of eyestrain, to deal with physiological reactions, and to set forth a number of scientific principles which have wide

231

practical application in the correction of adverse seeing conditions. Such study has wide practical value.

WHAT IS EYESTRAIN?

The term "eyestrain" is perhaps none too well chosen. However, its use is so common, even among scientists, that it has become indispensable in writing of what may more properly be called "ocular fatigue." In a broad sense, constant and even excessive use of the eyes is no more harmful than a corresponding use of other organs or muscles of the body. One seldom thinks of physical exercise as strain. There is little reason to conclude that a man who uses his eyes extensively during his working day is any worse off than a man who, during the same period, digs a ditch.

Except where there may be conditions of extreme brilliance or glare, the eyes are not easily "worn out." Indeed there is plenty of evidence to indicate that vision is improved with use. Many persons are of the false opinion that "eyestrain"—where it may be found to exist in some bad situation—has to do with fatigue of the nerves on the retina. On the contrary, it is of muscular origin. This will shortly be explained. It is almost impossible to "tire" the eyes by exposing them to reasonable changes in brightness. Obviously, direct peering at the sun will cause damage. Yet as Luckiesh states, "Since the compensating mechanism of the visual process may mediate brightness changes of perhaps a million to one, it is reasonable to assume that changes of less than a hundred to one do not tax the eyes sufficiently to induce ocular strain or any other human undesirable effects." The human eye may quite safely go about any normal tasks of seeing, as it has been doing for millions of years, and be all the better for its exertions—unless, of course, the tasks set upon it exceed the stress intended by nature.

232

The eyes of man are quite capable of prolonged work and hard work. To say that too much seeing causes eyestrain becomes as illogical as similar references to "earstrain," "touchstrain," or "tastestrain" because of too much hearing, touching, or tasting. If the eyes are abused, this is not as a rule traceable to overwork or overuse but rather to a harmful exposure to stimuli which make normal visual functions difficult or impossible.

FREQUENCY OF EYE DEFECTS

Figures compiled by the U.S. Public Health Service indicate that about 22 per cent of public school students have defective vision. In colleges the percentage rises to 40. A percentage of 50 is reached in persons between the ages of thirty and forty. At the age of fifty, defective vision reaches a frequency of 70 per cent. At the age of sixty, the frequency is above 90 per cent.

D. B. Harmon, however, writes of even higher percentages compiled during recent studies of elementary school children. He states that "59.0 per cent of the Anglo-American children in the elementary schools have refractive eye defects or various disturbances that are affecting or distorting their visual sensation." Like other authorities, Harmon has noted a relationship between faulty vision and other physical and psychological disturbances with an individual. For example, 62 per cent of school children with low physiological ages and low educational ages had visual defects. The backward child, not the bookish one, may need glasses.

THE CAUSES OF EYESTRAIN

Many authorities, particularly in the lighting field, unfairly quote figures on visual deficiency and imply that impaired eyesight is caused chiefly by difficult seeing tasks and by inadequate levels of illumination. It seems easy to convince the layman that his eyes will go bad if he uses them too much or if he doesn't have enough light over his tasks. However, it would be far more accurate to state that good eyesight springs first from heredity. Parents with good eyes are likely to have children with good eyes. Further than this, visual defects are to be traced to (1) serious illnesses, (2) poor diet, (3) critical seeing tasks which severely tax the eyes, (4) an environment which is extreme in glare or brightness contrasts, and (5) insufficient illumination.

It will be noted that in the above order of things, lighting is placed last. Indeed, its importance to safe and comfortable seeing is too frequently overrated. Too much light and too much glare are often worse than too little illumination. Besides, level of illumination is seldom the right criterion of an ideal seeing condition. In a very comprehensive study made by Ernst Simonson and Josef Brozek the conclusion was reached that, "In general, illumination engineers tend to exaggerate the effect of variations in the illumination level." These two investigators failed to note much difference in eyestrain under different light levels ranging from 5 to 300 foot-candles. After a very complete set of tests they wrote, "The only possible interpretation is that fatigue trends resulting from visual work must be produced by components which are common to all illumination levels. The illumination level is by no means the all-important variable for the development of visual fatigue."

Yet despite the fact that the human eye can do a prodigious job of seeing, it can be harmed by extreme glare, by excessive brightness extremes, by exposure to harmful fumes and harmful radiation. Tasks that require prolonged convergence of the eyes, that involve minute details, exacting mental judgment, and discrimination may all produce fatigue and directly as well as indirectly affect the human organism in general.

Where the eye is taxed, where seeing is attempted under severe tension or strain, a number of physiological and psychological reactions are to be observed.

The eye itself may increase its rate of blinking.

There may be a dilation of the pupil after several hours, even though the intensity of light may not change.

Power to hold the eyes in convergence, to distinguish small brightness differences, to focus for a clear image may be reduced.

There may be a reduction in sensitivity on the outer boundaries of vision. The eye may be less able to see clearly on the peripheral areas of the retina.

Most of these effects will disappear if the eyes are rested. However, prolonged abuse may result in permanent damage. The pathology of eyestrain has been treated at length by Ferree and Rand. The chief cause of distress is usually traceable to high and disturbing brilliancies in the field of view. Such brilliancies may constrict the pupillary opening and hence deprive the eye of sufficient light to see clearly. As a consequence, there may be unhealthy congestion within the blood vessels of the eye. In young persons these congestions may actually cause elongation of the eyeball and thus nearsightedness. As Ferree and Rand conclude, there may be disturbances in the mechanism of the eye, the iris and lens. There may as well be damage to the retina itself which may take the form of inflammation or detachments. "The eye has grown up under daylight. Under this condition only three adjustments have developed, and indeed only three are needed: the reaction of the pupil to regulate the amount of light entering the eye and to aid the lens in focusing the light from objects at different distances, and accommodation and convergence to bring the object on the principal axis of the lens and the image on the fovea. . . ." These adjustments tend to be coordinated. When they are separated, trouble is encountered. High brightness in the field of view, if isolated from the task, may cause disruption. The eye will thereupon struggle to set things right. *"This striving to clear up its vision by ineffectual maladjustments is the cause of what is commonly called eyestrain."*

OTHER MANIFESTATIONS

Where a wretched seeing condition may prevent the eye from seeing clearly, the eye will none the less try to do its best. Out-of-focus motion pictures, for example, may cause the lens of the eye to struggle without avail. When any kind of eyestrain persists, muscular tension throughout the body will be found to increase. Again, blood pressure and pulse rate may rise. The individual may experience headache, nausea, nervousness, and irritability.

Luckiesh has suggested a possible relationship between critical seeing tasks and the prevalence of heart disease in modern times. "A recent study of occupational morbidity and mortality by the United States Public Health Service revealed that in one company, with approximately 6,000 workers doing precision assembly of small parts, almost 80 per cent of the mortality cases in five years involved heart trouble. The trend with the rest of the 59,000 industrial workers whose occupational and illness records were studied was quite similar. It is conceivable that the reflex effects of critical seeing and the prevalence of mortality causes from heart trouble in occupations demanding critical seeing may be related."

At times the indication of eyestrain may be almost wholly mental or psychological. In one case study made by the author, nausea and illness among a group of women employees were

236

found to be caused by an inability to classify colors in a complicated electrical wiring task, not by insufficient light. Because management had stressed the need for accuracy, and because the employees had great difficulty in distinguishing certain colors from each other (orange from tan, blue from blue-green, etc.) the severe mental effort needed to perform the job wore out human patience and sent the workers to the plant dispensary to rest and recuperate.

That the mind will contribute to eyestrain may be commonly experienced when a person decides to read or to perform some difficult seeing task in extremely dim or extremely brilliant light. It is no strain to sit on a beach at noon or on a porch at night and gaze into distance. Yet an attempt to read under either of the above situations may promptly cause fatigue and distress until some adjustments are made.

Tremendous fear, as well, may raise havoc with the sense of sight. Psychological blindness has been encountered in soldiers. Although the eyes may be quite normal, the brain may pay no attention to the messages it receives. Thus while the eyes may "see," there is no vision because the sensations recorded in the brain have not the slightest meaning. Psychological blindness may follow sudden shock and may be restored through shock.

ILLUMINATION

Most living things, plants as well as animals, orient themselves to brightness. Harmon notes that posture disturbances in children may follow poor distribution of light within a classroom. The pupil may bend his spine, slant his shoulders, twist his head in an effort to see more easily. If such practices are maintained day after day, there may be visibly bad posture and even change in the normal shape of bone growth.

Amount of illumination is never the most important factor in establishing an ideal seeing condition. Ferree and Rand have stated, "If, for example, the light is well distributed in the field of vision and there are no extremes of surface brightness, our tests seem to indicate that the eye, so far as the problem of lighting is concerned, is practically independent of intensity." This is obviously true because of the phenomenon of color constancy and the fact that the eye, through millions of years of development, can adjust itself quite efficiently and effectively to widely different degrees of light intensity.

Aside from intensity, however, how is the eye affected by illuminants having different color qualities? The human eye has evolved under sunlight which is yellowish in tint. This region of the spectrum marks the point of highest visibility. Yellowish light is excellent light, creates clear images, is relatively free of aberration or blur, and is æsthetically pleasing.

Contrary to popular belief, ability to see clearly diminishes as the illumination approaches the blue end of the spectrum. Ferree and Rand write: "The clearest seeing, also the greatest speed, power to sustain, etc., are given by the wave lengths in the mid-region of the spectrum—the yellow, the orange-yellow and the greenish yellow." The colors least desirable in a light source are green, red, and blue, the last being the most objectionable.

Ordinary incandescent lamp bulbs and fluorescent tubes of 3500 degrees color temperature are wholly satisfactory for good and comfortable seeing. Because of the action of color on the focus of the eye, farsighted persons may prefer a warm tint and nearsighted persons a cool tint. Warm light will tend to make the lens of the eye convex and thus aid the farsighted eye. Conversely, cool light will tend to make the lens flatter and to aid the nearsighted eye.

Some authorities have suggested that fluorescent lamps and other light sources which emit ultraviolet radiation may be harmful through the rapid destruction of vitamins in the fluids of the eye—leading in turn to certain nutritional disturbances within the body. Such speculations have been hotly contested but still find occasional reference. As Luckiesh states, "There is no more fruitful field for quacks and quackery than in the field of light, color and radiant energy."

None the less, lights and light sources that differ markedly from sunlight or daylight are likely to be rejected by the average person. Whether the objection be psychological in origin or have its basis in a physiological effect as yet unknown, it is safe to conclude that illumination should, in color quality, be as like nature as possible.

BRIGHTNESS ENGINEERING

Luckiesh has written, "A visual task is inseparable from its environment. . . . High visibility, ease of seeing and good seeing conditions are overwhelmingly the result of good brightness engineering." Eyestrain thus finds its master not solely in illumination, nor in proper diet and medical care, but also in color and the ability of color to add efficiency and comfort to seeing. It is obvious, for example, that if great brightness extremes exist within the field of view, the pupil of the eye will be forced to undergo constant changes of adjustment. Areas too light in color may set up psychological distractions and pretty well defy concentration on other objects and tasks. "The eyes often adjust themselves to a bright peripheral object notwithstanding the fact that the attention is directed elsewhere" (Luckiesh). Seeing would be as difficult under this condition as would be the attempt to hear a speaker while someone kept ringing a bell.

To summarize the requirements of good seeing and to anticipate the principles of functional color and the case histories to be set forth in the next chapter, here are a series of general conclusions:

The problems of illumination, brightness, and color in the creation of ideal seeing conditions are complex. They cannot be solved from the standpoint of optics alone, for important physiological, neural, and psychological factors must all be considered.

Seeing efficiency and comfort are not to be assured merely through light intensity. In fact, it cannot authoritatively be said that dim light is any worse on the eyes than brilliant light. Without question the eye needs light in order to see, and high levels seem more desirable than low levels. However, high levels, without attendant adjustments in the brightness of the environment, often cause glare and unfavorable extremes which waste light and handicap vision.

Ferree and Rand have reported: "The presence of high brilliancies in the field of view produces a strong incentive for the eyes to fixate and accommodate for them, which incentive must be controlled by voluntary effort. The result of this opposition of voluntary control against strong reflex incentive is to tire the eye quickly and to make it lose the power to sustain the precision of adjustment needed for clear seeing of the work."

In the main, if the equipment of a room is dark in color and cannot be changed and if surrounding walls are pale in tint, light levels beyond 25 or 35 foot-candles may cause trouble. If higher brightnesses can be introduced (but not beyond reflectances of 60 per cent, except on ceilings) higher light levels may also be introduced and very excellent seeing conditions may be achieved.

Thus great increases of light intensity in average American offices, factories, and schoolrooms will not be practical unless a tremendous amount of cooperative effort in brightness engineering is shown by fabricators of flooring materials, desks, filing cabinets, machinery, woodwork, paints, etc.

Until then, and for average seeing tasks encountered today in average interiors, light intensities approaching 25 foot-candles are satisfactory. Fairly critical seeing tasks may be performed under 25 to 50 foot-candles.

In the opinion of the author, general room illumination should not—except under very carefully controlled conditions—exceed 100 foot-candles. Where high light intensity seems necessary, supplementary illumination sources should be introduced directly over the workplace or task.

On the matter of reflectance, one point should not be overlooked. Average human complexion among Caucasians reflects about 50 per cent of light. Because practically all interiors are engineered for human occupancy, wall tones (and the colors of floors, equipment or machines) should not be very high in brightness. If they are, human appearance will suffer. Halos may appear about faces, and skin tones may grow deep and muddy. Too, the compelling attraction of the bright surrounding may set up annoying distractions to make the concentration of attention on tasks quite difficult. For a really ideal interior, no colors should reflect less than 25 per cent nor more than 60 per cent (except ceilings).

Low brightness contrasts are desirable. Glare should be overcome. Seeing is at its best where the brightness of the task moderately exceeds the brightness of its surroundings. Monotony should be avoided. Careful study must be given to the psychologic aspects of vision, to such phenomena as color constancy. For the seeing process is in the brain, in the psychic make-up of the individual, as well as in the organ of sight.

CHAPTER 19

Functional Color

THE TERM "FUNCTIONAL COLOR" is generally applied to uses and applications of hue in which beauty or appearance are secondary to more practical purposes. Where color may be employed to aid visual acuity—as in a hospital surgery—it is obvious that an objective rather than subjective attitude must be taken; good vision must be served, not the likes and dislikes of an individual. In other words, a great number of color problems are to be handled through technical rather than artistic methods. Functional color is concerned with measurable facts. It is founded on research, on known visual reactions, on data which may be statistically analyzed. It differs from so-called "interior decoration" in that personal preferences or emotional attitudes are denied for well-ordered scientific prac-

242

tice. A further difference may be stressed as follows: *beauty* in a decorative color scheme has no criterion other than taste or opinion; *functionalism* in a color scheme is entirely dependent upon tangible evidence.

VISIBILITY

Visibility is one factor in color that may be readily measured. The ability to see clearly may be determined by experiment and test and requires neither feeling nor judgment. As has previously been mentioned, the eye sees best in white, yellowish, or yellowish green light and worst in blue light. Thus sunglasses are best when tinted either yellow or yellow-green. These colors may not only increase visibility and acuity by cutting down the excess brilliance of full sunlight, but they will screen out the disturbing influence of ultraviolet. In fact, on a sunny day yellow glasses may actually improve vision and help the eye to see more clearly into distance.

In light signals, bright lights are obviously more readily seen than dim lights. Where intensities are kept uniform, however, red light is the easiest to recognize, followed by green light, then yellow, then white. Blue and purple are not well focused by the eye and tend to appear blurred. Such radiation is also "scattered" by atmosphere.

As to the apparent size of colors, yellow and white will be seen as largest, then red, green, blue. The quality of dimension (nearness or farness) is directly influenced by the optics of the eye. Red, for example, focuses normally at a point behind the retina. To see it clearly, the lens of the eye grows fat (convex), pulling the color nearer. Conversely, blue is focused normally at a point in front of the retina, causing the lens to flatten out and push the color back. Walls writes, "Since the dioptric [refractive] apparatus ordinarily places the yellow focus in the visual-cell layer, we must actually *accommodate* when diverting our attention from a blue object to a red one at the same actual distance from the eye, and must relax accommodation upon looking back at the blue object."

Yellow is the color of highest visibility not only in light sources but in surface colors such as paints. Combined with black it is the most legible of all color combinations. Next in order are green on white, red on white, blue on white, and white on blue, with black on white sixth. This particular order of superiority, however, is better adapted to posters or road signs than to book papers. Where the problem may also involve *ease* of seeing (not visibility alone) other factors must be reckoned with. For one thing, a bright color such as yellow would tire the eyes after prolonged concentration and would create a disturbing afterimage.

TINTED BACKGROUNDS

A great deal of scientific study has been given to the development of ideal backgrounds for critical seeing tasks such as reading. One common assumption that a green tint is easy on the eyes has been disproved by several authorities. Ferree and Rand write, "Any toning of the paper towards green is unfavorable in that it increases the tendency to ocular fatigue and discomfort." As with light sources, papers or backgrounds are quite ideal when white. Where a tint might be desired the yellow, yellow-orange, or yellow-green region of the spectrum would be suitable. "All coloring is inferior to white if the printed characters are to be black" (Ferree and Rand). Next in order would be a pale ivory or cream, then a pale yellowish green. However, because legibility is directly related to degree of contrast, black on white or black on ivory are hardly to be excelled.

Visibility may differ as light intensity differs. In strong light, white objects or details on a black background seem most favorable. In weak light, black objects on a white ground are best. These facts were examined by the author during the Second World War in a study of instrument dials for the U.S. Navy. Under low levels of illumination· the white dial not only was easier to locate visually, but its markings could be more quickly read. In this connection Ferree and Rand have written, "Our results on speed of vision have shown that near the threshold of acuity, *i.e.,* for small visual angles and low intensities of illumination, speed of discrimination is higher for such objects as a black letter on white . . . than for a white letter on black."

COLOR CONDITIONING

The applied science known today as "color conditioning" is greatly concerned with problems of visibility, acuity, and ocular fatigue. It deals with seeing conditions encountered in factories, offices, schools, hospitals, and it seeks to give them perfection through the specification of tried scientific principles.

For a brief historical review, color conditioning had its beginning in the mid-twenties of this present century. At that time studies were made in hospitals to lessen glare and improve the vision of the surgeon. To accomplish this, new techniques were worked out whereby the degree of fatigue could be measured by instrumental means. Results were achieved in the control of brightness and hue that quite definitely established the value of color in aiding human efficiency and well-being.

As adapted to hospitals and schools—and later to industrial plants and offices—color conditioning was applied to increase production, improve quality of workmanship and normal skill, reduce "seconds" and "rejects," cut down accident frequencies, raise standards of plant housekeeping and machine maintenance, reduce absenteeism, and improve labor morale.

Tremendous impetus came during the war period when production had to be increased, when labor was scarce, when finer tolerances were demanded in product manufacture. The value of color conditioning was widely tested and accepted.

THE CASE AGAINST WHITE

The optical system of the human eye is regulated by the amount of light that enters it. This makes brightness an important factor in the action of seeing. While uniformity of brightness is highly desirable for efficient and comfortable vision, extreme departures from such uniformity cause trouble.

With illumination, for example, two lighting systems may deliver the same number of foot-candles on a working surface. Yet if in the one system the fixtures are exposed and if in the other system the fixtures are concealed, eye adjustments will differ. Where the fixtures are exposed, the pupil of the eye may be unduly constricted and seeing may be difficult and probably painful. In an authoritative study made by R. J. Lythgoe of England, it was found that visual acuity increases at a steady rate as the surrounding brightness is raised to equal the brightness of the task. However, where the surrounding brightness *exceeds* the brightness of the task, acuity immediately collapses. Luckiesh has stated, "It may be concluded that brightnesses somewhat lower than those of the central field are generally most desirable. All experimental evidence indicates that peripheral brightnesses higher than those of the central field are definitely undesirable."

Despite the fact that some lighting engineers may freely recommend white and off-white colors for working environments (to gain as much light as possible per watt consumed) the bright

246

environment is quite objectionable. White walls may close the pupil opening, make seeing difficult, and set up annoying distractions. For the sake of a 5 or 10 per cent increase in lighting efficiency, there may be a drop of 25 per cent or more in human efficiency. Where a working environment may have dark floors, dark equipment, or dark materials, wall colors must be soft in tone to have the seeing condition right.

A REVIEW OF PRINCIPLES

It is quite possible to set forth ideal brightness specifications for factory and office conditions. Ceilings—almost without exception—should be white. This will be essential to the efficiency of indirect lighting systems. In direct systems, the white overhead will reduce contrasts between fixtures and their surroundings. Being "neutral," white will also attract less psychological notice and hence prove nondistracting.

Upper walls (generally to a line level with the bottom of roof beams or trusses) should have a reflectance between 50 and 60 per cent (if floors and equipment are on the dark side) or between 60 and 70 per cent if most areas and surfaces in the interior are (or can be made) fairly light. Wall brightnesses higher than 70 per cent seem to be allowable only where the most perfect and modern lighting system is installed and accompanied by pale floors and equipment—or for unimportant spaces such as storage where critical seeing tasks are not performed. It must not be forgotten, however, that bright walls are by no means flattering to human appearance.

If a dado is required to conceal stains, the color tone should reflect not less than 25 per cent and perhaps not more than 40 per cent. Floors should reflect at least 25 per cent if such is practical. Machines, equipment, desks should have a reflectance factor between 25 and 40 per cent, lighter when the floor is light and deeper when the floor is dark.

These ratios and percentages have been successfully applied in numerous plants and thus have the benefit of widespread trial and research.

Certain refinements are also to be introduced. Window sash ought to be white or a light tint to lessen contrast with outside brightnesses. Machinery may be highlighted in accordance with the principles of du Pont three-dimensional seeing to reflect more light at important parts and concentrate the attention of the worker. In numerous fine seeing tasks, background shields may be constructed to (1) reflect light and provide immediate contrast with materials, (2) confine the vision of the worker and hold eye adjustments relatively stable, (3) blank off shadows or movements in the distance, and (4) give the worker a better sense of isolation. Normally such shields should cover from 45 degrees to 60 degrees of the visual field.

End-wall treatments in medium tones also have widespread application. Where most workers may be engaged at difficult eye tasks and may be so oriented as to face in the same direction, the wall ahead may be colored in a pleasing tint having a reflectance of from 25 to 40 per cent. The end wall will help to overcome an unfavorable constriction of the pupil. Upon glancing up, it will afford relaxation rather than the stimulation of glare. It will likewise relax the strain of prolonged convergence and be psychologically pleasing and restful. Here again is a principle widely and successfully employed in industry.

TYPES OF COLORS

For industrial purposes, soft, delicately grayish hues are best. They are lacking in aggression, less distracting, and they most effectively conceal dust and soiling. Ordinarily, primitive colors such as blue and yellow are tiresome. Where subtlety exists (bluish green, peach, etc.) a more comfortable environment will be found and one that will "wear well" over prolonged periods.

It is logical to use "cool" colors such as green or blue where the working condition exposes the employee to relatively high temperatures. Conversely, "warm" tones of ivory, cream, or peach are suitable to soften up a vaulty or chilly space and compensate for lack of natural light.

In purely casual spaces, such as washrooms, rest rooms, cafeterias, lighter and cleaner hues may be used. In view of average color preferences, blue becomes ideal for facilities devoted to men, and rose for facilities devoted to women. In stairwells and corridors, usually deprived of natural light, bright tones of yellow are effective. In storage areas, white is best and will make the most of existing lighting installations.

Where critical seeing tasks are performed, however, and where distractions are to be avoided, the best colors to use are soft variations of green, gray, and blue. Large, vaulty spaces may be enlivened with ivory, cream, or peach over all walls, or yellow over end walls. Gray machinery highlighted with buff on important parts and working areas will prove effective. Medium gray is also ideal for unimportant elements such as bins, racks, shelving. One must remember that color is more compelling than neutrality. Hence, if it is strategically applied, it can make order out of chaos, distinguish important from unimportant elements, and help the worker in his mental effort to concentrate on his task. In theory as well as practice, the purpose of color is not so much to "inspire" the worker; too much of this attitude may lead to distractions and irrelevancies. On the contrary, color becomes integral with the task, not foreign to it. Improved efficiency

249

and relief from fatigue become automatic because the human eye can see more easily, with less strain. Color is made to fit in rather than stand out. It contributes to better visibility and to an agreeable and cheerful frame of mind.

THE MEDICAL PROFESSION

Wherever possible the applied science of color conditioning deals with facts—production records, accident statistics, instrumental measurements of the eye. It is not promoted to sell paint or new equipment in brighter finish. It is intended to pay dividends in increased efficiency and the conservation of human energy. Hence it is of interest to review some of the more palpable facts of functional color and to quote the results of a few competent research studies.

The author has been privileged to present the scientific aspects of color conditioning before national conventions of the medical profession. Through books and special publications, the best principles of color have been assembled for use in the graduate training of ophthalmologists. By and large the medical profession recognizes that color is intimately related to safe and hygienic seeing. Physicians and surgeons in the field of vision are today devoting special attention to the industrial aspects of color in practically every leading medical school in America.

NATIONAL INDUSTRIAL CONFERENCE BOARD

A thorough investigation into the value of color in industry has been published by the National Industrial Conference Board. Over 350 companies which had used color on a small or large scale were asked to comment on a long series of questions. It was found, however, that many "companies were unprepared to

250

evaluate their programs primarily because of the difficulty involved in measuring the effects of a service as intangible as color."

Yet despite the newness of the science of color conditioning, the facts divulged were quite impressive.

64.7 per cent of companies stated that color had improved lighting.

27.9 per cent reported production increases.

30.9 per cent noted an improvement in the quality of work performed.

19.1 per cent commented favorably on reduced eyestrain and fatigue.

14.7 per cent credited color for reduced absenteeism. This is also an indication of better morale.

All in all, 75 per cent of companies were entirely or well satisfied with their color programs; 5.9 per cent were not satisfied; 19.1 per cent had no opinion one way or the other.

U.S. PUBLIC HEALTH SERVICE

A competent and reliable evaluation of color has been prepared by the Public Buildings Administration in Washington and the U.S. Public Health Service. This involved a two-year investigation of work production in a government office and was singular in that all details of it were carefully guided by authorities in the fields of vision, illumination, and color. Production data were assembled by the Bureau of Internal Revenue.

A controlled study was undertaken to measure the working efficiency of a group of employees using business machines. Three conditions were analyzed: (1) the original room; (2) the room with the addition of new lighting fixtures; (3) the room with the further addition of color.

251

The fact that uniform brightness is essential to efficient and comfortable seeing has been confirmed by the above report. Under the first condition, the highest brightness in the room measured 1,195; under the second condition it was 47, under the third condition it was 20. Even more significant, brightness ratios under the first condition were over 100 to 1. The addition of new lighting (condition 2) reduced the ratio to 40 to 1—this being still excessive. Where proper color conditioning was done (condition 3) the brightness ratio was lowered to an ideal 4.7 to 1.

As to worker efficiency, one task had an improvement of 37.4 per cent. However, a fair and conservative figure of 5.5 per cent has been set as the general improvement shown.

In cash value, this 5.5 per cent production improvement was equivalent to a saving on gross payroll of $13,229 among some 95 government employees. If this figure is a credible one—and the author fully believes that it is—one may state that right illumination and right color are worth about $139.25 annually per average employee in American industry today! An organization having 100 employees would thus realize a year's saving of $13,925. For 1,000 employees, the annual saving would be $139,-250. These dollar figures, of course, would apply only where the conditions before and after were comparable to those of the government study. However, because countless factories and offices are found that are as bad or worse, the dollar value of color is substantial and is hardly to be overlooked as a sound business investment.

SAFETY

A color code for safety was developed in 1944 by the writer in collaboration with du Pont. It was later accepted in substantial part as a national standard by the American Standards Association and has since had an impressive history. Its general organization is as follows:

Yellow (or yellow and black bands) is standard to mark strike-against, stumbling, or falling hazards. It is painted on obstructions, low beams, dead ends, the edges of platforms and pits. Being the color of highest visibility in the spectrum, it is conspicuous under all lighting conditions and well adapted to the above purposes.

Orange is standard for acute hazards likely to cut, crush, burn, or shock the worker. It is painted around the edges of cutting machines and rollers. On the inside areas of machine guards and electric switch boxes, it "shouts loudly" when such devices are removed or left open.

Green is standard to identify first aid equipment, cabinets for stretchers, gas masks, medicines, and the like.

Red is reserved entirely and exclusively for the marking of fire protection devices. It is painted on walls behind extinguishers, on floors to prevent obstruction, on valves and fittings for hose connections.

Blue is standard as a caution signal. The railroad industry employs it to mark cars which should not be moved. In factories it is placed as a symbol on equipment, elevators, machines, tanks, ovens, etc., cut down for repair. It may be used on switch control boxes as a silent and unobtrusive reminder for the worker to see that his machine is clear before he operates it.

White, gray, or black are standard for traffic control and good housekeeping. They are used for aisle marks, painted on waste receptacles. White corners and baseboards may be used to discourage littering and to get the sweeper to dig into corners.

This code was widely employed during the Second World War and is today mandatory in all shore establishments of the U.S.

Navy. In a release issued by the U.S. Army Service Forces, a reduction in accident frequencies was reported in some government plants from a rate of 46.14 to 5.58 per cent. In one quartermaster depot, disabling injuries were cut from 13.25 to 6.99 per cent.

A carefully supervised and installed safety color code similarly reduced accident frequencies 42.3 per cent for the New York Transit System, which employs 38,000 workers. In this instance the color application was supplemented by a concentrated program of safety training and has had very dramatic results. In terms of cash value, a 42.3 per cent reduction in accidents among 38,000 workers is equivalent to a saving of $500,000 in one year as figured by compensation insurance statistics.

Government records place an average value of $1,044 on every industrial accident. Obviously, adequate protection against loss of life or limb not only is imperative from the human standpoint but is financially sound as well.

No doubt as the factual story of color is further enlarged and as added case histories are assembled, practical applications will be broadened and increased. Man's control over his environment will be better and more intelligently directed. He will find many of his problems lessened, for color is sorely needed in many places and will be found to repay its investment many times over when put to the test.

CHAPTER 20

The Prescription of Color

A PRACTICAL ART and science of color holds great potential benefit. From a study of the therapeutic and psychological aspects of the hues of the spectrum, it becomes possible to exert greater control over color mediums and to attain many vital ends. Taste and temperament may be supplemented by a surer knowledge of the influences of color in human life. Where formerly an artist or decorator might search his soul for inspiration, he may now—if he will educate himself—write prescriptions which have a basis in fact rather than fancy and which add definite functions to beauty. Although the progress of research must be endless, it is possible today to summarize and apply a tremendous fund of available data and to improve upon the principles and practices of yesterday.

255

Where the use of color relates to human comfort and well-being, color may have no great intrinsic value unless it is tastefully and artistically employed. Red, for example, may be exciting to most persons. Yet if in a hospital or a home it is painted on bare walls, any physiological effect may be canceled by a natural revulsion for crudeness. Red—or any other hue—to be therapeutically or psychologically stimulating must also be æsthetically pleasing.

Needless to say, many tests of color have failed because the above requirement has not been met. To seat human beings in cubbyholes or booths finished in different hues and attempt to measure their reactions would be both ludicrous and futile. Unless the test procedure compares favorably with the eventual condition under which color will be applied, and unless it may be agreeably undertaken, the human equation may destroy the scientific one.

Many applications of color to factories, offices, schools have been unsuccessful because they have been "engineered" as if people were sensitive to blank areas of color alone and not also to form, proportion, harmony, and the like. Nor will color accomplish many marvels if other factors influencing the other senses—heat, cold, glare, noise, odor, fumes, physical and occupational hazards—are not simultaneously dealt with.

On the other hand, the prescription of color cannot lean too heavily on the artistic. Here too color has often failed. When its use is overdone, when the colors chosen are too bright, the combinations too "dramatic," the effect may be wholly out of place, and the observer may actually be distracted from his tasks or made uncomfortable in his environment.

Although the author has had extensive experience in the use of color to accomplish well-defined ends, he is quite aware of the fact that a great world of energy remains untouched. A tremendous opportunity exists today to build a new therapy of color totally divorced from the esoteric, to coordinate the efforts of the biologist, the ophthalmologist, the psychiatrist, and the psychologist, and to follow method rather than mere feeling in getting color to serve the best interests of humankind.

In a few crowded years the author has met problems of eyestrain in factories and institutions. He has employed color to cope with accidents. He has cooperated with educators, hospital administrators, organizations devoted to the prevention of blindness. Though he has performed little of pure research, he has had practical occasion to interpret and apply a large number of the findings and principles reviewed in this book.

Method is important in color specifications. Indeed, trial and error often seem needless in view of the mass of evidence that has come out of the medical field. If the spectrum is to be utilized intelligently and if the color artist or color engineer is to consider himself qualified to deal with human problems, then more of system and less of insight will be necessary. The capable persons will be those who have an understanding of the strange workings of color, its direct effects upon the organism, and its influence through vision. For with a background of research data, results will be easier to anticipate and assignments may be approached with greater reason and regularity.

THE EFFECTS OF THE MAJOR HUES

Here are a few notes on the efficacy of the major hues of the spectrum. They will serve to bring together some of the chief

257

points of this book and to define the outstanding qualities of individual colors for convenient reference.

The Significance of Red

Red is perhaps the most dominant and dynamic of colors. Its energy has a strong influence on the growth of plants. It has been found to accelerate the development of certain lower animals, to increase hormonal and sexual activity, and to heal wounds.

In its action upon the human organism, red tends to distract the equilibrium of the body. It has been prescribed to treat sunburn, inflammation, rheumatism. It will act to raise blood pressure and pulse rate but may be followed by a reversal of these effects after a period of time.

Psychologically, red is exciting and increases restlessness and nervous tension. It represents an attraction to stimulus and as such provides an excellent environment for the creation (but not execution) of ideas. Under the influence of red, time is overestimated and weights seem heavier. The color is most pronounced when strong light intensities are also involved. (Red is the first of all colors to fade out in dim illumination.)

Under practical stituations, however, pure red can seldom be used; the full hue is too imperious and has too strong an afterimage. Brilliant red has its value in commanding human attention, although a high frequency of color blindness among men introduces limitations. Modified forms of red—rose, maroon, pink—are beautiful and expressive, universally appealing, and deeply emotional. Variations of red are preferred by extroverts; therefore the color has a place in psychotherapy to bolster human moods and counteract melancholia. It helps to distract attention from within and to direct it outward.

Variations of Orange

Orange partakes of the same qualities as red. It is not generally preferred in its pure form but highly pleasing in its tints (peach, salmon) and shades (brown). For the most part tints of orange (peach) are ideal for the interiors of hospitals or homes, factories, or schools. The color is mellow, less primitive than red, and it therefore has a more "livable" charm. It has high appetite appeal and is quite suitable for food service. Where it may be reflected upon human skin, it casts a cheerful and flattering glow.

Yellow

Yellow has been said to have a favorable effect upon human metabolism. In many studies of the biological action of light, however, it is generally found to be neutral (together with yellow-green). Because of the high visibility of yellow, it serves many purposes in safety. The hue is sharply focused by the eye, cheerful and incandescent in appearance.

In color conditioning, yellow will tend to appear brighter than white. It thus is useful in meeting unfavorable conditions of dim illumination or large, vaulty spaces.

Greens in General

Yellow-green is generally neutral from the biological standpoint. Greens and blue-greens, however, are pacific and tend to reduce nervous and muscular tension. Psychologically, green represents a withdrawal from stimulus. It provides an ideal environment for sedentary tasks, concentration, and meditation.

Bluish greens lack a primitive quality and are both pleasing and "livable." The same virtues have been expressed for peach, and indeed the two hues beautifully enhance each other. Because

259

blue-green is complementary to the tint of average human complexion, it provides a very flattering background.

The Significance of Blue

Blue has qualities that are antithetical to red. It seems to retard the growth of plants, to decrease hormonal activity, and to inhibit the healing of wounds. In its action upon the human organism it lowers blood pressure and pulse rate, though this effect may later be reversed.

Under the influence of blue, time is underestimated and weights are judged as being lighter. Because the color has a naturally low saturation it may be used in almost any form— light, dark, pure, grayish. Being visually primary, however, it tends to be bleak if applied in too large an area. While blues are suitable for homes, they have not proved very successful in offices, industries, schools, hospitals, except as incidental areas and then in medium or deep tones. (Pale blue seems to "bother" human eyes and to give a blurred appearance to adjacent objects.)

Because blue is a difficult color to focus, it is objectionable as a light source and low in attention-value. Yet blue is associated with dim light, is restful and sedate, and is an outstanding favorite throughout the world.

Purple, Gray, White, and Black

Purple being a blend of red and blue, the two extremes of the spectrum, is more or less neutral biologically. It is not suitable for large areas because it disturbs the focus of the eye. Of all hues, it seems to be the one dominantly esthetic in its appeal.

White is the perfectly balanced color, clear and natural in its influence. Black is negative; gray is passive. All three are found to be emotionally neutral and fail to have much psycho-therapeutic application except where negation may be the particular expression desired.

MONOTONY VS. VARIETY

Just as warm colors are exciting and cool colors are tranquilizing, so is brightness stimulating and darkness relaxing. Change, variation, sequence are all vital in the use of color. In fact, no human sense—including vision—can respond consistently to fixed stimuli. Human sensations ebb and flow, probably because average experiences ebb and flow. The eye, like any other organ of the body, is in a constant state of fluctuation. Changes in the diameter of the pupil will take place even before an area of unvarying brightness. Images on the retina (or sounds in the ear) will seem to fade in and out, despite the fact that they actually may be constant.

If chaos and disorder are mentally and emotionally distressing, unrelieved monotony is probably worse. The theory is personal with the author, but the superstition that bizarre designs and gaudy colors will "drive people crazy" has less verity to it than the one that attributes the same effect to situations which are precisely the reverse. That is, any human being forced to work in an office or home surrounded by nothing but ivory or buff will hazard his good disposition and sanity even more. A circus is less likely to make a person neurotic than the tan waiting room of a railroad depot!

In this connection, colors of brilliant intensity arranged in garish patterns were used after the First World War to treat "shell shock" (now termed "battle fatigue"). The principle involved was simple enough: in some forms of mental illness the senses tend to have widened thresholds and to be easily upset and "set on edge." In such unfortunate persons, nervousness may be aggravated by monotony and relieved through excitation. Because bright color may equal the intensity of the person's own turbulence, it may be agreeably distracting and therefore restful and therapeutic.

THE IMPORTANCE OF SEQUENCE

After many of the facts of the physiological and psychological action of visible light are weighed, it would appear that color is most potent, most efficacious, and most therapeutic where there is sequence rather than sameness. The reader may recall that red had the immediate effect of increasing blood pressure and pulse rate *above* normal, but that after a period of time the blood pressure and pulse rate fell *below* normal. Similarly, noise caused a decrease in the apparent intensity of red colors but was followed later by a reversal of sensitivity.

On the other hand, blue lowers pulse rate but later causes it to rise. Dim light also tends to increase the sensitivity of the eye to blue colors.

Brightness, loudness, and stimulation of the senses in general are to be associated with the most active effects of red and all warm colors.

Dimness, quietness, and sedation of the senses in general are to be associated with the most active effects of blue and all cool colors.

Neutrality is found in yellow and yellow-green.

Here, then, are two hypothetical principles of color therapy:

For excitation, begin with warm colors, bright illumination, fairly loud but pleasing noises. Blood pressure and pulse rate should rise. Follow with *sudden* exposure to cool colors, dimmer illumination, and quietude. End with sudden restoration of the first condition or exposure to pale yellow or white in bright illumination.

For sedation, begin with cool colors, dim illumination, quiet environment. Blood pressure and pulse rate should drop. Follow *gradually* with shift to warm color, brighter illumination, and moderate sound. End with gradual restoration of first condition or exposure to pale yellow or white in dim illumination.

The author wishes to repeat that his two principles are sheer supposition and based on logic rather than clinical test. Yet the reverse effect encountered in the action of color should, in the above two procedures, neatly balance each other and lead to a prolonged rather than temporary state of animated or passive spirit.

Where dramatic and highly emotional effects are wanted from color sequences—such as in motion pictures—deep blue colors should be "cut" abruptly into bright red colors for maximum excitation. However, bright red colors should be "faded" or "dissolved" into soft, cool hues when more melancholy moods are desired. Red has fast tempo; blueness, and greenness are "slow."

COLOR SPECIFICATIONS

Hospitals

In applying color for psychotherapeutic purposes, simple devices may be safely and successfully followed. The lobby or reception room of the hospital, visited chiefly by visitors, should have a variety of hues both warm and cool, the object being to avoid any one specific "mood." Where the public may be exposed to such hue contrast, the effect will be pleasant and cheerful. Yet any precise reaction, either ecstatic or lugubrious, will be compromised. The general impression will be visual rather than emotional in quality.

Warm tones such as peach and rose are desirable for the maternity division where the patient may not be seriously ill and where a will to get well is the spirit to be encouraged.

Cool tones of blues, greens, grays become appropriate for chronic patients who should be reconciled to a more prolonged stay.

In the surgery, the walls should be green or blue-green to overcome glare, relax the eyes, and complement the red hue of human blood and tissue.

Lavender, cool yellows, and yellow-greens are to be avoided, such hues being "sickly" in aspect and casting unfavorable reflections which give human complexion a ghastly appearance.

Schools

Elementary schoolrooms are best "color conditioned" in warm tones of yellow, peach, pink. These colors are stimulating to young minds and are favorable for "emotionally determined actions," as Goldstein has noted. In secondary grades, tones of green, blue-green, blue, and gray are recommended to avoid emotional distraction and to aid mental concentration.

The impulsive nature of children is essentially related to warm hues. Maturity is to be associated with the cool region of the spectrum which seems to be conducive to thought.

Airplanes and Ships

Where color is meant to reduce apprehension or nervousness, as in air or ocean travel, moderately warm tones, such as peach, may be best for general areas.

First of all, a warm tint will counteract the blurring effect of wide expanses of blue which seem to distress the eye. Again, the warm tint, being moderately stimulating, will more nearly agree with the passenger's own mood. It will offer a "bright smile" and not a "glum frown."

For variety and harmony, blue-green may be further introduced, such as in carpeting or upholstery fabrics. This color will complement peach. When steadily fixated by the eye it has a pinkish afterimage that gives the objects of the world a mellow and attractive appearance.

Homes

Color in the home may be functionally considered. A convivial mood will follow the use of a warm tone in the living room. (Or if the owner wishes a more formal atmosphere, he or she may use blue.) Peach, the most appetizing of all tints, may be suitable for the dining room. The kitchen may be in cool tones of green or turquoise, such colors tending to shorten the apparent passage of time.

Yellow may be appropriate for rooms deprived of abundant natural light, for the basement and playroom. The den or library should be in some deep hue—warm or cool—to prevent the environment from distracting from the task or book. Bathrooms should be pink to give the skin a luminous glow through reflection. Bedrooms may be in any color, preferably of light tint. Strong contrasts and large patterns may encourage early rising. Late sleepers will value plain areas and less aggressive tones.

COLOR AND MEDICAL SCIENCE

Consciously or unconsciously, man has always held an innate faith in the efficacy of color. The great significance he has attached to it is everywhere evident in the surroundings of his life. For the hues of the spectrum have always been associated with his history and civilization.

Science may substitute protons and electrons for red and blue, but the appeal of color still persists. Those who have studied the growth of plants, the biological effects of color on lower organisms, the behavior of insects and animals, the physiological and psychological reactions of the human body, are aware that real "magic" exists.

Indeed, color has a required need in human life. It may be prescribed like medicines or drugs and its effects anticipated. Yet to work in this intelligent fashion, the qualities of the spectrum should be thoroughly understood. It is not enough to believe in the virtues of color; orderly and diligent research is needed to clarify its therapeutic values and to develop reliable techniques for its use.

The intimate role which color may play should become increasingly vital as man turns from an æsthetic and esoteric attitude to one more rational and clinical; as recognized medical science forgets its prejudices and appreciates that color is physiologically and psychologically beneficial and may be put to effective human service.

Part 5

NEW BIOLOGICAL AND PSYCHOLOGICAL FINDINGS

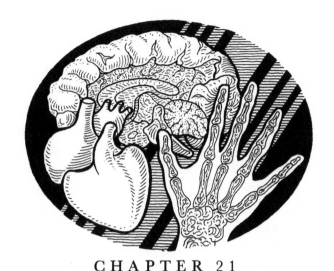

CHAPTER 21

*New Biological and Psychological Findings**

THE MEDICAL PROFESSION, with good reason, has always cast a suspicious eye on any claims for therapy in color. In the general "gestalt" of seeing, it is difficult to isolate psychic factors from physical or physiological ones. If you or I (or a puppy) respond gleefully to a sunny day, the same response cannot be claimed for everyone else. Red, which may appeal to you, may be rejected by another. And because practically all color experience is likely to be qualified and judged in personal terms, sound and objective data are not easy to gather.

Thus some researchers report positive results, while others report negative ones, and often in very similar tests. This clearly

* Part of the material in this section first appeared in "The Effects of Color on the Human Organism," by Faber Birren, *American Journal of Occupational Therapy,* XIII, 3, 1959.

indicates that the testing methods themselves must be scrutinized. Indeed, if the psychological or human conditions of a test lead to any sort of prejudice or mental interference, the physiological reactions may themselves be unfavorably affected. Many normal responses are often cancelled out by merely pointing them out. Is red a warm color, for example? It is by and large in the unconscious reaction of most of us. But ask a person to explain this peculiarity of red and he may end up doubting it completely.

There is little question that visible light and color influence and affect living things. Virtually all plant life thrives on visible light and is inhibited by infrared and ultraviolet energy. While medical science acknowledges physiological effects in this radiation beyond the two ends of the visible spectrum (infrared and ultraviolet), and makes therapeutic use of them, any admission of benefits for the particular wavelengths of light seen by the human eye has been very widely ignored or disregarded. It hardly stands to reason that visible light—the illumination under which the human race has flourished and to which its eyes are adjusted—should be without potency.

But reason and logic cannot suffice for facts. What seems to be evident is that the mystery of visible light, its physiological and psychophysiological importance, has been pretty well neglected. Thus to add to a very sparse record, the writer is happy to set forth some recent experimental results.

For sound research techniques and impressive quantitative data, the world of color psychology and medicine is indebted to the recent efforts of Robert Gerard. In an outstanding doctor's thesis in psychology for the University of California at Los Angeles, Gerard has painstakingly reviewed the whole area of light, color and their psychophysiological influences. Probably for the first time, he has tested the reactions of the entire organism, using advanced and modern techniques. Profiting from the experience of others, he has evolved new approaches and has come up with a number of significant facts.

Gerard set forth to ask and answer several questions: Is the response to color differential? That is, do such hues as red and blue arouse different feelings and emotions? Do they induce correlated changes in autonomic functions, brain activity and subjective feelings? Do the patterns of response correspond to the relative energy of the colored stimuli?

In his experiments, Gerard made use of red, blue and white lights transmitted on a diffusing screen. Brightness and spectral purity were balanced. Measurements were made of blood pressure, palmar conductance (electrodes in the palm of the hand which indicate arousal of the autonomic nervous system through reaction of the sweat glands), respiration rate, heart rate, muscular activation, frequency of eyeblinks, and brain waves by means of an electroencephalogram.

Affective responses, based on the personal experience, judgment and feeling of the subjects, were also recorded. These responses, incidentally, ran rather true to traditional form. On the subjective side, red was found somewhat disturbing to the more anxious subjects. In fact, the higher their chronic tension, the more they were affected physiologically by red. Blue had a reverse effect, for anxious subjects were calmed by it. From the point of view of clinical psychology, this may be an important finding, for it points to the possibility that blue may be effective as a tranquilizer in cases of tension and anxiety. In brief, there was a feeling of greater well-being and calm, more pleasant ideation with blue, and more tension, excitement and arousal with red. Both reactions may well hold implications for clinical practice.

On the physiological side, Gerard's results may be summarized as follows: Blood pressure for the most part increased under the influence of red light and decreased under blue light. In palmar conductance, both colors produced immediate increases. However, arousal after a period of time was consistently higher for red than for blue. "Respiratory movements increased during exposure to red light, and decreased during blue illumination." With heart rate, no appreciable differences were found between the stimulation of red and blue. Frequency of eyeblinks increased during exposure to red light and decreased during exposure to blue light.

Regarding cortical activation, the brain was markedly affected upon the introduction of all three lights (red, blue and white). With time, however (up to 10 minutes), activation remained consistently greater for red than for blue.

It should be appreciated, of course, that in palmar conductance and cortical activation, any stimulus is likely to show effects. What is significant as to color is that red consistently showed a more pronounced pattern over blue, both upon the introduction of this stimulus and after a period of time.

Gerard is extremely modest in the interpretation of his results. He proposes that psychophysical activation tends to increase with wavelength from blue to red and from low to high stimulus. Gerard's caution regarding all the implications of his tests is commendable. He worked with normal subjects and, in all his writings, points out the need for more research. The medical profession is quite aware of the fact that because color has such a strong emotional impact, it is not always easy to be strictly impartial in dealing with it. Gerard is aware of this and has maintained an admirable objectivity.

In its effects, blue seems to hold particular merits. Gerard's thesis states: "The results obtained with blue light suggest trying out its use as an adjunct or supplemental form of therapy in the alleviation of various conditions."

It might act as a relaxant and tranquilizer to dampen psychophysiological arousal in anxious individuals, since this effect was marked in the more anxious subjects.

Because blue lowers blood pressure, it may have possiblities in the treatment of hypertension.

The general relaxation and relief from tension experienced by the subjects suggests that blue may be of help in alleviating muscle spasms, and perhaps also torticollis and tremors.

Because it reduced eyeblink frequency and is subjectively experienced as soothing, it might have some advantages in eye irritations.

Because of its restful effects, dim blue illumination might be "conducive to sleep in cases of insomnia."

It might further contribute to the *subjective* relief of pain due to its reported sedative action.

In Gerard's findings, red and white stimulations were pretty much the same. From this it may be assumed that red and other "warm" colors are more related to excitation in general. Blue and other "cool" colors, however, may be more specific in their particular effects. Yet red might be useful in arousing persons troubled with reactive depression or neurasthenia. It may have value in increasing muscular tonus or blood pressure in hypotensive individuals. While white light is physiologically stimulating, it may also be psychologically boring. In other words, stimulation by itself does not tell the whole story. Such boredom (with white) might prove irritating and hence be reflected in physiological arousal. On the other hand, arousal with red seems to go along with feelings of aggression, sex, fear of injury. Autonomic reactions may be similar, but to the subject there may be a world of difference.

What is further needed, as Gerard has pointed out, is more study as to the differential effects of color, orange and yellow as well as red, and green and violet as well as blue.

Next I should like to refer to the recent work of John Ott as described in his book MY IVORY CELLAR (Twentieth Century Press, Chicago, 1958). Ott is America's foremost time-lapse photographer. Many of his findings are phenomenal and his time-lapse methods are working their way into medical research. "The principle of time-lapse photography is very simple. It is just the opposite of slow-motion pictures, with which most people may be more familiar. In place of slowing motion down, it speeds up many times faster than normal such subjects as a flower opening, or the complete growth of a plant on the screen in a few seconds." If the reader has seen these engaging effects on television or in Walt Disney's *Secrets of Life,* he has made acquaintance with John Ott's talents and skills.

Through time-lapse photography, Ott has caused primroses to dance to a waltz and tiger lilies to Dixieland jazz. This has been accomplished through the control of light and moisture on which the plants thrive and comport themselves.

Although it is generally recognized that visible light is conducive to plant growth, and that ultraviolet and infrared light contribute little or nothing, Ott found ultraviolet energy necessary, for example, for the normal growth of corn and the reddening of apples. He confirmed the importance of length of day in controlling the flowering of such plants as chrysanthemums and poinsettias, a practice that is now common among commercial growers.

And what about the effects of different wavelengths of light? With morning glories, a night-blooming flower, Ott discovered that red light caused trouble, and that through the use of blue filters over his photographic light sources, this red could be filtered out and flowering encouraged.

With the pumpkin, which has both male and female flowers, differential effects for color were quite pronounced. Fluorescent light, slightly warm in tint, produced male flowers and withered female. Ott concludes: "The fact that either male or female flowers can be brought forth by controlling slight variations in color of wavelength opens up some interesting possibilities for investigation."

In animals also, control of length of day is important. Brown stoats which turn to white ermine in winter (short days) can be turned to white in mid-summer if exposure to light is properly reduced. Mink can be given heavy winter pelts in July or any other month, practically at will.

Ott reports on the raising of chinchillas which seemed to persist in having male offspring when ordinary incandescent lamps were used for supplementary light, and female offspring when daylight bluish bulbs were employed. He concludes that these findings indicate that the sex of the offspring can be influenced well along in the pregnancy.

As to birds: "It is now known that the lengthening night period causes certain glandular changes in birds that are responsible for their seasonal migration." Supplementary light is commonly used in poultry raising to stimulate egg production. "Originally it was thought this merely kept the hens awake longer, but more recent research has proved that increased egg production is attained as a result of the light reacting through the chicken's eye on its pituitary gland."

In this connection, the English biologist, Sir Solly Zuckerman, has reported greater virility among city birds than in their country cousins. As Zuckerman relates, "I remember in the late twenties or thirties Rowan came over here from British Columbia to study the effect of the illumination, the advertising lighting, in Trafalgar Square and Piccadilly Circus on the starlings. As a control he used starlings he collected in a wood near Oxford. On alternate nights he collected birds from Oxford and from London, and he found that the birds he collected in London—by means of a lot of dangerous work on the parapets of the National Gallery, I recall—had active reproductive organs at a time when those of the birds from the country were completely atrophied or non-functional."

Even though some of Ott's work is in the hypothetical realm and further research is needed to support his theories, one is struck by the rich potentiality of his approach.

Among other findings of the last decade are those of A. Kelner. The medical profession has been impressed by his discovery that visible light may reverse or arrest the injurious effects of ultraviolet light. Two other investigators, A. F. Rieck and S. D. Carlson, have shown that the death rate in albino mice brought about by severe exposure to ultraviolet may be substantially reduced when visible light is used as a palliative. In what is called photogenic epilepsy, flickering red light is more likely to induce radical brain waves than other colors. C. Van Buskirk reports that in several cases the wearing of eyeglasses which cut off the red end of the spectrum reduced the frequency of clinical seizures, even though medication was discontinued.

For many years it has been my profession to work with color and with people in all walks of life. I have kept abreast of color research in the fields of medical therapy, ophthalmology and psychology and I have endeavored to put to wholly practical use some of the more theoretical findings of the scientific specialist. In all my activities I have tried to adhere to the best scientific practice and to avoid the purely speculative views which so often beset those dealing with the highly temperamental, esthetic (and often occult) medium of color. With an eye to sound research and practical experience, my conclusions concerning the use of color in everyday life are as follows:

1. There is in color and light what might be called a centrifugal action—away from the organism to its environment. With high levels of illumination, warm and luminous colors in the surroundings (yellow, peach, pink), the body tends to direct its attention outward. There is increased activation in general, alertness, outward orientation. Such an environment is conducive to muscular effort, action and cheerful spirit. It is a good setting for factories, schools, homes where manual tasks are performed or where sports are engaged in.

2. On the other hand, color and light may have a centripetal action—away from the environment and toward the organism. With softer surroundings, cooler hues (gray, blue, green, turquoise) and lower brightness, there is less distraction and a person is better able to concentrate on difficult visual and mental tasks. Good inward orientation is furthered. Here is an appropriate setting for sedentary occupations requiring severe use of the eyes or brain—offices, study rooms, fine assembly in industry.

3. The wise color practice expressed in items 1 and 2 above, however, is not always observed. Lighting engineers, for example, are likely to deal with human environments in terms of light intensity and brightness alone. These are obviously important, but without attention to color as well the truly ideal condition is not realized. Today high levels of *general* illumination are often specified where critical seeing is necessary. While it may be granted that the eye needs a lot of light to see clearly, if this necessity leads to high brightness in the surroundings, the organism may be

279

seriously handicapped. Brightness not only will draw attention from a task; it may defy good visual adjustment and concentration. If intense *general* illumination is required, at least the surroundings ought to be suppressed in tone. Better still, the general illumination should be moderate, and localized light sources should be added and directed immediately over the task. This will put attention where it belongs and eliminate distractions in the outer fields of view. To make a point, note how often a person will close his eyes when trying to solve a complex mental problem; the impulse here is to get rid of the environment completely.

4. In the psychological realm, experimental work in schools and hospitals has emphasized further strategies with color. Outwardly integrated persons, "nervous" persons, small children will find relaxation in an actively colored environment. The reason is a very simple one: visual (and emotional) excitement in the environment will effectively "match" the spirits of such persons and thereupon set them at ease. Attempts to pacify them through color or anything else may only serve to "bottle up" such spirits to a bursting point.

5. Conversely, inwardly integrated persons will ordinarily prefer a more sedate environment—and it will provide the equanimity they innately prefer. A quiet soul told to wear a red dress or a red tie may by no means respond according to the usual pattern. On the contrary, such boldness may make him increasingly shy and embarrassed. In the case of mental disturbance, however, reverse policies may be necessary. A person with an inordinate craving for bloody red—which might lead to trouble—probably should be exposed to blue in order to counteract his temper. The melancholy person, who is tolerant only of drabness, probably should be exposed to red to animate him, physiologically as well as psychically.

And so research in color goes on and perhaps will continue to be pursued indefinitely. If that which is purely physical and biological can be combined with that which is so definitely emotional and psychical, then man's future will be a bright one indeed.

Bibliography

Altogether, several hundred volumes, articles, and reports have been examined in the writing of this book over the past several years. In many instances, however, too little has been gleaned from them to warrant inclusion in this bibliography. The items listed below are the ones that have been most profitably consulted. Thus they hold major significance and constitute a rich source of reference on the therapeutic and psychological aspects of color.

Abbott, Arthur G.: *The Color of Life,* McGraw-Hill Book Company, Inc., New York, 1947.

Allen, Frank, and Manuel Schwartz: The Effect of Stimulation of the Senses of Vision, Hearing, Taste, and Smell Upon the Sensibility of the Organs of Vision, *Journal of General Physiology,* September 20, 1940.

Babbitt, Edwin D.: *The Principles of Light and Color,* published by the author, East Orange, N. J., 1896.

Bagnall, Oscar: *The Origin and Properties of the Human Aura,* E. P. Dutton & Co., Inc., New York, 1937.

Bartley, S. Howard: "Visual Sensation and Its Dependence on the Neurophysiology of the Optic Pathway." See Klüver, *Visual Mechanisms.*

Birren, Faber: Color and Psychotherapy, *Modern Hospital,* August-September, 1946

Birren, Faber: *Functional Color,* Crimson Press, New York, 1937.

Birren, Faber: The Ophthalmic Aspects of Illumination, Brightness and Color, *Transactions of the American Academy of Ophthalmology and Otolaryngology,* May-June, 1948.

Birren, Faber: The Specification of Illumination and Color in Industry, *Transactions of the American Academy of Ophthalmology and Otolaryngology,* January-February, 1947.

Birren, Faber: *The Story of Color,* Crimson Press, Westport, Conn., 1941.

Bissonnette, T. H.: Experimental Modification of Breeding Cycles in Goats, *Physiological Zoology,* July, 1941.

Bissonnette, T. H., and A. G. Csech: Modified Sexual Photoperiodicity in Cottontail Rabbits, *Biological Bulletin,* December, 1939.

Bissonnette, T. H., and A. P. R. Wadlund: Spermatogenesis in Sturnus Vulgaris: Refractory Period and Acceleration in Relation to Wave Length and Rate of Increase of Light Ration, *Journal of Morphology and Physiology,* December, 1931.

Blum, Harold Francis: *Photodynamic Action and Diseases Caused by Light,* Reinhold Publishing Corporation, New York, 1941.

Boring, Edwin G.: *Sensation and Perception in the History of Experimental Psychology,* Appleton-Century-Crofts, Inc., New York, 1942.

Bragg, Sir William: *The Universe of Light,* The Macmillan Company, New York, 1934.

Brombach, T. A.: *Visual Fields,* Distinguished Service Foundation of Optometry, Fall River, Mass., 1936.

Bucke, Richard Maurice: *Cosmic Consciousness,* University Books, Inc., New Hyde Park, N. Y., 1961.

Budge, E. A. Wallis: *Amulets and Talismans,* University Books, Inc., New Hyde Park, N. Y., 1961.

Celsus on Medicine, C. Cox, London, 1831.

Detwiler, Samuel R.: *Vertebrate Photoreceptors,* The Macmillan Company, New York, 1943.

Deutsch, Felix: Psycho-Physical Reactions of the Vascular System to Influence of Light and to Impression Gained Through Light, *Folia Clinica Orientalia,* Vol. I, Fasc. 3 and 4, 1937.

Duggar, Benjamin M. (Editor): *Biological Effects of Radiation,* McGraw-Hill Book Company, Inc., New York, 1936.

Eaves, A. Osborne: *The Colour Cure,* Philip Wellby, London, 1901.

Ellinger, Friedrich: *The Biologic Fundamentals of Radiation Therapy,* Elsevier Publishing Co., Inc., New York, 1941.

Emery, Marguerite: Color Therapy, *Occupational Therapy and Rehabilitation,* February, 1942.

Evans, Ralph M.: *An Introduction to Color,* John Wiley & Sons, Inc., New York, 1948.

Eysenck, H. J.: A Critical and Experimental Study of Colour Preferences, *American Journal of Psychology*, July, 1941.

Farnsworth, Dean: "Investigation on Corrective Training of Color Blindness," Publication 472, National Society for the Prevention of Blindness, New York, 1947.

Fergusson, James: *A History of Architecture in All Countries*, John Murray, London, 1893.

Ferree, C. E., and Gertrude Rand: Lighting and the Hygiene of the Eye, *Archives of Ophthalmology*, July, 1929.

Ferree, C. E., and Gertrude Rand: Lighting in Its Relation to the Eye, *Proceedings of the American Philosophical Society*, Vol. LVII, No. 5, 1918.

Frazer, J. G.: *The Golden Bough*, Macmillan & Company, Ltd., London, 1911.

Galton, Francis: *Inquiries into Human Faculty*, Macmillan & Company, Ltd., London, 1883.

Gellhorn, E.: "Anoxia in Relation to the Visual System." See Klüver, *Visual Mechanisms*.

Goethe's Theory of Colours, translated by Charles Eastlake, John Murray, London, 1840.

Goldstein, Kurt: *The Organism*, American Book Company, New York, 1939.

Goldstein, Kurt: Some Experimental Observations Concerning the Influence of Color on the Function of the Organism, *Occupational Therapy and Rehabilitation*, June, 1942.

Gruner, O. Cameron: *A Treatise on the Canon of Medicine of Avicenna*, Luzac & Co., London, 1930.

Guilford, J. P.: The Affective Value of Color as a Function of Hue, Tint, and Chroma, *Journal of Experimental Psychology*, June, 1934.

Guilford, J. P.: A Study in Psychodynamics, *Psychometrika*, March, 1939.

Haggard, Howard W.: *Devils, Drugs and Doctors*, Harper & Brothers, New York, 1929.

Hall, Manly P.: *An Encyclopedic Outline of Masonic, Hermetic, Qabbalistic and Rosicrucian Symbolical Philosophy*, H. S. Crocker Co., San Francisco, 1928.

Hall, Percy: *Ultra-Violet Rays in the Treatment and Cure of Disease,* The C. V. Mosby Company, Medical Publishers, St. Louis, 1928.

Hardy, LeGrand H., and Gertrude Rand: Elementary Illumination for the Ophthalmologist, *Archives of Ophthalmology,* January, 1945.

Harmon, D. B.: Lighting and Child Development, *Illuminating Engineering,* April, 1945.

Harmon, D. B.: Lighting and the Eye, *Illuminating Engineering,* September, 1944.

Hartmann, Franz: *Magic, White and Black,* Metaphysical Publishing Co New York, 1890.

Hecht, Selig, and Yun Hsia: Dark Adaptation Following Light Adaptation to Red and White Lights, *Journal of the Optical Society of America,* April, 1945.

Helson, Harry: Fundamental Problems in Color Vision. I. The Principle Governing Changes in Hue, Saturation, and Lightness of Non-Selective Samples in Chromatic Illumination, *Journal of Experimental Psychology,* November, 1938.

Helson, Harry: Fundamental Problems in Color Vision. II. Hue, Lightness, and Saturation of Selective Samples in Chromatic Illumination, *Journal of Experimental Psychology,* January, 1940.

Hessey, J. Dodson: *Colour in the Treatment of Disease,* Rider & Co., London.

Hill, Justina: *Germs and Man,* G. P. Putnam's Sons, New York, 1940.

Howat, R. Douglas: *Elements of Chromotherapy,* Actinic Press, London, 1938.

"Influence of Lighting, Eyesight, and Environment Upon Work Production," Report of a two-year study made jointly by the Public Buildings Administration and U. S. Public Health Service, Washington, 1947.

Iredell, C. E.: *Colour and Cancer,* H. K. Lewis & Co., London, 1930.

Jaensch, E. R.: *Eidetic Imagery,* Kegan Paul, Trench, Trubner & Co., London, 1930.

Jayne, Walter Addison: *The Healing Gods of Ancient Civilizations,* Yale University Press, New Haven, 1925.

Jeans, Sir James: *The Mysterious Universe,* The Macmillan Company, New York, 1932.

286

Johnston, Earl S.: *Sun Rays and Plant Life,* 1936 Report of Smithsonian Institution.

Judd, Deane B.: Color Vision, *Medical Physics,* Year Book Publishers, Inc., Chicago, 1944.

Judd, Deane B.: Facts of Color-Blindness, *Journal of the Optical Society of America,* June, 1943.

Judd, Deane B.: "Hue, Saturation, and Lightness of Surface Colors with Chromatic Illumination," Research Paper RP1285, National Bureau of Standards, 1940.

Kandinsky, Wassily: *The Art of Spiritual Harmony,* Houghton Mifflin Company, Boston, 1914.

Karwoski, Theodore F., and Henry S. Odbert: *Color-Music, Psychological Monographs,* Vol. 50, No. 2, 1938, Ohio State University, Columbus.

Katz, David: *The World of Colour,* Kegan Paul, Trench, Trubner & Co., London, 1935.

Kilner, Walter J.: *The Human Atmosphere,* Rebman Co., New York, 1911.

Klüver, Heinrich (Editor): *Visual Mechanisms,* Cattell and Company, Incorporated, Lancaster, Pa., 1942.

Kovacs, Richard: *Electrotherapy and Light Therapy,* Lea & Febiger, Philadelphia, 1935.

Krause, A. C.: "The Photochemistry of Visual Purple." See Klüver, *Visual Mechanisms.*

Kravkov, S. V.: Color Vision and Autonomic Nervous System, *Journal of the Optical Society of America,* June, 1942.

Kravkov, S. V., and L. P. Galochkina: Effect of a Constant Current on Vision, *Journal of the Optical Society of America,* March, 1947.

Kuhn, Hedwig S.: *Industrial Ophthalmology,* The C. V. Mosby Company, Medical Publishers, St. Louis, 1944.

Leadbeater, C. W.: *The Astral Plane,* Theosophical Publishing Society, London, 1905.

Leadbeater, C. W.: *Man Visible and Invisible,* Theosophical Publishing Society, London, 1920.

Levi, Eliphas: *The History of Magic,* William Rider & Son, London, 1922.

Logan, H. L.: The Anatomy of Visual Efficiency, *Illuminating Engineering,* December, 1941.

Logan, H. L.: Light for Living, *Illuminating Engineering,* March, 1947.

Luckiesh, M.: Brightness Engineering, *Illuminating Engineering,* February, 1944.

Luckiesh, M.: *Light, Vision and Seeing,* D. Van Nostrand Company, Inc., New York, 1944.

Luckiesh, M.: *The Science of Seeing,* D. Van Nostrand Company, Inc., New York, 1937.

Luckiesh, M., and A. H. Taylor: A Summary of Researches in Seeing at Low Brightness Levels, *Illuminating Engineering,* April, 1943.

Lutz, Frank E.: Invisible Colors of Flowers and Butterflies, *Natural History,* November-December, 1933.

Maier, N. R. F., and T. C. Schneirla: *Principles of Animal Psychology,* McGraw-Hill Book Company, Inc., New York, 1935.

Menju, Kotaro: Effect of the Visible Light upon the Secretion of Milk, *Japanese Journal of Obstetrics and Gynecology,* June, 1940.

Mosse, Eric P.: Color Therapy, *Occupational Therapy and Rehabilitation,* February, 1942.

Ostwald, Wilhelm: *Colour Science,* Winsor & Newton Limited, London 1931.

Panchadasi, Swami: *The Human Aura,* Yoga Publication Society, Chicago, 1915.

Pancoast, S.: *Blue and Red Light,* J. M. Stoddart & Co., Philadelphia, 1877.

Papyrus Ebers, translated by W. Bryan, Geoffrey Bles, Ltd., London, 1930.

Pleasanton, A. J.: *Blue and Sun-Lights,* Claxton, Remsen & Haffelfinger, Philadelphia, 1876.

Podolsky, Edward: *The Doctor Prescribes Colors,* National Library Press, New York, 1938.

Polyak, S. L.: *The Retina,* University of Chicago Press, Chicago, 1941.

Porter, L. C., and G. F. Prideaux: War on Insect Invaders, *Magazine of Light,* April 25, 1942.

Prescott, Blake Daniels: The Psychological Analysis of Light and Color, *Occupational Therapy and Rehabilitation,* June, 1942.

Pressey, Sidney L.: The Influence of Color upon Mental and Motor Efficiency, *American Journal of Psychology,* July, 1921.

Read, John: *Prelude to Chemistry,* The Macmillan Company, New York, 1937.

Redgrove, H. Stanley: *Alchemy: Ancient and Modern,* William Rider & Son, London, 1922.

Reeder, J. E., Jr.: The Psychogenic Color Field, *American Journal of Ophthalmology*, April, 1944.

Rickers-Ovsiankina, Maria: "Some Theoretical Considerations Regarding the Rorschach Method," Rorschach Research Exchange, April, 1943.

Rubin, Herbert E., and Elias Katz: Auroratone Films for the Treatment of Psychotic Depressions in an Army General Hospital, *Journal of Clinical Psychology*, October, 1946.

Sander, C. G.: *Colour in Health and Disease*, C. W. Daniel Co., London, 1926.

Simonson, Ernst, and Josef Brozek: Effects of Illumination Level on Visual Performance and Fatigue, *Journal of the Optical Society of America*, April, 1948.

Singer, Charles: *From Magic to Medicine*, Ernest Benn, Ltd., London, 1928.

Sloan, Raymond P.: *Hospital Color and Decoration*, Physicians' Record Co., Chicago, 1944.

Solandt, D. Y., and C. H. Best: Night Vision, *Canadian Medical Association Journal*, July, 1943.

Southall, James P. C.: *Introduction to Physiological Optics*, Oxford University Press, New York, 1937.

Tassman, I. S.: *The Eye Manifestations of Internal Diseases*, The C. V. Mosby Company, Medical Publishers, St. Louis, 1946.

Thomson, J. Arthur: *The Outline of Science*, G. P. Putnam's Sons, New York, 1937.

Townsend, Charles Haskins: *Records of Changes in Color Among Fishes*, New York Zoological Society, New York, 1930.

Vollmer, Herman: Studies in Biological Effect of Colored Light, *Archives of Physical Therapy*, April, 1938.

Waite, Arthur Edward: *The Book of Ceremonial Magic*, University Books, Inc., New Hyde Park, N. Y., 1961.

Waite, Arthur Edward: *The Hermetic and Alchemical Writings of Paracelsus*, James Elliot & Co., London, 1894.

Waite, Arthur Edward: *The Occult Sciences*, E. P. Dutton & Co., Inc., New York, 1923.

Waite, Arthur Edward: *The Secret Tradition in Alchemy*, Kegan Paul, Trench, Trubner & Co., London, 1926.

Wald, George: "Visual System and the Vitamins A." See Klüver, *Visual Mechanisms*.

Walls, G. L.: The Basis of Night Vision, *Illuminating Engineering*, February, 1944.

Walls, G. L.: *The Vertebrate Eye*, Cranbrook Press, Bloomfield Hills, Mich., 1942.

Walls, G. L.: "The Visual Cells and Their History." See Klüver, *Visual Mechanisms*.

Werner, Heinz: *Comparative Psychology of Mental Development*, Follett Publishing Company, Chicago, 1948.

White, George Starr: *The Story of the Human Aura*, published by the author, Los Angeles, 1928.

Williams, C. A. S.: *Outlines of Chinese Symbolism*, Customs College Press, Peiping, China, 1931.

Wolfram, E.: *The Occult Causes of Disease*, Rider & Co., London, 1930.

Woolley, C. Leonard: *Ur of the Chaldees*, Charles Scribner's Sons, New York, 1930.

Wright, W. D.: *The Measurement of Colour*, Adam Hilger, Ltd., London, 1944.

Wright, W. D.: *Researches on Normal and Defective Colour Vision*, The C. V. Mosby Company, Medical Publishers, St. Louis, 1947.

Yogo, Eizo: The Effect of the Visible Light upon the Vegetative Nervous System, *Japanese Journal of Obstetrics and Gynecology*, June, 1940.

Additional Bibliography

FOR REVISED EDITION

Birren, Faber: *Selling Color to People*, University Books, Inc.,New Hyde Park, N. Y., 1956.

Budge, E. A. Wallis: *The Book of the Dead*, University Books, Inc., New Hyde Park, N. Y., 1960.

Budge, E. A. Wallis: *Osiris:* The Egyptian Religion of Resurrection, University Books, Inc., New Hyde Park, N. Y., 1961.

Deck of 78 Tarot Cards, in four colors, University Books, Inc., New Hyde Park, N. Y., 1960.

Gerard, Robert: *Differential Effects of Colored Lights on Psychophysiological Functions,* Doctoral dissertation on file with librarian, U. of Calif., Los Angeles, 1957.

Gerard, Robert: Color and Emotional Arousal, *American Psychologist,* July, 1958.

Grillot de Givry, Emile: *A Pictorial Anthology of Witchcraft, Magic and Alchemy,* University Books, Inc., New Hyde Park, N. Y., 1958.

Kelner, A.: Revival by Light, *Scientific American,* May, 1951.

Mead, G. R. S.: *Fragments of a Faith Forgotten,* University Books, Inc., New Hyde Park, N. Y., 1960.

Ott, John: *My Ivory Cellar,* Twentieth Century Press, Chicago 1958.

Rieck, A. F., and Carlson, S. D.: Photorecovery from the Effects of Ultraviolet Radiation in the Albino Mouse, *J. Cell & Comparative Physiology,* 46, 1955.

Tyrrell, G. N. M.: *Science and Psychical Phenomena* and *Apparitions,* University Books, Inc., New Hyde Park, N. Y., 1961.

Van Buskirk, C., et al: The Effect of Different Modalities of Light on the Activation of the EEG, *EEG Clin. Neurophysiology,* 4, 1952.

Waite, Arthur Edward: *The Holy Kabbalah,* University Books, Inc., New Hyde Park, N. Y., 1960.

Waite, Arthur Edward: *The Pictorial Key to the Tarot,* University Books, Inc., New Hyde Park, N. Y., 1960.

Index

294

Maier, N. R. F., 91, 126
Mariotte, Friar, 215
Mast, S. O., 97
Menju, Dr. Kotaro, 127
Mental disorders, color treatment of, 158, 159
Mental efficiency, influence of color on, 121
Mental hospitals, use of color in, 158–160
Metabolism, affected by light and color, 132, 151
Method in color, 257
Metzger, A., 131, 145
Michelson, Albert A., 165
Mitogenetic energy, 89
Mizutani, Dr. S., 128
Mohammedans, preference of, for green, 5
Moleschott, 109
Monotony vs. variety, 261
Morrison, Beulah M., 177
Mosquitoes, color preferences of, 95
  likes and dislikes of, 94
Mosse, Eric P., 160
Motor efficiency, influence of color on, 121
Müller, 220
Murphy, Gardner, 200
Muscular reactions, light tonus in, 130, 142
Music, and color, 157, 163
  comparisons of, dimensions in, 164
  keys of, likened to colors, 163
Mysticism, 3

N

Natume, Dr. M., 128
Nebuchadnezzar, temple of, 10
Nervous system, affected by colors, 169
Neurotics, response of, to color, 119, 151

Newhall, S. M., 168
Newstead, R., 95
Newton, Isaac, 70, 163
Night vision, 224
  and color, 227
  rapid breathing as aid to, 228
Numerals in colors, 194
Nuttall, G. H. F., 95

O

Occupational hazards, 256
Ocular fatigue, 232
Odbert, Henry S., 163
Odors and colors, 166
Odyssey, The, color symbolism in, 4
O'Neill, John, 199
Optics, 207
Ostwald, Wilhelm, 183
Oxygen tension of blood, 224

P

Palette, theatrical, 141
Panchadasi, Swami, 43, 44, 46
Pancoast, S., 52, 53
Paracelsus, 24, 25, 28, 46
Pasteur, 26
Pawnee priest, 6
Perry, L. J., 94, 95
Persians, color therapy of, 17
Personality, color relationships of, 171
Personality tests, color, motion, and time in, 165
Philosopher's stone, 24
Phlogiston, 28
Photobiology, 122
Photosensitivity, 76
Photosynthesis, 88
Pincussen, 132
Pirenne, 103
Planck, Max, 70
Planets, color superstitions about, 9–11, 25

Library of the Mystic Arts
A LIBRARY OF ANCIENT AND MODERN CLASSICS

3. THE ORIGINS OF CHRISTIANITY by F. C. Coneybeare. This absorbing volume takes a bold course away from the traditional and conventional story of Jesus; Paul's decisive role is made clear. **$6.00**

4. EGYPTIAN MAGIC by Sir Wallis Budge. The Egyptian priest made darkness as well as light his realm; his power was exercised by names, spells, enchantments, amulets, pictures and ceremonies accompanied by potent words to be spoken in a certain manner. Nothing was beyond the means of the magician well versed in these formulae. Illustrated. **$5.00**

4a. EGYPTIAN RELIGION by Sir Wallis Budge. Numerous illustrations from the great collection made by Sir Wallis have been added to the original edition to make this as much a picture story as it is an exposition. Much of the book consists of selections from the celebrated Book of the Dead; Egyptian religion centered on death and the after-life when man's soul passed in judgment before Osiris, god of resurrection and (if he had lived virtuously) passed into the delights of the green fields of the underworld.. **$5.00**

5. MAGIC AND MYSTERY IN TIBET by Alexandra David-Neel. "Precisely the person to explore Tibet . . . absolutely fearless. Her accounts of Tibetan religious ceremonies and beliefs are the fullest and best we have."—The New Yorker. Illustrated. **$6.00**

5a. INITIATIONS AND INITIATES IN TIBET by Alexandra David-Neel. To readers of Magic and Mystery in Tibet this book comes as a welcome sequel. It presents a wealth of factual information and detailed observations, not only the author's own considerable findings, but many secrets imparted to her by renowned gurus—including the frequently misinterpreted dubthabs rites that aim at bringing the gods and demons into submission—and spiritual exercises employed by novice and initiate alike. **$5.00**

6. THE PARTING OF THE WAY—Lao Tzu and the Taoist Movement by Holmes Welch. There is entertaining exposition on the search for the Isles of the Blest; Chinese Yoga; alchemy; the Dionysian Rites for the Salvation of Souls; sexual orgies; church states defended by Taoist armies; cult of drunkenness. **$5.00**

7. A PICTORIAL ANTHOLOGY OF WITCH-CRAFT, MAGIC AND ALCHEMY by Emile Grillot de Givry. "A unique volume," says Pastoral Psychology magazine, "written with a rare appreciation of the psychological and emotional needs which account for mankind's preoccupation with demons, witches, magicians. An unusual source book." Large format, 376 illustrations. **$10.00**

8. DOWN THERE—A Study in Satanism by Joris-Karl Huysmans, translated by Keene Wallis. Considered the classic novel on satanism. **$5.00**

9. THE SACRED FIRE—The Story of Sex in Religion by B. Z. Goldberg. The sexual symbolism underlying expressions of faith from prehistoric farmers to present-day evangelists is examined in the light of wide anthropological, historical and sociological evidence. Illustrated. **$7.50**

10. JESUS by Charles Guignebert. The author held the chair in the History of Christianity at the Sorbonne. He impartially sums up the results of a century and a half of Biblical criticism and the result has the effect of a blockbuster. "The genuine teaching of Jesus did not survive him," is but one of the fascinating conclusions he comes to. **$7.50**

11. POLTERGEISTS by Sir Sacheverell Sitwell. The noisy and prankish ghosts you read about in newspapers are Mr. Sitwell's subject. He leaves little doubt that poltergeists exist and that no purely natural explanation can account for them. **$5.75**

12. WORTH LIVING FOR by Eva Bartok. This is the autobiography of the famous Hungarian film star. It is an eloquent testimonial to the spiritual fulfillment to be found in Subud. The climax of the book is Eva Bartok's meetings with Pak Subuh, the Indonesian founder of Subud. **$3.50**

13. CONCERNING SUBUD, The Story Of A New Spiritual Force by John G. Bennett. Since 1920 Bennett has been known as a writer and speaker for Gurdjieff's system. Here is the story of Pak Subuh's spiritual ministry since 1923. **$3.95**

14. THE JEWISH WORLD IN THE TIME OF JESUS by Charles Guignebert. The Old Testament closes hundreds of years before Jesus, the New is written long after his death. What, then, do most of us know about his Jewish world? Nothing! Now here is that world—its Essenes, gnostics, magicians, angels and demons, hermetic books and Messiahs. **$6.00**

15. THE TRAINING OF THE ZEN BUDDHIST MONK by Daisetz Teitaro Suzuki. The clearest introduction to Zen that one could hope for, by the dean of the interpreters to the Western world. 27 illustrations. **$5.00**

16. THE SELECTED WRITINGS OF THE MARQUIS DE SADE. Now available, the famed controversial works only researchers could see on the restricted shelves. Selected and translated with an introduction by Leonard de Saint-Yves. $4.95

17. AN ENCYCLOPAEDIA OF OCCULTISM by Lewis Spence. A Compendium of Information on the Occult Sciences, Occult Personalities, Psychic Science, Demonology, Magic, Spiritism, Mysticism and Metaphysics. More than 2500 entries and articles. 488 double-column pages size 8 x 10". Alphabetically arranged with an eleven-page Master Index. Deluxe Edition, bound in buckram and elephant-hide and boxed. $15.00

18. THE PICTORIAL KEY TO THE TAROT by Arthur Edward Waite. Being fragments of a secret tradition under the veil of divination. With 78 plates in full color, illustrating the Greater and Lesser Arcana, from designs by Pamela Colman Smith. $7.50

19. SEVENTY-EIGHT TAROT CARDS IN FULL COLOR. Created by Pamela Colman Smith and Arthur Edward Waite. $5.00

21. COSMIC CONSCIOUSNESS by R. M. Bucke, M.D. One of the great classics of mystical experience, written sixty years ago but still ahead of its time. Neither supernatural nor supranormal, cosmic consciousness is the emergence of a new human faculty which is placing the people of the next epoch as far above us as we are above the simple consciousness of animals. $5.95

22. THE HOLY KABBALAH by A. E. Waite with an introduction by Kenneth Rexroth. A study of the secret tradition in Israel as unfolded by Sons of the Doctrine for the benefit and consolation of the Elect dispersed through the lands and ages of The Greater Exile. $10.00

23. THE HAUNTED MIND by Nandor Fodor. From his practice as a psychoanalyst and psychic researcher, Dr. Fodor has selected some 20 cases as the most interesting. They include mediumship, levitation, communication after death. $5.00

24. THE BOOK OF THE DEAD—The Hieroglyphic Transcript of the Papyrus of ANI, the Translation into English and An Introduction by E. A. Wallis Budge, Late Keeper of the Egyptian and Assyrian Antiquities in The British Museum. The Book Of The Dead is the great collection of texts which the ancient Egyptian scribes composed for the benefit of the dead—spells and incantations, hymns and litanies, magical formulae and names, words of power and prayers, cut or painted on walls of pyramids and tombs, and painted on coffins and sarcophagi and rolls of papyri. Illustrated. $12.50

26. FRAGMENTS OF A FAITH FORGOTTEN — The Gnostics: A Contribution to the Study of the Origins of Christianity by G. R. S. Mead. Until recently, almost all we knew about the Gnostics we were told by the Church Fathers who had burned the Gnostic literature. Gnosticism found in G. R. S. Mead a true and disinterested scholar; he made available to the English-speaking world his translations of Gnostic texts which had survived in Coptic in Ethiopia and in Egypt. FRAGMENTS OF A FAITH FORGOTTEN is an anthology of these Gnostic texts together with Mead's explanations. The Introduction by Kenneth Rexroth is correctly called "A Primer of Gnosticism." $10.00

25. THE VAMPIRE: His Kith and Kin by Montague Summers, author of THE HISTORY OF WITCHCRAFT and THE GEOGRAPHY OF WITCHCRAFT. The fascination of this theme has deep roots in human history. "Vampire" comes from a Slavonic word and this belief has had a peculiar intensity among the Slavonic peoples. "The fuller knowledge of these horrors reached western Europe in detail during the Eighteenth Century." $6.00

27. THE SIDDUR: The Traditional Jewish Prayer Book. An entirely new translation by Dr. David de Sola Pool, Rabbi Emeritus of the Spanish and Portuguese Synagogue of New York City. Translation approved by the Rabbinical Council of America. English and Hebrew on facing pages. A deluxe edition, 7¼ x 10¼ inches, approximately 900 pages, three-piece library binding, sturdy, printed slipcase. $17.50

28. CAGLIOSTRO by W. R. H. Trowbridge. Cagliostro figures as one of the great pioneers in every serious account of hypnotism and telepathy, magic and alchemy, precognition and spiritualism, psychic healing and modern mysticism. Yet the simplest facts about his life and his teachings remain bitterly disputed now, two hundred years after he was born. Savant or scoundrel! Here is the true role of this splendid, tragic figure! $6.50

29. AMULETS AND TALISMANS by E. A. Wallis Budge. The original texts with translations and descriptions of a long series of Egyptian, Sumerian, Assyrian, Hebrew, Christian, Gnostic and Muslim Amulets and Talismans and Magical Figures, with chapters on the Evil Eye, the origin of the Amulet, the Pentagon, the Swastika, the Cross (Pagan and Christian), the properties of Stones, Rings, Divination, Numbers, the Kabbalah, Ancient Astrology, etc. $10.00

30. SCIENCE and PSYCHICAL PHENOMENA and APPARITIONS by G. N. M. Tyrrell. These two famous classics of psychical research are now bound together in one volume. They are the best introduction to the subject. $7.50

31. THE BOOK OF CEREMONIAL MAGIC by A. E. Waite. Readers have met the distinguished author before; he wrote THE HOLY KABBALAH and THE PICTORIAL KEY TO THE TAROT. The present book is a complete Grimoire. Part I, the Literature of Ceremonial Magic, provides the key passages from the principal texts of the 14th, 15th and 16th centuries. Part II contains the complete Grimoire, the best source of magical procedure extant. 9 plates and numerous line drawings. $10.00

33. OSIRIS: The Egyptian Religion of Resurrection by E. A. Wallis Budge. Frazer's Golden Bough has made us familiar with a god who dies each year that he and his worshippers may live anew. Attis, Adonis, Osiris are the great examples. But Frazer only whetted our appetite. It was Sir Wallis Budge who gave us the definitive study of Osiris in depth. Much of it is startling indeed. Egyptian religion in its cruelty, its cannibalism, its bloodthirstiness, its general coloring, is African through and through. Osiris himself is both the father and the slain. It is his son Horus who is the living and victorious Savior. Isis brings the drowned Osiris to land, miraculously has intercourse and secures seed from the dead man, suckles Horus in hiding in the wilderness who, "when his arm grew strong," triumphs over Osiris' brother and slayer, Set, and Osiris is resurrected as god-man. Nearly 900 pages plus 14 pages of plates, 212 illustrations, and hundreds of hieroglyphic reproductions and transcriptions. $15.00

CPSIA information can be obtained
at www.ICGtesting.com
Printed in the USA
LVHW021003101118
596660LV00001B/223

9 781425 424107